Singing for Life

Singing for Life

HIV/AIDS and Music in Uganda

Gregory Barz

Foreword by Jim Wooten, *Nightline,*
ABC News Senior Correspondent

Routledge
Taylor & Francis Group
New York   London

Published in 2006 by
Routledge
Taylor & Francis Group
270 Madison Avenue
New York, NY 10016

Published in Great Britain by
Routledge
Taylor & Francis Group
2 Park Square
Milton Park, Abingdon
Oxon OX14 4RN

Printed in the United States of America on acid-free paper
10 9 8 7 6 5 4 3 2 1

International Standard Book Number-10: 0-415-97289-2 (Hardcover) 0-415-97290-6 (Softcover)
International Standard Book Number-13: 978-0-415-97289-5 (Hardcover) 978-0-415-97290-1 (Softcover)
Library of Congress Card Number 2005013959

Library of Congress Cataloging-in-Publication Data

Barz, Gregory F., 1960-
　　Singing for life : HIV/AIDS and music in Uganda / Gregory Barz ; foreword by Jim Wooten.
　　　　p. cm.
　　Includes bibliographical references and index.
　　ISBN 0-415-97289-2 (hardback : alk. paper) -- ISBN 0-415-97290-6 (pbk. : alk. paper)
　　1. Music therapy-Uganda. 2. AIDS (Disease)--Prevention-Uganda. 3. AIDS (Disease)--Songs and music. 4. AIDS (Disease)--Drama. 5. AIDS (Disease)--Religious aspects. I. Title.

ML3920.B25 2005
362.196'9792'0096761--dc22   2005013959

Taylor & Francis Group
is the Academic Division of Informa plc.

Visit the Taylor & Francis Web site at
http://www.taylorandfrancis.com

and the Routledge Web site at
http://www.routledge-ny.com

In music there is talking, but somehow in a different way. In music there is also drama.
So, you may sing about something and at the same time you are acting.
People can hear what you are saying and also see a picture, you see?
So they may think about what you are telling them when they actually see an example of it.
So people can catch stories and pick messages better than merely telling it to them.
—Walya Sulaiman, PADA
People Against AIDS Development Association
Iganga, Uganda

For Vincent, Godfrey, Noelina, and Patrick:
They say that some people walk along the paths in order to begin a journey.
Others create the paths and enjoy the journey home.

For Mona, Simon, and Lucy:
They say that some people journey in order to find themselves.
Others revel in the people they meet along the way.

Lyii woowe, we are invaded, *yaaye,* we struggle
We wail, we do not know where to turn
Hey, you there, listen to this lamentation sounding the warning
Many are asleep and others are on beds
They are not guilty of anything, but are victims of the disaster, the mass murder
This word has a dangerous origin, all diseases are hidden within it
This contagion destroyed the man with whom I struggled
If it is a spell you could look for a "doctor"
But, see here, your friend has become death and you cannot trust each other
We no longer trust our God and there is nothing to do
The one gone out to work cannot trust the one at home
The keeper of the home just sits waiting for the disease to come home
The hearts of children are afraid to be left alone as orphans
If the disease begins in your womb, then you will bury them continuously
When it begins in a family, it is like an ambush
You cannot know who will be the one to get it today
It begins slowly, gnawing away and shows up after three years
It does not wait to grow but begins right away to grip you, alluding and hiding
You cannot know those who are infected after a day, a week, or a month
When it takes your lover your heart melts, you expect to leave life
Many diseases come, and worry is the first
Everywhere you go you picture yourself leaving your family
Poverty is number two, you need to feed well, but body weaknesses
come one by one
Then you begin slimming immediately
It shames us, my friends, to look at ourselves and wonder when we will die
The one lying on the bed considers himself lucky and wonders why
it still spares him
But, we are all invaded by *mukenenya,* such a deadly disease
There is no solution for us all, let us weep
Nobody will be spared from the crying
See the doctors, it causes them to decay helplessly
The professors, ha! It does not even trust them
Oh, this is terrible, why does it take the babies?
For sure we are at a loss while it eats us to the last person
We have come out today with medicine in our songs
Listen, it means abstinence is the first medicine
Listen, youth, never give away your life
You who are still children, know that life is more important
Be patient as you look for a trustworthy marriage partner
Before you decide, go for the test
If you are both healthy then be faithful to each other
You will preserve your life for long
People will wonder if that is the provision for your journey
To survive *Slim,* stop lovemaking, do not try at all
If you decide to have the pleasure, condoms are available so use them
Use them like shoes

—Bright Women Actresses
Bwaise, Uganda

CONTENTS

FOREWORD

IN THESE PAGES there is a gathering of such rare and poetic wisdom that those unfamiliar with Africa, with its traditions, with its music or with its problems—specifically the overwhelming problem of HIV/AIDS—will take from their reading not merely new information (although there is a wealth of that) but the priceless gift of inspiration as well.

As the president of Uganda, Yoweri Museveni, has urgently explained, the threat of the deadly virus to the people of his country and to the continent is so grave and so immediate that warnings must not simply be given, not simply announced, they must be shouted—and in this scholarly but noble collection and compilation of poetry, songs, and drama, ethnomusicologist Gregory Barz records many of the Ugandan voices now being raised across that nation. They are the voices of young women such as Aida Namulinda of the Bright Women Actresses, of Florence Kumunhyu of Maboni Nabanji (a traditional healer or witch doctor), of Noelina Namukisa, and of scores of others, all of which amount to a collective shout being heard in their villages, in their towns, in their cities, in their schools, and in their churches. Together these voices form a choir which, in a way previously unexplored, is not only *singing for life* but *saving lives* as well by educating thousands who would otherwise be unaware of the elementary facts of HIV/AIDS, of how it is transmitted, of its effects on the body, and of how it is prevented.

My own experiences with Africans who live with HIV or are dying with AIDS have persuaded me that, until a vaccine is developed or until antiretroviral drugs are available in large quantities to patients there, the focus of the continent's political, medical, and religious leadership ought to be on prevention, and the key to prevention is education—and education takes many forms. As Faustus Baziri, an AIDS activist, put it to Barz:

There are a lot of informations. But one of them is health education. We educate the community. We pass on the message. Music is an organized sound, eh? So, through this sound we send messages to people, and it is quite attractive. As they come to listen they learn.

And it is not only Ugandans who are listening. There will surely now be many others who *listen*, so to speak, to the lessons captured within these pages.

Jim Wooten
Nightline, ABC News
Author, *We Are All the Same: A Story of a Boy's Courage and a Mother's Love*

ACKNOWLEDGMENTS

SINGING FOR LIFE IS A SONG OF PRAISE for the efforts of so many people who work tirelessly in the field of HIV/AIDS health-care education, care, and counseling in Uganda. Two individuals in particular—Noelina Namukisa, executive director of Meeting Point Kampala (MPKLA) and Vincent Wandera, director of Good Shepherd Support Action Centre Kampala (GOSSACE)—confirmed for me on countless occasions that "living positively" with HIV was not merely a goal, but rather a necessity in Uganda for survival and for moving forward. The compassion, love, and energy with which Noelina and Vincent engage the humanity of AIDS-related issues in rural and urban Ugandan communities among HIV-positive children and adults continue to move me deeply. Thus, it is to the tireless, ongoing work of providing care for People Living with HIV/AIDS (PLWHAs) by Noelina and Vincent that I dedicate this study.

There are many others who assisted and guided the field research in Uganda that supports the data and ethnographic materials represented in this study. Centurio Balikoowa has been my colleague since I first stepped off the plane at the Entebbe Airport in the 1990s. Today he is a teacher, a friend, and a colleague. Stephen Bwoye was a student in the Department of Music, Dance, and Drama at Makerere University in Kampala when we first began working together. Bwoye was extremely helpful by providing translations from Luganda, Lusoga, and other languages of eastern Uganda. Composer and educator Justinian Tamusuza has been my host on several occasions in Uganda. His guidance has led me to many wonderful people without whom I would not have had the rich experiences I took in. Sylvia Tamusuza continues to inspire me with her work and her passion for Ugandan traditional expressive culture. Kitogo George Ndugwa, an impressive young musician, assisted me, leading me in many new and unexpected directions. Chris Ssebunya Senyonjo Mubende, an education major at Makerere University, also provided cultural translations of many popular songs. Dr. Peter Mudiope and Dr. Alex Muganzi Muganga facilitated many of the interviews in rural villages, providing valuable medical information to villagers and me.

I am indebted to the support and assistance of John Turner, John Dick, Paul Epp, Lee Ann O'Neal, Jonathan Rodgers, Jack Rutledge, Jeff Sheehan, and Nathan Hoeft, all undergraduates at Vanderbilt University who assisted me with documentation and recording at various times in Uganda and in the United States. Patrick Anguzu and Noelina Namukisa of Meeting Point Kampala have become a part of my family, fostering and facilitating my efforts and championing this project from the beginning. Vincent Wandera and Godfrey Mukasa, also of GOSSACE, have moved beyond mere colleagues in their friendship and guidance of my efforts.

The field research that supports this study began in 1999 and continues to this day. The Uganda National Council for Science and Technology Research granted clearance for the ongoing project (UNCST File No. SS1368), as did the President's Office of the Republic of Uganda. Funding for the research was provided by two grants from the Vanderbilt University Research Council, from Mark Wait, dean of the Blair School of Music at Vanderbilt University, and as a Senior Fulbright Research Fellow as part of the AIDS and AIDS-Related Research of the African Regional Research Program. Vanderbilt University also provided additional grants for two extensive research trips to Uganda. I am grateful for their continuing support of this project. Many of the ideas, especially those pertaining to memory, presented in this study draw on my experiences as a fellow in the Robert Penn Warren Center for the Humanities at Vanderbilt University. I am grateful to my fellow "fellows," who encouraged, supported, and informed my work. While in Uganda I was an affiliate of the Makerere University Institute of Social Research (MISR), and I thank Patrick Mulindwa of MISR for facilitating many aspects of this productive affiliation. Dean Wait has been tireless in his enthusiasm for this project. He was one of the first people to "get" the importance and value of this project. His encouragement and support have allowed me to take this work in so many nuanced directions.

My ethnomusicology and musicology colleagues at Vanderbilt have encouraged me since I arrived at the Blair School in 1998. Joy Calico, Dale Cockrell, Cynthia Cyrus, Stan Link, James Lovensheimer, Melanie Lowe, Michael Rose, and Helena Simonett have each contributed their support of my ongoing research efforts and have covered for me in so many ways. Dennis Clark, music librarian *par excellence* at the Anne Potter Wilson Music Library at the Blair School of Music and codirector of the Global

Music Archive, has been patient and indefatigable in his efforts to support this publication. Other members of the Wilson Music Library—Rodger Coleman, Robert Rich, Catherine Gick, and Michael Jones have contributed tirelessly to the seemingly endless research demands, materials collection, and InterLibrary Loan requests this project demanded. I am grateful for their contributions and count myself blessed to have access to such a highly competent and motivated staff.

All photographs included in this text (unless otherwise noted) are by Jonathan Rodgers, a student of mine at Vanderbilt who traveled with me one summer to Uganda as a research assistant. I continue to be moved by Jonathan's artistry. He very quietly worked in the background, approaching his own understanding of the very desperate situations we encountered. His images are profound and they tell their own stories. I am honored to have them in this book and hope they help to communicate something of the beauty of everyday life in Uganda to the reader.

Jim Roberts engineered and mastered the compact disc accompanying this book at Kalimba Studio in Nashville. Jim's sense of humor—in addition to his engagement of the sound materials and his unending patience—made the recording production experience meaningful.

Mona Christenson Barz has provided an endless reserve of support for (and patience with) this project—support in the form of her ongoing encouragement for me to engage these issues to whatever extreme I felt necessary, and patience when losing touch with me for weeks on end during trips to Africa. Her participation in the field research during one of my extended periods in Uganda was truly a blessing, as was the presence of my children—Simon and Lucy. The time we spent together in Uganda presented many opportunities and opened communities to me in unexpected ways while providing a much-needed perspective on the complexities of everyday life in the field.

ACRONYMS USED IN THE TEXT

ACHAP	African Comprehensive HIV/AIDS Partnerships (Botswana)
AIC	AIDS Information Center
AIDS	Acquired Immunodeficiency Syndrome
ANC	Antenatal Clinic Attenders
ARVs	Antiretroviral drugs
AWOFS	AIDS Widow Orphans Family Support, Nsambya Hospital, Kampala
BAPET	Bwakeddempulira AIDS Patients Educational Team
BUDEA	Buwolomera Development Association
CBO	Community-Based Organization
CDC	Centers for Disease Control
FGM	Female Genital Mutilation
FSW	Female Sex Worker
GOSSACE	Good Shepherd Support Action Centre
GPA	Global Programme on AIDS
HIV	Human Immunodeficiency Virus
IDAAC	Integrated Development Activities and AIDS Concern, Iganga
IMAU	Islamic Medical Association of Uganda
IGA	Income-Generating Activity
LC	Local Counsel
MPK	Meeting Point Kampala
MTCT	Mother-to-Child Transmission
MUDINET	Mukono District Network of People Living with HIV/AIDS
NACWOLA	National Community of Women Living with HIV/AIDS

NGO	Non-Governmental Organization
NRM	National Resistance Movement
PADA	People with AIDS Development Association, Iganga
PHA	
(or PHAs)	People Living with HIV/AIDS
PLI	Philly Lutaaya Initiative
PLWHA	
(PLWHAs)	People Living with HIV/AIDS
PMTC	Parent of Mother to Child Transmission
PTC	Post Test Club
PWA	Person with AIDS (older term than PLWHA)
SIDA	*Syndrome immuno-déficitaire acquis* (French translation for "AIDS")
TASGA	Tokamalirawo AIDS Support Group Awareness
TASO	The AIDS Support Organization
TB	Tuberculosis
TFD	Theatre for Development
THETA	Traditional and Modern Health Practitioners Together Against AIDS and Other Diseases
UNAIDS	Joint United Nations Program on HIV/AIDS
UNASO	Uganda Network of AIDS Service Organisations
UNICEF	United Nations Children's Fund
VCT	Volunteer Counseling and Testing
VOLSET	Voluntary Service Trust Team
WHO	World Health Organization

RECORDED SELECTIONS
ON THE COMPACT DISC

Track 1   *"Anjorina"* (*"Angelina"*)
           1. Students at Kibuye Primary School, Kampala
           2. Ensemble led by Okello Michael
           (With permission by Centurio Balikoowa and Okello Michael)

Track 2   *"Bakabitandika nk'onigambo"* ("It all started as a rumor")
           Kashenyi Nursery School Children
           (With permission by Dr. Alex Muganzi Muganga)

Track 3   *"Luno olumbe lwa twidhira"* ("This disease came for us")
           BUDEA, Buwolomera Development Association
           (With permission by Florence Kumunhyu)

Track 4   *"Omukazi omoteguu"* ("A married woman who does not
           respond to instruction from her husband")
           Vilimina Nakiranda, voice and *akadongo*
           (With permission by Vilimina Nakiranda)

Track 5   "TASO is going forward with positive living"
           TASO Mulago Drama Group
           (With permission by Tony Kasule)

Track 6   *"Olumbe lwa Silumu"* ("This disease of AIDS")
           Aida Namulinda
           (With permission by Aida Namulinda)

LIST OF FIGURES

ORTHOGRAPHY

LUGANDA (oluGanda, sometimes spelled LuGanda) is a Bantu language native to the Buganda people and belongs to the Nyoro-Ganda linguistic Bantu family, according to Malcolm Guthrie's linguistic classification scheme (1967–71). It is generally spoken and understood north of Lake Victoria's northwestern shore in Uganda's Buganda Province. Luganda, while not an official language of state, is spoken widely in many outlying areas of Uganda.

The Luganda alphabet is composed of twenty-four letters:
        seventeen consonants: b, p, v, f, m, d, t, l, r, n, z, s, j, c, g, k, ŋ
        five vowels: a, e, i, o, u
        two semi-vowels: w, y

Since ŋ consonant does not appear on standard computer keyboards, it is frequently replaced by the letter combination ng'. (The apostrophe is frequently left off in contemporary orthography, leading to confusion with the distinct and different sound arising from the letter combination ng.) The letter combination ny is also treated as a unique consonant.

PRELUDE

"Those Who Do Not Listen to Our Songs and Change Their Behavior Will Land in Problems"

MZEE MATA IS A SEVENTY-YEAR-OLD *akadongo* (lamellophone, "thumb piano") player, blind since birth, who lives in Iganga, one of the principal towns located along the Jinja Road in the eastern Busoga region of Uganda. Mzee Mata—whose singing and playing style is recognizable throughout the country—is perhaps best known for having composed and recorded a song widely played on the radio extolling the merits of the nation's newly ratified constitution in 1962. People remember Mzee Mata and the educational outreach of his political song. I first met and recorded Mata in the 1990s when he performed songs for me that seemed strange at the time—these songs told stories of strange fruits enveloping entire communities, strange insects eating farm animals, and even stranger references to brooms that were sweeping their way through villages. What follows is a transcription of a more recent conversation with Mzee Mata in which he reflects on the position of music, dance, and drama in local medical outreach efforts pertaining to HIV/AIDS education and prevention in his area of the country.

The following is an English translation of a conversation with Mzee Mata in the Lusoga language held in Kasokoso in Iganga town in the eastern region of Uganda on June 12, 2004.

> My names are Mzee Nasani Byansi Mata. I am the leader of the lo-
> cal Busoga National Actors Mata Group which I started in Iganga
> way back in 1952. The group's original goal was merely to entertain
> people, to make people happy by entertaining them, but later our
> goals became more commercial and also more educational. Our

principal aim has always been to achieve some good income for ourselves, but unfortunately what I get is really very little. So, you can say that we have not yet achieved our aims.

Music has really helped in controlling and preventing AIDS not only in this area, but also throughout the country. People who listen to us, well they normally change and adapt their behavior. Those who do not listen do not learn. Music has played a very big role in my own community. There are songs sometimes that tell people how to protect themselves, and for those who are already sick there are songs about how to live happy and live positively. For those who have not yet got AIDS there are songs about how to be careful as they move around. Music has helped people throughout the region, preventing them from catching the virus. We even use songs to advise people how to use condoms, especially in those areas where things are not so good in terms of information about health care. We tell them that they should use condoms in order to prevent catching AIDS.

Some traditional healers just give out herbs, just as you go to get tablets from clinics or hospitals. But others use music to call the ancestors to come and solve the problems. They often use music in such settings. Very many people at the grassroots have now formed groups that mirror my own group's efforts to educate, and in response to my songs people now go out and compose, also using music to change and prevent people from catching AIDS. Music controls AIDS. We have really struggled for this country, Uganda.

Unfortunately I have a feeling that AIDS has no cure, so those who do not listen to our songs and change their behavior will land in problems. Women and the youth must fight back against AIDS with their music. The youth normally listen to music and should therefore listen to we musicians who advise them to change their behavior. Those who do not listen often land in problems.

I purposely open this text with the voice of Mzee Mata and the rather direct connection this performer makes between his personal efforts as a rural musician and the greater goal of behavioral change. Music, dance, and drama have been (and continue to be) deep cultural resources and instruments of survival in the confrontation with the ongoing HIV/AID crisis in Uganda. For culture bearers such as Mata, singing, dancing, and performing represent not only a means for maintaining traditional expressive culture, but perhaps more importantly, a function as medical intervention in communities that look to and depend on the strength and cultural solidarity of musicians, dancers, and actors.

Singing for Life is a book that responds to the pleas of Mzee Mata and others to listen to the musicians, to listen to the songs of hope and healing regarding HIV/AIDS … to listen and change behavior.

Introduction

"MUSIC IS TAKEN AS A MEDICINE"

Singing for Life in a Time of AIDS

ETHNOMUSICOLOGISTS, much like our not-so-distant cousins—journalists, *griots*, poets, folksingers, novelists—are singers of tales. We often travel far (to Africa in my case) in order to fulfill a deep-seeded curiosity about how others are in the world musically. We return home laden with equipment bags packed with stories, experiences, and memories. We compete to present our findings at academic conferences where each of us listens intently, learning from each other as if attempting to put together a challenging jigsaw puzzle of the world's musical cultures and traditions. In our classrooms we teach and pass along these stories, writing articles and books about our experiences along the way, convinced that the world will be a better place for the sharing of our memories and of our cultural awareness. Many of us—myself included—feel that in our privilege to share in and make meaning out of the musical lives of people around the world, we are the most fortunate of all storytellers.

But as I return to the country of Uganda each year—sometimes for brief periods, other times for longer stays—I realize that it is not the music that motivates me; in fact it never has been. Rather it has been the stories of people with whom I am privileged to spend time that inspire me to write. As an ethnomusicologist I am drawn not only to musical performances, but to the stories of individual lives and the cultural dramas that develop out of those lives, especially in response to the contemporary global AIDS pandemic.

This book is an attempt to add my own story to those of many others—Aida, Vincent, Maboni, Noelina, Florence, Apofia, Godfrey, Ruth, Peter, Hajji, Alex, and Mata—as they recount and detail their relationships to HIV/AIDS in Africa. Each engages in battles within separate spheres of influence, advocating for individual rights, access to better medical care, and the empowerment of those who are HIV positive. Individually, these path breakers often work anonymously in their distinct spheres without anyone taking note of them. Collectively, however, they impress.

My presence in the story that follows is as complicated as it is simple. As a now middle-aged ethnomusicologist I have long given up on objectivity; I am strongly affected by what I have experienced in Uganda and thus my stories reveal a rather personal engagement concerning how I came to know what I know about HIV/AIDS in Africa. In the singing of this tale, therefore, I find it tiresome to feign unemotional detachment; those reactions to perceived authorial reflexivity, subjectivity, and perhaps even self-indulgence that will likely be raised by many readers are thus understandable. My stance, however, is not one without power, and I do not pretend to adopt a defensive posture. I am present in this story as I am in the lives of friends—colleagues, informants, collaborators—who continue to expect and demand my presence in their work and in their efforts to affect change. I am well aware of the potential harm the insertion of myself into this narrative can cause, but I trust that the risk far outweighs the prospect of damage.

I also realize that this book—an ethnography of experiences of music among those living positively with HIV in Uganda—is perhaps not the most judicious way of telling this story. Any attempt on my part to analyze, reflect on, illustrate, transcribe, or narrate the lives of those out front in the grassroots working tirelessly to affect change may very well accomplish the opposite by obfuscating the everyday nonmusical efforts of the individuals documented in this study. Yet, faced with the dilemma of representation, I choose to embrace the tool of my trade, ethnography, not only because I can write, but for my own sense of partnership and solidarity with the individuals detailed in this study, I have to write. I only hope that within the inherently flawed medium of academic ethnography that some truth of the lives of those actively engaged in the struggle with AIDS will come through the text.

Singing for Life presents a cultural analysis of hope and healing regarding HIV/AIDS in Africa. It is a series of stories about the infusion of medical interventions specific to HIV/AIDS within musical performances—songs, dramas, and dances—in Uganda, East Africa. The contemporary performances documented in this study reflect a social phenomenon in Uganda in which music now often focuses on gender- and health-related issues specific to women and youths by drawing on song texts that warn against participation in risky sexual environments or engagement of unprotected sexual behavior. Such performances frequently assume didactic functions—educating a broad spectrum of society, outlining support networks available within local or regional communities, and providing information concerning the availability of condoms and VCT (Volunteer Counseling and Testing; see Vaderpuye and Amegatcher 2003).[1] Music, dance, and drama have become the principal tools of many local initiatives and media that disseminate information, mobilize resources, and raise societal consciousness regarding issues related to HIV/AIDS. Critical responses by women in particular to the AIDS pandemic in the form of musical performances are one of the most significant means of constructing localized knowledge concerning disease prevention and health-care education in this area of the world.[2]

The stories that follow underscore the immediate need for medical ethnomusicology to focus on disease, healing, as well as on the application of local herbs and traditional medicines by healers, herbalists, and health-care practitioners in sub-Saharan Africa. The ability of expressive culture in Uganda to contribute to health-care initiatives is deeply embedded within musical performance. Indigenous conceptualizations of music in Uganda often describe the ability of performances to both communicate information and affect social behavior. Song texts, for example, frequently suggest interventions that both encourage medical analysis—"singing about HIV helps people learn about the need to go for testing"—and take the form of medical treatment itself—"Music is taken as medicine. Even if one is in pain they will begin getting back some life if there is music. Even the bereaved or those in shrines, music is there. So, music is both medicine and education."

In addition to providing a general readership opportunities to reflect on these issues, this study has the potential to persuade governmental and non-governmental organizations of the power and efficacy of musical performance as a forum for medical interventions by highlighting the efforts of women, men, and youths throughout Uganda to combat the HIV virus and AIDS disease in ways in which private multinational and multilateral NGOs have been either challenged or unsuccessful. The case studies presented in this book, for example, demonstrate the link between the recent decline in Uganda's infection rate and the introduction of grassroots interventions of rural women's groups in response to the largely unsuccessful, inaccessible, and expensive efforts based on Western medical models. Only when supported and encouraged by performances drawing on localized musical traditions have medical initiatives taken root and flourished in local health-care systems leading many to a much needed and much deserved peace of the body.

I have engaged East African expressive culture—music, dance, and drama—since first assuming a position as lecturer in the Department of Art, Music, and Theatre at the University of Dar es Salaam, Tanzania, in 1992 while simultaneously completing my doctoral fieldwork. At that time my field research centered primarily on the contemporary post-colonial (and post-mission) processes of musical indigenization occurring within Lutheran churches along the Indian Ocean coast.[3] Since 1999 I have worked primarily in Uganda (with peripheral research efforts in western Kenya and northwest Tanzania) to support the work of the present study on HIV/AIDS. My field research in Uganda has ranged from intensive work in rural village areas to long-term field research based in Kampala—the nation's capital—allowing for frequent trips to visit consultants and drama groups in outlying areas of the country.

GENERAL OVERVIEW OF THE BOOK

Today in Uganda, only 10 percent of the population has access to medical facilities; there is only one doctor for every twenty thousand people (as compared to the 1:400 ratio in the United States). While infection rates have fallen in Uganda, down from 30 percent to 5 percent in the past ten years, two million orphans and one million persons living with AIDS represent a need for care that cannot be met by currently available *medical* resources. Less than 2 percent of those who need antiretroviral drugs can afford them, and treatment costs, while much lower today than just a few years ago, still overwhelm the government's annual health allotment of $10 per person. Given these conditions, music's contributions to intervention and palliative care are a humane and necessary option. Music often mitigates the socioeconomic effects of illness by directly supporting caregivers, controlling pain, and providing counseling.

HIV/AIDS in sub-Saharan Africa is a widespread phenomenon that is largely the result of deep cultural issues related to the politics of local and regional economies as well as to conflicts between local and foreign health-care systems. Efforts within the past decade to address the pandemic in Africa have dealt with HIV/AIDS principally as a medical concern—despite the fact that funding agencies continue to be confronted with the dense meanings supporting the indigenization of AIDS in local African contexts. HIV/AIDS is, sadly, more than a medical crisis in Africa. It continues to impact rural and urban development efforts significantly, causing massive socioeconomic challenges throughout the continent. Women are especially at risk in many parts of Africa due to general poverty, lack of access to education, and subordinate positions within marital and sexual relationships. Only a small proportion of women are in a position to rely on the availability of condoms let alone embrace "safer sex" practices, and fewer still are able to approach the theme of the latest American-backed funding initiative, "abstinence" (see Grundfest Schoeft 1997, 329).

AIDS in many African countries is a societal concern that impacts the transmission of the very cultural issues that could normally intervene. Gone, for example, are the "aunties" in many villages, female family members who have historically contributed to the cultural education of young female family members on issues of sexuality and reproduction. Yet, when cultural institutions fail in their efforts to affect social change, artists step in. When technologies and organizational systems disappoint, musicians sing and dance, thereby creating meaning out of chaotic lives. If one person can make a difference in the ongoing struggle with AIDS in Uganda it will be a musician, a dancer, or an actor.[4] One such activist, Walya Sulaiman, is a Muslim living outside of Iganga town. Since diagnosed with HIV almost ten years ago, Sulaiman has dedicated what is left of his life to educating and counseling other Muslims through his group, PADA (People with AIDS Development Association). Although his community group receives no funding and no media attention, all strive to "live positively" rather than live as "HIV positive." According to Sulaiman, drama is inherent in musical performance, so that within the act of singing the historical tradition of conveying information is reinforced. As such, music is a more affective medical intervention than the outreach efforts of doctors and health-care workers. Most Ugandans openly deny consulting spiritual and traditional health-care practitioners. Many urban residents and those affiliated with faith communities publicly denounce the efforts of tradition healers. Privately, however, people avail themselves of multiple healing systems, especially when HIV is involved. In a conversation with Maboni Nabanji, a respected traditional healer—or "witch doctor" as he prefers—I asked about treatment in his healing practice (see Figure 1.1). His response—"Singing is the main form of treatment we witch doctors employ. We play drums and other instruments during the process of diagnosis to discern whether a patient has AIDS, familial spirits, or other possession."

In order to communicate effectively in villages the term *kayovu* is adopted in several of the songs performed Walya Sulaiman's group, PADA, to refer to AIDS. *Kayovu*, a banana weevil, is an insect that eats fruit from the inside out. Similarly, in performance the witch doctor Maboni Nabanji frequently refers to HIV as *ffene*, or jackfruit to suggest how one can get stuck in the sticky fruit, unable to wash or scrape the virus off.

Figure Introduction I.1 Spirit possession ceremony led by Maboni Nabanji (playing *nsasi* rattles, far left) along with other traditional healers.

Such linguistic localizations occur frequently in songs, enabling cultural meanings of HIV/AIDS to be understood at deep levels. In a country where there are so few trained medical doctors, traditional healers, witch doctors, and herbalists fill a very specific need regarding HIV/AIDS, and the fact that many of the interventions offered by healers such as Nabanji surface within musical performances surprises no one except those culturally distanced from traditional, rural practice.

The epidemiology of AIDS[5] in Uganda is enhanced when the deep cultural layers that contribute to diagnosis and care are acknowledged. These observations represent efforts to combat AIDS that governments and private organizations find inaccessible. External funds rarely trickle down to villages. Performances depicting jackfruit and banana weevils facilitate a deeper engagement with HIV/AIDS, and it is within such musical exchanges that medical interventions enter a community and stick.

Singing for Life is deliberately constructed to allow the reader multiple points of entry into the text, thus allowing for variance of interest and knowledge. The book presents a series of case studies framed within individual chapters that as a whole contribute to an understanding of the many ways Ugandan groups and individuals draw on musical and dramatic performances in their everyday lives as they interact with, understand, fight, and reconcile the position of HIV/AIDS in their lives. These case studies are supported by the introduction of a theme that draws on song texts, interviews, testimonies, and published reflections in order to establish a direct connection between music and local medical interventions regarding HIV/AIDS.

With the end of this prodromus I take a much needed and anticipatory gulp of air before launching directly into the story of *Singing for Life* in which the lives of those who have affected me so deeply in the development of my own responses to HIV/AIDS in Africa are introduced.

1

HIV/AIDS, JACKFRUIT, AND BANANA WEEVILS
Music and Medical Interventions in Uganda

I can hear wailing and people crying for help
We are all in danger, Ugandans
Let us pull up our socks—those who are still alive
Let us fight the disease that wants to destroy us
Many diseases have come to torture and mercilessly kill both the old and the young
Now is the time for those of us who can see into the future to stand and fight our hunters
Woe to us, woe to parents who bury their offspring
Our heads drip with pain
Who will bury us?
Who will help us when we are old, in the future when our bones are brittle?
Ah, wasteland, those villages that used to be inhabited

—Song performed at Meeting Point Kampala, Uganda

AT THE TIME OF THIS WRITING, 38 million people are infected with the HIV virus worldwide. Of this figure, over two-thirds, nearly 67 percent—or roughly 25.3 million children and adults—live in sub-Saharan Africa. Moving beyond the charts and diagrams that map global HIV infection rates, many more are *affected* by the HIV virus in African countries such as Uganda, where orphaned children, spouses, and entire communities suffer the affects of this deadly disease. According to a recent United Nations report, the *best* statistics among African nations reflect only a stabilization of overall infection rates. Such data are often eclipsed, however, by the staggering rise of HIV infections rates in countries such as South Africa, Namibia, Zimbabwe, Swaziland, and Botswana.[6] HIV

9

prevalence rates in sub-Saharan Africa confound any reasonable attempt to comprehend infection rates. As recent UNAIDS (Joint United Nations Program on HIV/AIDS) statistics demonstrate, the majority of Africans live in a world grossly out of sync with global infection rates. By the end of 2003, the *UNAIDS 2004 Report on the Global AIDS Epidemic* issued the following estimates for HIV and AIDS prevalence by geographic area:

North America	1,000,000
Caribbean	430,000
Latin America	1,600,000
Western Europe	580,000
North Africa and Middle East	480,000
Eastern Europe and Central Asia	900,000
East Asia	900,000
South and South-East Asia	6,500,000
Oceania	32,000
Sub-Saharan Africa	*25,000,000*

One country, however, continues to stand out since its initial, alarming infection rates were first documented—Uganda. The Republic of Uganda in East Africa, bordering Lake Victoria, stands outside all attempts to confound HIV infection rates. It is the single sub-Saharan African country that has successfully demonstrated a remarkable, constant decline in overall infection rates over the past years (see Table 1.1).

What makes Uganda unique in this regard? There are many ways to respond to this question due to the fact that many factors have contributed to the remarkable decline experienced in Uganda. *Singing for Life* focuses on a comprehensive, critical contribution that has developed as a significant response since start—music. Men, women, and children, traditional healers, witch doctors, and herbalists, as well as urban and rural residents alike all *sing* their response to AIDS, and have done so for quite some time. From the start, many Ugandans adopted the task of spreading information about the virus and disease within contexts of indigenous and newer popular forms of music, dance, and drama. Singing and dancing have, therefore, been among the earliest medical interventions introduced in the country concerning HIV. Within songs and dramas, Ugandans educate, care for, and console one another through music, and they have done so for decades.

> Most studies of prevention programmes in low and middle-income countries indicate that effective behaviour-change projects include educational and communications components, using a range of media, from traditional theatre and music, to global television and radio networks (Merson et al. 2000). Countries that have significantly reduced rates of

Table 1.1 UNAIDS Estimates of Adult (15–49 years) HIV Prevalence Rates 1997–2001.

Country	1997	1999	2001	Difference in Rates 1999–2001
Botswana	25.1%	35.8%	38.8%	3%
Burkina Faso	7.2	6.4	6.5	0.16
Burundi	8.3	11.3	8.3	−3
Cameroon	4.9	7.7	11.8	4.1
Central African Rep.	10.8	13.8	12.9	−0.9
Congo	7.8	6.4	9.7	3.3
Cote d'Ivoire	10.1	10.8	9.7	−1.1
Dem. Rep. of Congo	4.4	5.1	4.9	−0.2
Ethiopia	9.3	10.6	6.4	−4.2
Ghana	2.4	3.6	3	−0.6
Kenya	11.6	14	15	1
Lesotho	8.4	23.6	31	7.4
Malawi	14.9	16	15	−1
Mozambique	14.2	13.2	13	−0.2
Namibia	19.9	19.5	22.5	3
Nigeria	4.1	15.1	5.8	0.7
Rwanda	12.8	11.2	8.9	−2.3
South Africa	12.9	19.9	20.1	0.2
Swaziland	18.5	25.3	33.4	8.1
Togo	8.5	6	6	0
Uganda	9.5	8.3	5	−3.3
Tanzania	9.4	8.1	7.8	−0.3
Zambia	19.1	20	21.5	1.5
Zimbabwe	25.8	25.1	33.7	8.6

Source: UNAIDS (cited in R. Bennell 2003, 2).

new infections have typically invested heavily in AIDS education and awareness initiatives. (quoted in *UNAIDS 2004 Report on the Global AIDS Epidemic,* 14)

The popular response to HIV in Africa—often translated in dramatic fluctuations in pie charts and statistical diagrams—confounds many in the scientific communities as more Ugandans adopt positive behavioral changes in response to the *threat* of the AIDS pandemic.[7] I provide several definitions that help ground my usage of terms such as "pandemic" and "epidemic" throughout this text:

An *epidemic* is a rate of disease that reaches unexpectedly high levels, affecting a large number of people in a relatively short time. Epidemic is a relative concept: a small absolute number of cases of a disease is considered an epidemic if the disease incidence is usually very low. In contrast, a disease (such as malaria) is considered *endemic* if it is continuously present in a population but at low or moderate levels, while a *pandemic* describes epidemics of world-wide proportions, such as influenza in 1918 or HIV/AIDS today. (Barfield 1977, 150, quoted in Barnett and Whiteside 2002, 25, emphasis added)

UGANDA'S UNIQUE RESPONSE

A fertile, landlocked, water-rich nation of twenty-five million people, Uganda is currently governed by the National Resistance Movement—or NRM—a political organization[8] led by President Yoweri Kaguta Museveni. Nearly one-third of the population—and well over one-half of the total female population—is undereducated. The average fertility rate is seven children per woman in Uganda. The majority of the population exists on US$60 per month. It is estimated that 1.1 million Ugandans currently live with HIV or AIDS. Each year approximately 110,000 individuals die from the disease, which is transmitted for the most part through heterosexual intercourse.[9]

President Museveni seized control of the country in a bush war ending in 1986, and he promptly sent his soldiers to Cuba for further military training. The Cuba-based soldiers underwent routine physical examinations shortly after their arrival and it was soon revealed that over one-third of the troops were in fact HIV positive. As Greg Behrman suggests, Museveni rejected the early denial of AIDS demonstrated by other African countries and embraced an open, multisectoral response:

> The country's leader, Yoweri Museveni, had only recently seized the reins of political authority via military coup in January 1986. Having replaced the notorious despot Milton Obote, Museveni's regime was green and not yet entirely stable when he started to receive deeply disturbing reports from senior military officials. Fidel Castro, it seemed, citing incidence of mysterious, debilitating, and seemingly infectious disease, was returning Ugandan soldiers from Cuba, where for years they had gone to be trained. The reports jolted Museveni, still enormously reliant on the strength and stability of his military. It was the bulwark of his fledgling regime. Unlike almost all of his political contemporaries around the continent, Museveni did not indulge in denial. Losing little time, he launched an ambitious multisectoral—government, industry, religion, and civil society—effort aimed at combating the disease. Early acknowledgment and leadership would, over the following decade, make Uganda the archetypal success story. Museveni's early and comprehensive response helped curb the pandemic. (2004, 43)

The Ugandan president, new to his leadership of the country, had no formal health-care training or medical expertise. Realizing that he was in the middle of a severe medical catastrophe, Museveni launched a tireless campaign—with little outside funding or support—to address the scourge of AIDS in his country. At the time, AIDS was more often referred to as *Slim* (a verbal truncation of *Silimu*), due to the wasting effects the disease had on patients. The program established by Museveni became known as "ABC," and has subsequently been embraced by the Bush administration as the "answer" to addressing the AIDS crisis not only for Uganda, but for Africa as a whole.[10] According to Behrman, the ABC program "called on people, first to *abstain* from non-marital sex. If they wouldn't abstain, they must *be faithful*…if they wouldn't be faithful, they must use a *condom*" (2004, 113).

Practice **A**bstinence
Be faithful[11]
Use **C**ondoms

The ABC program has penetrated deep into the programming and curricular initiatives of educational institutions throughout the country, through national mandates for primary and secondary school education. An excellent example of how far this program has reached can be seen in the simple drama I recorded in the western town of Ishaka at the Kashenyi Model Primary School (see Figure 1.1). The English translation is transcribed below.

Kashenyi Model Primary School, Ishaka
Drama

Knock on the door
Father: Oh my children, please come in. Good evening Shira (Sheila).
Sheila: Good evening, Father.
Father: Good evening, Pete.
Peter: Good evening, Daddy.
Father: Mamaa Shira? Mamaa Shira?
Mother: Eee?
Father: Poor woman! Do you respond to your husband like that? Pete and Shira are back from school. Come with a drink.
Mother: Oh my children, welcome back from school. Good evening Shira and Peter.
Peter and Sheila: Good evening Mummy.
Mother: How was the day at school?
Peter and Sheila: Fine.
Father: Shira, what have you learned at school today?
Sheila: We learned about plants and animals.
Father: What about you, Peter?
Peter: We learned about a new disease called AIDS.

Father: What? AIDS? What does it stand for?

Peter: AIDS stands for Acquired Immune Deficiency Syndrome. It is a deadly disease caused by a virus called HIV. It has the following features—pneumonia, lung infection, cancer of skin and mouth, severe diarrhea, nerve disorders, and brain damage. Our teacher also said that the disease can be prevented by abstaining from sex, proper condom use, avoiding sex before marriage, avoiding sharp and piercing instruments such as razor blades, needles, and pins and by using sterilized needles and safe blood during transfusions.

Father: Thank you.

Billboards erected by government agencies in the late 1980s used images of coffins along with skulls and crossbones to make as strong a point as possible. Radio and television were used to broadcast messages specifically in line with the politically sanctioned ABC plan. In every public appearance, Museveni devoted a section of his speeches to ABC, regardless of the venue or subject of his speech. The government's militaristic all-out assault on AIDS has in large part been highly effective. The infection rate, at one time as high as 30 percent in Uganda,[12] has been lowered to its current level of 5 percent:

> One exception is Uganda, which has gained worldwide acclaim for its success in slowing down HIV's spread due to a high level of engagement by civil society and the government's own prevention efforts. There,

Figure 1.1 Children at the Kashenyi Model Primary School, Ishaka.

adult HIV seroprevalence rates have dropped from a peak of 18 percent in 1995 to around 5 percent at the end of 2001. The Bush administration has touted the Uganda prevention model, one that stresses sexual abstinence and monogamy, as a model for the world. Ironically, Uganda bears the sad distinction of having more AIDS orphans than any other country in Africa. In this county of 21 million, one in every ten people is a child orphaned by AIDS. That's an important reason why Ugandan civil society responded so strongly to the threat of AIDS, and why public health officials there were quick to embrace a program to prevent mother-to-child transmission (MTCT) of HIV. (D'Adesky 2004, 142)

In retrospect, this praise seems laudatory. Yet, at the time of Museveni's initial interventions there was considerable concern in the world community that failure on Museveni's part to control the fast-growing virus in Uganda would only worsen other African situations. Norman Hearst, professor of epidemiology at the University of California, San Francisco, reflects on the historical reception of Museveni's ABC plan:

Fortunately for Uganda, there weren't a lot of foreign experts telling them how to do things in the late 1980s and early 1990s. So they did things their own way. That's when Museveni was going around with his bullhorn telling people about "zero grazing" and, in the circles I travel (the so-called AIDS experts), everybody thought he was a clown, a buffoon. Everybody made fun of him. Well, it turns out he was exactly right, and we were all wrong. (quoted in McIlhaney 2004)

Yet "abstinence" and "faithfulness" are problematic concepts when promoting so-called "zero grazing." The suggestion implied is that the lack of faithfulness—perhaps grazing outside one's pasture—must necessarily result in something we all too comfortably label "promiscuity," which historian Maryinez Lyons suggests is problematic when applied to Ugandan contexts:

How objective is a term which includes among its meanings the notions of "indiscriminate," "haphazard," "casual" or "accidental" in connection with social relations? In fact, I suggest that the term cannot be used scientifically because it implies a notion of "standards," be they ethical, moral, legal, or scientific, to which no society could subscribe in unison. (Lyons 1997, 136)

With similar rhetoric, Cindy Patton questions the usefulness of campaigns that promote faithfulness in African contexts when "[I]n many African nations, the Global Programme on AIDS (GPA), national health ministries, nongovernmental organizations (NGOs), and local activists promoted a 'return to monogamy' instead of exploring the complex class, migration, and cultural patterns that concretely framed the epidemic" (2002, xii).

In a recent issue of the journal *Science,* Stoneburner and Low-Beer noted that, more than access to condoms, the great progress of the system adopted in Uganda for AIDS prevention was largely due to the effective transmission of medical and social information through well-established traditional social networks:

> Despite limited resources, Uganda has shown a 70% decline in HIV prevalence since the early 1990s, linked to a 60% reduction in casual sex. The response in Uganda appears to be distinctly associated with communication about acquired immunodeficiency syndrome (AIDS) through social network.... The Ugandan success is equivalent to a vaccine of 80% effectiveness. (2004, 714)

Molecular Biologist Helen Epstein focuses on the success in Uganda with promoting fidelity in sexual relations, particularly on the reduction of sexual partners among Ugandan men:

> Newspapers, theaters, singing groups and ordinary people spread the same message...Uganda's women's movement, one of the oldest and most dynamic in Africa, galvanized around issues of domestic abuse, rape and H.I.V. The anger of the activists, and the eloquent sorrow of women throughout the country who nursed the sick and helped neighbors cope, was a harsh reproach to promiscuous men. So was their gossip, a highly efficient method of spreading any public health message. (2004, 56)

Despite the very real need to address issues of men's roles in sexual relationships, AIDS is increasingly a woman's issue in the developing world,[13] with thirteen infected women in sub-Saharan Africa for every ten infected men according to the latest report from the United Nations. Delaying and abstaining from sexual activities and using condoms—the central tenets of the ABC plan adopted in Uganda and elsewhere—can be of limited affect with young girls and adult women. Young girls in particular are targeted quite heavily by organizations such as the Straight Talk Foundation in Uganda, organizations that use media and school-based initiatives to communicate social skills and healthy life choices. *Young Talk*, the magazine published by Straight Talk includes a cartoon strip, "Sara," the title character who serves as a role model for many Ugandan girls (see Mckee et al. 2003). For many women and girls, issues of power—cultural and economic—and the social dominance of men combine to jeopardize many women's attempts to negotiate safe health practices, specifically regarding condom usage. Issues surrounding the use of condoms by clients of female sex workers (FSWs), for example, highlight the cultural difficulties accompanying global expectations of health patterns. A recent study undertaken in the Nyanza Province of western Kenya attempted to survey condom use by regular clients of

FSWs. As the excerpt below indicates, the consistency of condom usage among FSWs and their clients (either casual or regular) problematizes our understanding of the depth with which the ABC plan can (or cannot) penetrate the grassroots in East Africa:

> [C]ondom use with regular or steady FSWs is very low, because regular sex workers are treated as wives, with whom using a condom is unacceptable because it tends to signal a lack of trust. This finding is confirmed by studies among sex workers: FSWs rarely use condoms with their boyfriends or regular partners. When a distinction is made between regular and one-time clients, they use condoms less often with regular clients than with one-time clients, but more than with boyfriends. The comparisons show that it is common in sub-Saharan Africa for clients to have steady FSWs and that this is often linked with low condom use....[T]his study in Nyanza province in Kenya revealed that clients of FSWs engage in high-risk behavior by maintaining several steady FSWs, with whom they often do not use condoms. Interventions therefore should target clients in bars, nightclubs, and lodges and should focus on convincing them to use condoms, with casual as well as steady FSW partners. (Voeten et al. 2002, 451)

Conflicting social and religious systems are often central to the aid and educational outreach efforts offered to African countries in the form of relief. In a recent interview with Gerry McCarthy in the online magazine *The Social Edge.com*, Diane Stinton relayed the distantiation that exists between life at the grassroots in rural East Africa and the moral and ethical values of foreign NGOs:

> A common sight in Kenya today is to see huge, brand-new four-wheel drive vehicles labeled this NGO or that NGO addressing AIDS. Also: there are regular conferences in five-star hotels for the so-called experts addressing HIV/AIDS. But what accountability is there in terms of what they're actually accomplishing on the ground? I also see many faith-based organizations doing tremendous work at the grassroots level. They're truly impacting their communities in the fight against AIDS. Yet often these organizations are not able to access funding from overseas, because they don't subscribe to the same agendas and values. One example: the use of condoms. (quoted in McCarthy 2004)

Similarly, in many remote Ugandan villages, women are in a powerless position regarding condom usage, even if they practice safe sex. Along the shores of Lake Victoria, for example, fishermen often come up from the lake and either buy sex from young girls or rape them, thereby reinserting the virus into the local population. The following personal field note illustrates the genesis of my own response to confronting the role of women within Museveni's ABC plan.

Three villages in one day. Every woman I met today openly pro-claimed that she was HIV positive. Every single one! By the end of the day I began to anticipate the response: "My name is so-and-so, and I am living positively with HIV." I asked Florence Kumunhyu, leader of BUDEA [Buwolomera Development Association], if every single woman in her village was infected, why then did they bother singing? Why bother dancing? She paused before responding to me, and her words moved me so much so that all I could do was nod my head: "Well, this singing is all we have left to give our daughters. At the same time we have to encourage the men to stop the cycle. We cannot give up or otherwise the cycle will never be broken."

I thought long and hard about my experiences in Buwolomera Village and the other two villages today along the long ride back to Iganga. The farming villages had no access to education or health care. Even if people wanted to leave the village for blood testing, the roads were all but impassable. There was no electricity, so how could one listen to radio broadcasts carrying messages about HIV/AIDS awareness unless one owned a portable—how then could one afford the cells [batteries]? When I asked a group of women in Buwolomera whether a medical doctor, nurse, or health-care professional had ever visited any of the villages in the area, they all shook their heads, indicating that none had. Everyone must make there way to town at considerable expense, I was told.

Florence told me that in order to entice men to listen to their performances, they have deliberately placed their messages within traditional cultural contexts that men are typically attracted to—song and dance. "Men will come and hear the drumming. They will come and watch the dancing," according to Florence....If messages can be communicated in such a subtle yet direct way, then these women are not only clever, they're saving lives.

For several decades the AIDS pandemic has been interpreted and reinter-preted in disparate local African contexts, and as the virus has strength-ened, been abated, uncoiled, and held in check across the continent, significant sectors of overall populations have been destroyed and entire generations have been wiped out, according to Emma Guest:

> Deadlier than war, deadlier even than malaria, AIDS is silently tearing Africa apart. The epidemic is throwing millions of households into tur-moil. Often the middle generation is wiped out, and children and the elderly are left to fend for themselves. (2003, ix)

The history of the public health crisis in Africa is still shallow in the memo-ries of many communities. Baseless rumors, obsolete and inappropriate healing practices, as well as misinformation passed along specifically by popular musicians have all combined to lead to the further spread of the virus. This is beginning to change, however. Localized graphic descriptions and slang terms for AIDS still abound in regional music, but those terms are often now clarifying rather than obfuscating the message. As mentioned earlier, AIDS can be locally interpreted by referencing aspects of the natural environment, such as a "banana weevil," an insect that eats its fruit from the inside out, or a "broom" or "sweeper," referring to the power the disease has to brush aside entire villages, or even "jackfruit," a way of likening the sticky fruit that is hard to wipe off one's hands to HIV.

"This baggage is too heavy," Walya Sulaiman cautions in a traditional song sung by members of PADA (People with AIDS Development Association) in Iganga town, after they enumerate several of the physical responses to the progression of the virus.

"Eitulilimuki?" ("What is in the luggage?")
PADA (People with AIDS Development Association)
Walya Sulaiman, leader

Someone wants to kill you
On arrival it comes with its own baggage
That one who wants to kill, when he comes he brings with him luggage
Those who are listening while you stand, find someplace to sit
And you here, those already seated, relax and I will narrate
The goal of my being here is to share with you some of this luggage
The goal of my being here is to narrate my sad experience
I did not want to die, but because of this luggage
I did not want to get sick, but because of this luggage
This baggage is too heavy, you cannot lift it
This baggage is too big, you cannot lift it
It really came for me, a poor man

This *Silimu* is wrong, it is a wrong disease
When it wants to make you sick, it sends opportunistic infections[14]
You feel headache, as it resolves the ears start to hurt
When the pain in the ears subsides, again backache sets in
As the backache subsides, again abdominal upset comes
As the abdominal upset resolves itself, profuse diarrhea begins
This *Silimu* is a real disease, it is a wrong disease indeed
It is after us, killing us
It selects by choice
When it arrives in a village, it selects indiscriminately
It has taken good men, it has taken good women
It has taken even young children, it has taken the rich people

> But even with the poor, this AIDS does not discriminate
> It came for me here, even though I am poor man
> Gentlemen, I ask you to safeguard yourselves against the disease

> Ladies, I urge you to safeguard yourselves against the disease
> I also urge you children to safeguard yourselves
> This disease is very bad
> I urge you politicians to help those victims within your reach
> I urge you relatives to take care of those patients within your reach
> Children, I urge you to safeguard yourselves against the disease
> It came for me, sincerely, I am here, a poor man, it came for me

This song resonates closely with the key theme of the 2002 World AIDS Day celebration—"AIDS has no cure, AIDS is a reality, AIDS does not discriminate." Walya Sulaiman—like so many others in Uganda—sing their songs for anyone who will listen. If there are children present, all the better. Sulaiman believes that in order for true social change regarding sexual behavior to occur, Uganda's children need to grow up in an informed world, one in which they have the necessary tools to fight the disease. Children suffer the most today in many African cultures. The future is not bright for many of the younger generation in Uganda, South Africa, and other countries torn apart by HIV/AIDS, creating a conflict according to Jeff Gow and Chris Desmond with the basic humanity of children:

> The impacts of the HIV/AIDS epidemic on children are numerous. Children will be infected, become ill and die, others will live to see their parents or other loved ones become increasingly sick and eventually succumb. Still more children will be affected by the impacts on the health, education and welfare system and all children will be affected in one way or another by widespread adult deaths and the broader economic implications of the epidemic. These impacts are violations of the basic rights of children. Many of these children already live in poverty and HIV/AIDS will serve only to make their bad situation worse. (2002, 207).

During the course of my field research trips I have often recorded the songs of schoolchildren, whether in Kampala, Uganda's capital city, or deep in the rural interior. On a recent trip to Kampala, a group of children at Kibuye Primary School presented a musical performance to me in preparation for the nation-wide annual school music competitions. Dressed in school uniforms but barefoot, dozens of young boys and girls carried an ensemble of musical instruments into a large classroom—panpipes, *akadongo* (lamellophones, "thumb pianos"), *engalabe* (long drums), *madinda* (xylophones), *adungu* (bow harps), and the *baakisimba* drum and other drums. As the performance began, I recognized "Anjorina" (also referred to as "Angelina"), a popular tune that I had heard several groups perform in the recent past. Performed in the style of the Acholi people of northern Uganda, specifically from the area of Gulu, "Anjorina"—included as Track 1—today appeals to audiences far beyond its original ethnic borders. The lyrics warn Anjorina to be careful how she holds her long, slender neck in public. Track 1 includes two performances of "Anjorina," opening with the Kibuye schoolchildren led by Centurio Balikoowa, followed by a group performance led by Okello Michael. "Anjorina" is an example of music's ability to transcend original contexts in order to become a part of everyday HIV/AIDS discourse.

> *Anjorina ye*   Angelina, eee
> *Kopucetwot Anying*   Let the program begin

Track 1 "Anjorina" ("Angelina")
  1. **Students at Kibuye Primary School, Kampala (Centurio Balikoowa, Tumwesigye, Amuza, Yusuf, Kagwa, Nasanga, and Doreen)**
  2. **Group performance led by Okello Michael**

Performances of "Anjorina" are intended to entertain as well as to educate young girls how not to be perceived as overtly sexual, suggesting that women should avoid tilting their heads in ways that can be possibly misconstrued as provocative. After the performance of "Anjorina" concluded I asked the school's principal why the students chose to sing this particular piece. "That's funny," he responded. "By singing 'Anjorina' you might think that we are merely teaching the children Ugandan culture through the music, but in fact, by being present in the room the children themselves are in a position to 'pick' the message. *You too* got the message, didn't you?"

A few years earlier, in the remote town of Ishaka in the western Bushenyi region of the country, my research team was engaged in an interview with a group of schoolchildren, ranging in age from six to sixteen, concerning ways in which AIDS awareness had penetrated the educational curriculum in Bushenyi when we were interrupted by a procession of preschool students marching across the schoolyard. As they passed, the young students' teachers asked what we were discussing. Hearing the topic, the head of the nursery school spoke to the children who quickly formed a chorus to sing for us. The young children sang several songs for us, such as the one included as Track 2, about condoms, blood testing, and the use of unsterilized instruments. The translation of one of their songs, "It All Started as a Rumor," below demonstrates a highly nuanced and scientific knowledge of the HIV virus.

Track 2 **"Bakabitandika nk'onigambo" ("It all started as a rumor")**
Kashenyi Nursery School Children

It all started as a rumor
The disease continued spreading
The rumors continued spreading
It all started as a rumor
The virus continued spreading as well
AIDS has become a serious problem!
Let us tell you the story of a person who refused to listen
Those who could spread the messages did so about AIDS
It is transmitted by unsafe blood transfusions
Unsterilized instruments
and unprotected sexual intercourse
One person, however, refused to hear
He went to a shop
Bought a dress for his girlfriend
Bought the most recent lotions—"Mufti and Revlon"
He bought these things at extravagantly high prices
When all he was buying was AIDS!
The man became infected with HIV
He lost all his charisma and strong will
He started selling his property looking for a cure!
AIDS cannot be cured in villages
Neither can medical doctors cure it!
The only cure is death and the hoe
Young boys and girls, we hope you have heard our message
Men and women, you can make the right choices or not
Adulterous and promiscuous people, you have nowhere to go
AIDS is finishing you
Ask God to forgive you

African children come to know AIDS under the most painful of circumstances. As I recorded these nursery school children—mostly two-, three-, or four-year-olds—I could not help but think of my own children, one just two years old at the time. What do children of this age know of condoms and the sex act in Europe and North America? What do they know about sharing unsterilized needles and blood transfusions? The head teacher of the preschoolers told me afterward that in order for medical information to *stick*, it has to be repeated and ingrained at a very early age. "And what better way for children to learn how to survive than by learning musical messages by rote." Leaving rural Bushenyi on the all-day drive back to Kampala on overcrowded buses I reflected not on the medical issues raised in the musical sounds of this seemingly innocent song, but on the problematic message inserted in the song's final line—"Ask God to forgive you." I remember being confused, knowing full well the power of such loudly proclaimed—and repeatedly internalized—religious sentiment, even when sung by innocent children.

Trained as an anthropologist and ethnomusicologist, I have often found myself on unfamiliar ground in my field research in Uganda—and not infrequently in the thick of a highly charged, political, and at times life-and-death international debate. In my graduate-school training during the so-called anthropological "crisis of representation," in which all authority and privilege to represent "the Other" was questioned, I—like many others—began to question our ability to research and observe subjects objectively, take innocent field notes, leave no footprints, do no harm, or refrain from meddling. Despite all original intentions, I now often find myself involved and immersed in political issues related to HIV/AIDS in Uganda. Invited to a national musical event while recently in Kampala, I sat in the audience as the director of the Ugandan AIDS Commission personally thanked me, the "American professor," for "teaching us that music, dance and drama are the most effective tools for fighting AIDS in our country." By restating the director's proclamation I by no means mean to suggest that it was "I" who brought this phenomenon to the attention of many of the groups with whom I have worked. Quite the opposite. I have merely been persistent in noting such occurrences and have engaged discussions that highlight such issues, such as demonstrated in Florence Mahoro's column in the *AIC News*: "Educational talks help members improve their knowledge of HIV/AIDS, Reproductive Health and other health-related issues like PMTCT (Prevention of Mother to Child Transmission) and Anti-retroviral drugs…Drama provides therapy for the members involved in the rehearsals and performances and those who watch the shows" (2002, 16). In fact, I was dumbstruck by the Uganda AIDS Commission medical director's statement. I had never publicly stated, "This is what you should be doing!" I have merely been relentless in the pursuit of answers to my questions, as I have tried to identify key issues at play for individuals and communities.

MORE THAN A MEDICAL CRISIS

It bears repeating that HIV/AIDS in sub-Saharan Africa is a widespread social phenomenon largely resulting from deep cultural issues related to conflicts between local and foreign health care systems. In Africa HIV/AIDS has principally been a medical concern, despite the indigenization of AIDS in local African contexts.

Musical testimonies such as that offered by Walya Sulaiman as the soloist in "Akawa kangema" and by the women of BUDEA in Buwolomera Village—whose performance of " Luno olumbe lwa twidhira" is included on Track 3—do more than merely entertain local village residents. The songs performed by PADA, BUDEA, and other groups in Uganda are compelling interventions in communities that embrace multiple medical, spiritual, and societal truths regarding HIV/AIDS. In the text to "Akawa kangema" given below, Walya Sulaiman and members of PADA sing about the spread of HIV/AIDS in the village in the form of a personal testimony (see Figure 1.2).

"[Akawa] Kangema" ("I caught the virus")
Walya Sulaiman and members of PADA

I caught the virus at home and then I had a problem
I caught the virus at home and thought I was dying
Relax, as I narrate this point
This point is very strong
I used to spend my days at home mourning the disease and in fear
I used to spend my days at home thinking of nothing but suicide
But then I would remember my children
There was a day when my sister came to my home and told me
That I should go to IDAAC[15] in Iganga
IDAAC looks after many AIDS victims
What follows I narrated to my aunt
My aunt later stopped me from going to IDAAC
She stopped me from even trying to go to IDAAC or TASO[16]
Saying that people who go there, their years are cut off
The drugs they give out from there (IDAAC and TASO)
They bear the sign of a spade and of a grave on the cover
When you take their drugs you spend only a limited time on earth
My aunt convinced me, and I was banned from going to either IDAAC
or TASO
But friends, what rescued me was sensitization and counseling
I used to fear drugs, but after PADA taught me I no longer fear
I used to fear food, but after PADA taught me I no longer fear
I used to fear IDAAC, but after PADA taught me I went to IDAAC
I used to fear TASO, but after PADA taught me I went to TASO
But my aunt, sincerely that aunt of mine
She tried to convince me that the tablets kill very fast
That their food facilitates your death
She is the one who has killed you
When she stopped you from going for sensitization and counseling
She is the one who had killed you
When she stopped you from going where there is peace

Figure 1.2 Walya Sulaiman and members of PADA.

On Track 3 the members of BUDEA empathize with the sorrow felt by many in the community, but urge all to assume responsibility for individual knowledge of the disease:

Track 3 "Luno olumbe lwa twidhira" ["This disease came for us"] Buwolomera Development Association (BUDEA)

Introductory Comments
What is the club I hear is in Buwolomera?
Buwolomera Development Association, in short BUDEA.
Why was this association established?
To uplift the situations of those who are sick,
And to educate the people in the community, starting here in Buwolomera.
Do you think that Buwolomera has the highest number of AIDS patients?
No, but when Jesus came, he said that you should always start with your people.

Song Starts
Solo—What has she said?
Chorus—How can I walk with Jesus, how can I walk alone?
Solo—Sincerely this disease is it!
Chorus—This disease came for us.
Sincerely Ugandans, our friends, we are in sorrow.
It has combined the adults with the young.
More so, it is a shameful disease to talk about.

Solo—If you have knowledge about the disease, please tell us.
Chorus—Do not say that we are no longer scared.
Talking about it brings more sorrows,
But since you asked us to tell you properly, then you sit comfortably and we will tell you.
This disease, sincerely it came to finish us.
Solo—Sincerely the disease!
Chorus—This disease came for us.
Sincerely Ugandans, our friends, we are in sorrow.
It has combined the adults with the young.
More so it's a shameful disease to talk about.
When you catch the virus it is fearful,
But when we catch it we are no longer ashamed.
When we came to know about it we felt more sorrows.
Now that we are use to it we no longer have problems.
Even you people here.
We are telling you that when you catch it, you need to know.
You can maintain yourself and push ahead for some drugs.
Solo—Sincerely this disease!
Chorus—This disease came for us.
Sincerely Ugandans, our friends, we are in sorrow.
It has combined the adults with the young.
More so, it is a shameful disease to talk about.
Solo—What shall we girls do who have not married?
Chorus—It is still a problem.
More so, there is no treatment.
But, those who are unmarried should take a HIV test with their lovers.
And take the HIV test with those they are to marry.
Solo—Sincerely this disease!
Chorus—This disease came for us.
Sincerely Ugandans, our friends, we are in sorrow.
It has combined the adults with the young.
More so, it is a shameful disease to talk about.
Solo—Where are you from you fellows who have this problem?
Chorus—We are from Iganga, here in Buwolomera.
The disease has us, and we have no peace.
But now we have come out with our sorrow so that you people who are still lucky can give us a hand.
Solo—Like you distinguished guests sitting here.
Chorus—Wololo, the outcry is directed to you.
But now we have come out with our sorrow so that you people who are still lucky can give us a hand.
Solo—Like you distinguished guests who have reached us.
We are asking you to give us a hand.

According to Sulaiman, drama has long been an intrinsic aspect of the dissemination of information in his area of the country, and it is often within performances of dances, dramas, and songs such as that given above in Track 3 that historical traditions for conveying information are reinforced and maintained. As such, doctors and health-care workers often recognize music as a more localized and thus more affective medical intervention than outreach efforts taking the form of lectures and seminars.

In addition to acknowledging a variety of interventions regarding HIV/AIDS, most Ugandans juggle a wide range of acceptance of and tolerance for spiritual and traditional health-care practitioners. Many urban residents and those affiliated with faith-based communities in rural communities often publicly denounce the efforts of tradition healers regarding HIV/AIDS. Publicly, this is certainly true. Privately, however, people often avail themselves of a variety of healing systems, especially when HIV is involved. And there is often less stigma attached to seeking the counsel of traditional healers than people admit, as the following excerpt from the newsletter of the Uganda Network of AIDS Service Organisations suggests:

> [T]raditional health practitioners are known, trusted and respected as key members of the community in most regions of this planet. As in many other African countries, healers vastly outnumber biomedical workers in Uganda. As indigenous resource persons, healers command respect and a unique knowledge that can positively influence protective health behavior. ("THETA—Working with Traditional Healers to Increase Access to HIV/AIDS Prevention and Care in Uganda" 2002, 6)

Hajji Ssentamu, director of BAPET (Bwakeddempulira AIDS Patients Educational Team; see Figure 1.3) is another tradition healer—or "traditional *doctor*" as he prefers—who believes in the power of music to "pound the message home," as he suggests, that is, music is able to confirm for him that critical health-care information "lasts in the brain." Ssentamu, like others, has participated in the training programs offered by THETA (Traditional and Modern Health Practitioners Together Against AIDS and Other Diseases; see chapter 5 for more details on THETA) and holds strong the view that music has the ability to communicate the disadvantages of AIDS, as well as ways in which one can avoid the disease and how to live positively once one is diagnosed with HIV. In addition, Ssentamu feels that after positive test results are confirmed, musical and dramatic performances can be used to counsel, especially to highlight the fact that it is a "crime," in his words, to pass the virus along to others once one's HIV status is known.

Ssentamu collaborates with all social service units present in his community as do many others at the grassroots that deal with HIV/AIDS from

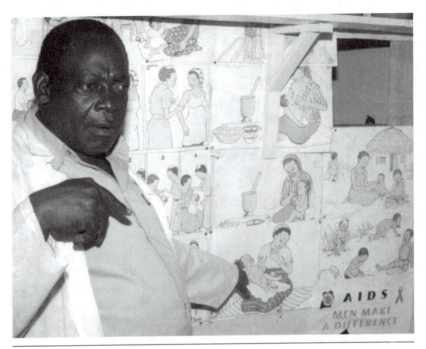

Figure 1.3 Hajji Ssentamu, BAPET.

the standpoint of traditional healing. He has formed a performing group comprised of local youth, clients, families of clients, and local residents to help him communicate his messages. In the following excerpt from an interview, Ssentamu relates the frustrations of conflicting philosophical approaches to HIV/AIDS that exist between religious and faith healers, as well as a sadness for the overwhelming medical needs of his community and country:

> *Ssentamu—Here in Uganda, it is we traditional healers who have helped the government of Uganda in treating AIDS with our traditional herbs. This is because people in Masindi and everywhere else use the medicine. Unfortunately the government has not yet thought about us down here, the herbalists. For that reason we have our <u>kiganda</u> drums [drums of the Baganda people]. Actually even though we are the most active people, we are the people working with the most hardships.*
>
> *We work together with THETA and other organizations in Kisenyi. I deal with many medical outreach centers when a patient comes to me complaining of fever or diarrhea. I send my patients out to them for a blood test so that I can treat someone from an informed*

position. Here in Uganda there is no disease that heals completely. When fever heals it soon comes back. A diabetic patient lives on injections, while one's blood pressure fluctuates between high and low. Even with this virus [HIV] there is no one who can claim to heal it. We just need to fight it until we weaken it so that people can live longer. As for me, I do not deal with those claiming to heal AIDS.

The AIDS situation in Uganda has been on a declining trend recently, but some evangelical groups may in fact undo that progress. We tell them that there is no medicine for AIDS, that it is just being kept down for a short time. But when preaching in public, some of the evangelicals say they are able to heal AIDS, asking people to come forward to be prayed for. I had five patients who went to the late Balabyekubo. They came back claiming they had been healed completely and have resumed making love to others saying they will not need my medicine. I warned them, but after only three months one died while another one got ill. So, if we did not have "confusers" claiming that in Luke, chapter four in the Bible, AIDS can be healed, well . . . we will be on a better course only when people are better informed. There are also witch doctors whose primary objective is money. An AIDS victim will usually pay anything as long as healing is promised, even five hundred thousand shillings. They will pay it.

Since I am a doctor and herbalist, I feel for the patients so much, just as you see these certificates for the support group—diarrhea, diabetes. Unlike AIDS, I can successfully treat those conditions. The one from THETA certifies my support group and says that I can give counseling services. We need assistance from those NGOs and organizations because we must accomplish so much without the government's financial assistance. That shows how I feel for my country. The organizations that assist NGOs should consider us in their programs instead of giving more only to TASO, an older, more mature NGO.

What I know about AIDS is that one should not delay. When fever comes one should go to the hospital for treatment. The same way for syphilis. But the first generation of AIDS victims was stigmatized. When people saw an AIDS patient, oh my goodness! AIDS was so shocking for us! People would experience shock in addition to the pain. It used to be considered disgusting. Even preachers would say, "let us pray for our friends who were tempted by the devil and got infected with AIDS," and they would pray this way in public!

The witch doctors' job is mostly to wrestle with ancestral spirits. One needs to know something about science, to be taught about medicine, before one can give counseling or treatment to AIDS patients.

You have to know how the virus is transmitted and how one can avoid getting infected so that by the time you collect the herbs, you know what you are up against and what you are able to treat and what you are not able to treat.

The problem with we traditional herbalists is that most of our patients die from extreme poverty. Once a patient is dismissed from work, his family might abandon him. The wife might think he could possibly infect the children. So we get such people and attempt to remodel their lives anew. I do not have much assistance that I can offer to them. They need to work on their own sustenance. We need sewing machines or something else that can bring in money for patients, such as with TASO. But with these smaller groups, there are a large number of people. Many of them have failed to be treated by TASO so they come here, maybe when there is no more assistance available at TASO.

The biggest number of people suffering is down here in the villages. They are poor. They come to us when they do not have anything else. They come with three or five thousand shillings for any assistance we can offer so that they can live longer.

During a performance of Ssentamu's drama group, a young woman turned to me as we sat next to each other on a bench watching a dance performance and pointed to several older women who had joined the vigorous dancing taking place. "You see, professor, we *dance our disease.* There is nothing else we can do." I was reminded of observations made on several occasions by Barbara Browning (1998, 15), specifically regarding the ability of dance to politicize or heighten awareness of issues that either cannot be voiced or will not be readily apparent: "In *Samba: Resistance in Motion,* I argued that…'*it is the suspension or silencing of a beat which provokes movement.*' My argument there was that dance often articulates apolitical consciousness which has been silenced" (208, 28n). As I watched the elderly women dance while Ssentamu met with patients, I found myself listening not to silent beats, but to the deafening sound of silence of the collective disease.

THE POLITICS OF KNOWLEDGE—FIELDWORK, ETHNOMUSICOLOGY, REPRESENTATION

Because of the sensitive nature of my field research, necessary precautions have been adopted throughout this text to protect individual or group anonymity when necessary; one's HIV status remains a serious matter in Uganda as stigmatization, although fought aggressively, is still a very present reality for many in the society, especially among children. Often, however, I transcribe and represent the voice of an individual who is "living positively," that is someone who has discarded the burden associated with the label of being HIV positive and adopted an "open" approach to his or her sero blood status. (The cultural phenomenon of "positive living" and how it differs from being "HIV positive" is discussed in greater detail in chapter 2). Many, if not most, of my field colleagues in Uganda are living positively and would find it odd if I hid their identities or masked or changed their names. Those who I represent with their real names are, therefore, individuals who feel that an even greater contribution can be made by appearing as themselves in this text, whether HIV+ or HIV–. All understood this issue of representation while working with me and all whose real names are given supported the efforts to publish this study.

Singing for Life was intended from the start to reach several different audiences. While it draws heavily from the ethnographic theory and practice of the academic disciplines of ethnomusicology and anthropology, the chapters were conceptualized and written with a general readership in mind, hence no single disciplinary language of obfuscation is adopted. Those interested in elements of African expressive culture will find the case studies and recorded musical examples of interest. For others more interested in analyses of indigenous health-care responses and initiatives in which music, dance, and drama function as medical interventions, there are entire sections devoted to such. For those curious about emergent cultural theories, sections are included that document ways in which music is mapped on to local cultural beliefs by many communities.

Ethnomusicologists have long grappled with defining, rejecting, and re-defining the fundamental tenets of their discipline. One principle long embraced, however, maintains that the production of knowledge (and the representation of meaning derived from knowledge) should be drawn from lived experience (through a process often labeled "participant observation"), and that such experience is derived from time spent in a place referred to rather simply and in an unproblemitized way as "the field." Separation from one's "home" occurs in the field within encounters with "the Other," representing for many the creation of a sacred, albeit empty space. In such a conceptualization of field research, this empty space leaves a void that allows for the acquisition (and hopefully exchange) of understanding gained through familiarity. Yet fieldworkers are seldom unburdened with the weight of intent and expectation. Whether it is a graduate student collecting data to support degree-writing requirements or the institutionally funded fieldworker conducting vetted and sponsored research, each carries expectations for the outcome of their efforts. Anticipated results that developed out of my earliest interactions with rural and urban communities in Uganda were just as overt;

I specifically approached the efforts of those fighting for social change regarding health care in such a way that the only sincere representation available to me would easily (and surely rightfully) appeal not only to academic audiences, but also to donor, relief, religious, and aid-giving agencies in both public and private sectors. As a way of addressing this goal *Singing for Life* was purposefully conceptualized in such a way as to introduce a variety of voices that communicate within a variety of styles. When writing from the perspective of a scholar and cultural theorist, I deliberately chose not, therefore, to eschew the concomitant masks of cultural advocate and health-care activist at any point. To do so would be academically disingenuous and not take into account the responsibilities I have assumed in the maintenance of relationships (personal and medical) with many key field colleagues in Uganda.

Today, ethnomusicologists increasingly represent musical phenomena as products of the personal experiences of the ethnomusicologist emerging from within relationships in the field. No scholars do this more effectively than Michelle Kisliuk in her insightful ethnography based on experiences with the Central African BaAka people (1997) and Carol Babiracki in her studies of the "self" versus the "Other" and gender issues in terms of field relationships in India (1997). Yet the fact that writer-scholars of ethnographic texts affect, encourage, or even acknowledge changes, problems, or issues that may arise due to our presence are seldom admitted and only rarely documented (for a recent, thorough treatment of this issue see Cooley 2003). Motivation that might easily be labeled as activistic in its agenda is seldom embraced for fear, I assume, that accusations of "going native" or losing one's objectivity (or, indeed, not being "scientific" enough to maintain one's academic position) might be attached to the fieldwork efforts of a particular ethnomusicologist. That ethnomusicology can (and should?) be an ideologically messy affair hardly needs to be stated. Ethnomusicologists have the responsibility to become entangled—if not embedded—within the "politics of knowledge," as anthropologists Susan Reynolds Whyte and Harriet Birungi suggest, with the intent of "causing eyes and ears to open in ways that they might not have before" (2000, 144). Thus, the goal of participant-observation as a field research methodology in ethnomusicology can (and often does) very easily extend beyond reflection to embrace engagement, involving active participation in initiatives that focus on issues of authority, public interest, and the quality and condition of human lives, perhaps politicizing to a greater extent that which anthropologist Mary Catherine Bateson refers to (perhaps stated oversimply) as "the disciplined use of a species of informal learning" (2003, B5).

My field research in Uganda has ranged from intensive work in rural village networks to long-term "living" in Kampala—the nation's capital—allowing for frequent trips to visit consultants and drama groups in outlying areas. The variety of approaches to fieldwork modalities adopted (as outlined throughout this text) in my research range from living with colleagues in Uganda to having colleagues live and stay with me in the United States, adding several additional layers to the contemporary adage of many a fieldworker, "there is no *there* there." In fact, as Daniel Reed points out in his recent ethnography of Dan Ge performance in Côte d'Ivoire, the parameters of research are wide, and fieldwork is never really over (just as it surely never really begins): "Fieldwork is, in reality, just living—albeit a specially framed and focused kind of living—that does not end when we return from some metaphoric 'field'" (2003, 8).

One of the most interesting twists that occurred in my field research is surely a normative occurrence for many ethnomusicologists. Ugandan musician Centurio Balikoowa has been my principal collaborator and research colleague over the years. Our joint activities have included intensive interviewing, recording, and working in remote village communities. Balikoowa, a secondary school teacher in Kampala and trainer for many school musical groups, has come to the United States to perform and work with "my" students in "my" university, while I have devoted a substantial amount of print space dedicated to telling "his" story (and by extension, "my" story; see the chapter on Balikoowa in Barz 2004, *Music in East Africa*). We have become coauthors of a monograph on Ugandan music (among other efforts), and our colleagueship has led to a friendship that moves beyond the cliché of being—in his words—brothers. The twist I mentioned earlier involves the fact that in addition to being a research colleague, Balikoowa has also been my music teacher from the start. Much, if not all, that I know about Ugandan musical performance has been filtered through some form of interaction with Balikoowa. Balikoowa taught me my *endingidi* (tubefiddle) repertoire, my *ntongoli* (bowl-lyre) playing style is a product of Balikoowa's tutelage, and my knowledge of *amadinda/embaire* (xylophone) performance traditions draws on my experiences playing alongside of Balikoowa. My research in village performance contexts has not only been informed by the participation of Balikoowa, but my understanding of and appreciate for the musical traditions that I have studied have also been filtered through my experiences of learning through Balikoowa.

With Balikoowa and a team of medical doctors a research methodology was designed to approach issues related to the Ugandan use of traditional and modern forms of music, dance, and drama to address the country's devastation due to the HIV/AIDS pandemic. Various permutations of this methodology were adapted for differing circumstances during the course of fieldwork as I interviewed and interacted with individuals and groups, as well as documented dramas, musical performances, and historical dances. As my research became increasingly focused on the use of music as medical intervention, a series of questionnaires was devised in consultation with health-care professionals—doctors, clinicians, and nurses—who both vetted the research methodology and participated in the data collection. My documentation of 150 interviews consisting of DAT recordings, digital videos, and photographs (both 35mm and digital) serves as the source for much of my analysis and interpretation in tandem with both my experiences and those of my research colleagues. The documentation frequently served as a tool for reflection among research colleagues allowing collective interpretation to occur, as well as affording opportunities for "in the field" translation.

"YES, THIS IS AFRICA, BUT IT'S NOT ALWAYS ABOUT RHYTHM"

Since the topic of this study is intentionally broad in theoretical and territorial scope, the specifics of musical performance may not seem, at first glance, to be among the most essential elements for analysis. This does not mean, however, that the explicitly sonic aspects of performance do not dictate a community's response to messages, information, and sentiment. Quite the contrary. After working for weeks transcribing and notating musical and dramatic performances in the eastern Busoga region of Uganda, Centurio Balikoowa responded to my query about a particular dance rhythm: "Yes, this is Africa, but it's not always about rhythm, Professor." Balikoowa was agitated in his response, and when I asked him to explain what he meant he made it clear that our work together among a plurality of women's groups, youth groups, NGOs, and health outreach programs was in his mind more about determining a community's initiatives and *responses* to music, dance, and drama, and not really *about* the performances themselves, not about music-as-sound.[17]

About midway through my first field research trip to Uganda, I began to suspect that the sonic aspects of expressive culture that were so intriguing to me and that are so very central to many of the groups and individuals with whom I had been working, would be much less important in the representation of the larger theoretical phenomenon represented in this study. As I continued to crisscross the countryside, entering and exiting distinct cultural communities, it became increasingly clear to me that more important than an individual community's choice of musical selection was the phenomenon of the use of music, dance, and drama in the first place. I am convinced that telling this broader story is much more important at this point in time. There is room, welcome space in fact, for more detailed documentation and nuanced case studies of similar phenomena within an individual culture, ethnic group, or even city or community. Thus, when specific sonic elements of music—rhythms, melodies, etc.—do appear in the text it is with the intent of demonstrating an example of how *one* group or individual addresses a musical issues and thus should not be globalized from the local example.

At the time of Balikoowa's statement about rhythm I thought long and hard about its implications for my research study. Of course I understood what he meant, but for some reason it still made me uncomfortable. Several days later, while drinking a room temperature Chairman's ESB (Extra-Strong Brew) at the Rest Easy Hotel in Iganga town, I returned to the issue of "African rhythm" and suggested to Balikoowa that in fact he might be right. Our research efforts had from the start clearly been about the "issue" and not about the "sound" of the issue. But, I asked him to consider whether the women with whom we had been working for the past weeks made specific *localized* choices about what music and which dances to include in their dramas. I asked if the women used specific *localized* musical instruments and played and tuned them in *locally* distinct ways. Finally I asked if women drummed in specific, *localized* ways, yes "rhythms," to attract others to their performances. After a pause, we both agreed and came to terms with ways in which communities make specific cultural choices when performing. And as Balikoowa ordered two more Chairman's, he brought the conversation to a close: *"Yeah, I guess in fact it is a bit funny to think of this research as having **everything** to do with rhythm and music while at the same time having **nothing** to do with it at all."*

PATHS, ROUTES, AND DIRECTIONS

There are several different approaches one can take through this text. The logic of the linear progression that I have laid out may appeal to some while others will choose alternate, more circuitous routes through the text—and this may very well lead to unexpected ways of understanding the materials. *Singing for Life* presents a series of case studies framed within individual chapters that as a whole contribute to an understanding of the many ways Ugandan groups and individuals draw on musical and dramatic performances in their everyday lives to interact with, understand, fight, and reconcile the position of HIV/AIDS in contemporary

Uganda cultures. These case studies are supported in each chapter by the introduction of a specific theme that draws on song texts, interviews, testimonies, and published reflections in order to establish a direct connection between music and medical interventions.

Interspersed between the chapters are interludes that present extended excerpts from interviews with musicians or health-care workers, artwork, testimonies, or song texts. The inclusion of these interludes—presented as much as possible without significant reflection or interpretation—is meant to provide the reader with opportunities to experience several of the profound voices of individuals who work tirelessly at the grassroots to affect change in the lives of those who are already HIV positive as well as those who may still have a fighting chance to avoid infection.

The stories of individuals and communities included in this book are presented in a variety of ways in order to illustrate the complexities of the subject matter with compassion and consideration of the rights for anonymity of an individual. The inclusion of first-person reflections and personal field notes are not meant to distract. Rather the intention is to draw the reader deeper into the experiences of the social phenomena as others and I have experienced them. Other voices in the text are presented in direct English translation excerpted from interviews, in quotation from a previous publication, the inclusion of song texts, and the translation and transcription of dramatic texts. Interviews, dramas, songs and other musical performances that appear in the text thus represent experience in both direct and indirect ways.

Chapter 2, "What You Sing Nourishes Your Body Like Food," introduces issues relating music to the study of HIV/AIDS in Africa in general and in Uganda in specific. In addition, the Ugandan concept of "positive living"—rather than living one's life as merely "HIV positive"—is underscored. An attempt is also made in this chapter to problematize the term "music" by invoking its varying meanings and exploring the different ways music is used, received, and understood among Ugandans. The meaning of music is exploded in this way to allow room for localized understandings of the power of music to heal and to persuade others to allow healing to occur. In addition, the concept of an academic disciplinary approach labeled "medical ethnomusicology" is introduced and defined, providing a foundation for exploring how such academic nomenclature can expose human experiences of local health issues to new and different levels of cultural understanding. Immediately following this chapter is an interlude that presents a portion of an interview with the young Ugandan doctor Alex Muganzi Muganga. The doctor—my companion and field colleague on many research trips to rural villages—provides details concerning the history of HIV/AIDS in Uganda and a valuable interpretation of the history of the AIDS pandemic in sub-Saharan Africa.

Chapter 3, "No One Will Listen To Us Unless We Bring Our Drums! AIDS and Women's Music Performance in Uganda," provides case studies that demonstrate the use of music as medical intervention particularly among women's groups. Song texts are translated and various foci of the performances are analyzed in order to approach the persuasive power adopted by many women in Uganda today. Women and women's indemnity groups are forced to confront the HIV virus and AIDS disease in ways in which local governments and private multinational and multilateral NGOs are challenged.[18] Throughout this chapter the *link* between the recent decline in Uganda's HIV infection rate and the grassroots efforts of rural women's groups is shown to be never far beneath the surface. A transcribed interlude is presented following chapter 3 in which the women of Nawaikoke Village perform a powerful song about strength and healing.

Chapter 4, "'Today We Have Naming of Parts': Languaging AIDS Through Music," focuses on the mobilization of youth groups in the country and on their efforts to educate and counsel their peers. Several performances of testimonies are analyzed; in addition, song and drama texts are translated and demonstrated to be quite different from the oral texts used by nonyouth groups. The primary thrust of this chapter presents a detailed analysis of how indigenized terminologies related to HIV and AIDS have emerged and are maintained in local performances. In addition, this chapter's "naming of parts" is extended to include a discussion of the localization of understandings surrounding condoms and other interventions among youth in Uganda. Following this chapter an interlude is included in which members of the Bukato Youth Fellowship reflect on the power of music, dance, and drama to motivate young people to respond to interventions that could lead to behavioral change.

Chapter 5, "'Singing in a Language AIDS Can Hear': Music, AIDS, and Religion," introduces issues related to the involvement of Ugandan religious and faith-based initiatives in HIV/AIDS care and counseling. Issues related to HIV/AIDS are problematic for many religious institutions, but the case studies in this chapter demonstrate specific examples of individuals and organizations that have taken the matter in their own hands. *Slim* was originally conceptualized as a "strange" disease, and initial reactions were of fear and denial. The epidemic resulted in numerous other reactions; among them was the belief that AIDS was a form of punishment or curse from God. Institutionalized faith-based communities initially assumed only a minor role, if at all, in HIV prevention due to the belief held by different churches that the disease was a form of divinely induced punishment. Only when church leaders, elders, and other influential people in church hierarchies started dying did churches begin addressing the issue. A former archbishop of Uganda suggested that churches must begin to "speak a language that AIDS can hear." Music and dancing now more than ever facilitate opportunities to connect with spiritual lives, to get outside of one's self and one's wounded body, to reach out, and to communicate a unique and positive attitude. In response, this chapter explores the often-interdependent roles of traditional healers, churches, and mosques in musical performances of faith, hope, and healing regarding HIV/AIDS. At the conclusion of this chapter an interlude highlights a conversation with the lively and passionate director of VOLSET (Voluntary Service Trust Team), Francis Baziri who discusses ways in which music and drama support the grassroots efforts of his team to educate local communities about HIV/AIDS.

Chapter 6, "Re-Memorying Memory: HIV/AIDS and the Performance of Cultural Memory" addresses issues related to memory within an ongoing process of engagement and change by introducing cases in which multiple memories, or multiple ways of "memorying" are engaged within musical performances. Changes in and adaptation of memory—a process referred to rather inelegantly as "re-memorying"—often combine active memory work with intentional manipulation. Positioning memory within a social activity (the act of "re-memorying") engaged in the present suggests that the passive notion of "collective memory" may be an artificial construction. The need to remember—to maintain and disseminate objects of social memory—is forefronted in the lives of many Ugandans, women specifically, as many confront their own mortality and impending deaths of those around them. In this chapter I approach ways in which re-memorying functions within musical performances. Memory-as-process is inherently performative, and it is within the *performance* of memory, as Paul Connerton suggests, that memory is activated when it is recalled, conveyed, and sustained (1991). Efforts to preserve and maintain what are typically labeled "collective memories"—what Marita Sturken, Mieke Bal, and others refer to more directly as "cultural memories"—often result in a performative effort in Uganda, within songs, dances, or dramas: "cultural recall is not merely something of which you happen to be a bearer but something that you actually *perform*, even if, in many instances, such acts are not consciously and willfully contrived" (Bal 1997, vii). Yet, within any performance of cultural memory a reshaping of the past occurs, thus changing any future and present understanding of the past.

Figure 1.4 Member of the TASO Drama Group offers her personal testimony in a sensitization outreach effort.

A final interlude leads directly into the book's conclusion by introducing the voices of a group of TASO counselors—all members of the TASO Drama Group—as they perform their personal testimonies (see Figure 1.4).

The oral art of the testimony persuades many who listen to adopt behavioral changes and to seek health-care counseling. Such testimonies clearly indicate that all forms of communication (direct and indirect) are taken seriously by youth, especially those who take the leap of joining the TASO Drama Group, a very public way of acknowledging one's HIV status.

Interlude 1
Testimony — Florence Kumunhyu

Figure Interlude 1.1 Florence Kumunhyu—Founder, Coordinator, BUDEA (Buwolomera Development Association), Buwolomera Village.

I first got sick in 1988, and soon thereafter in 1990 my husband died. In October of 1990 I decided to enroll in a counselor-training course to become a HIV/AIDS counseling aide with IDAAC [Integrated Development Activities and AIDS Concern] in Iganga town. At the same time I was consulting with the LC [Local Council] leaders as to whether they would allow me to start my work by sensitizing the Buwolomera village community about HIV/AIDS, which they happily agreed to. But at that time in the early 1990s there was a still a significant degree of stigma and shame in our village area. In the beginning it was so difficult because for every person I attempted to talk to or when I called at their home, the other members of our community would think that the person to whom I was talking must also be HIV positive since I was the first person in my village to declare openly that I had tested positive for the virus.

As time went on, people started responding, and the numbers continue to grow today as you can see from those gathered around us here in the village. I started the main activities of BUDEA in October of 2000, while the drama group started the following month, November of 2000. With the help of IDAAC we were able to start a poultry farm as a successful IGA [Income Generating Activity] to support our efforts. We sold the first birds and bought groundnut seeds, which we planted. Right now, the drama club has fifty-six members and we sing and perform dramas for anyone who will listen. We even perform for those who will not listen.[19]

2

"WHAT YOU SING NOURISHES YOUR BODY LIKE FOOD"

The solidarity of women in rural African communities may be their
greatest source of strength for coping with the AIDS epidemic…

—P. Ulin 1992, 64 (quoted in Baylies 2004, 1)

INTRODUCTION

DURING A VISIT SEVERAL YEARS AGO to the village of Kibaale in the
Busiki district of the eastern Busoga region of Uganda, I noticed a woman
approach the family compound of Centurio Balikoowa, my Ugandan
research colleague, where I was conducting field research. The woman
carried a small *akadongo* (or *akogo*, a plucked lamellophone, a musical
instrument often referred to as a "thumb piano") slung across her shoulder
as she made her way toward us along the pathway through the banana
fields that led from a neighboring village. Several hours later, I concluded
a recording session with the local male *embaire* (xylophone) musicians of
the village and I noticed that the woman with the *akadongo* had joined
the seated village residents listening to the impromptu performance.

Before putting my recording equipment away, I asked Balikoowa about
the woman and more specifically about the musical instrument she carried. He shrugged his shoulders saying that he was also curious because
he had never heard a "lady *akadongo* player." Vilimina Nakiranda (see
Figure 2.1) introduced herself to me as the leader of the local Bakuseka
Majja Women's Group and asked if we would also like to record *her* and

41

her songs. The recordings I made of Vilimina singing about HIV/AIDS on that day back in 1999 represent the starting point of a long journey for me. It was then that I began listening, questioning, and approaching music in Uganda in a significantly different way. The song lyrics below are an excerpt from "Omukazi Omotegeuu," one of the many songs I recorded with Vilimina that day in Kibaale Village and can be heard on Track 4.

Track 4 "Omukazi omoteguu" ["A married women who does not respond to instruction from her husband"]
Vilimina Nakiranda, voice and *akadongo*

We ladies, we used to sit behind the houses
The real truth is that we used to cry from behind there
We used to put on only half a *gomesi* [traditional Ugandan women's dress]
We used to drink water in gourds that were already drunk from
But these days we eat using forks because we are now civilized
We now drink water in cups
We also sit on chairs very well
We even cross one leg and we are happy
I have come to advise you
Stop complaining
Marriage issues are not easy things to discuss openly
The first thing you fight about is washing the trousers
Well, stop fighting
Things are different nowadays
There are those youth and others who keep fooling around with their bodies
They do not listen to their friends
You, children, you better change your behavior
What I am telling you is very important and may help your family
What makes me sad is that the youth do not listen to advice
When you tell them not to get married to older women they do not listen
When you tell them that AIDS is killing everybody
Even me, I am going to die with you, ladies
I am advising you because AIDS came to kill everybody
I want you to abstain from sex and keep yourself safe
AIDS came to kill us
I am advising the youth to keep themselves safe
Stop shaming us
These young boys are so difficult to understand
We do not want you to shame us
We women learned the *endongo*[20] some time ago
We women now even play the *engalabe*[21]
We put on the leg rattles

In "Omukazi Omoteguu" Vilimina Nakiranda sings about several dramatic social shifts that have been experienced within women's culture in Kibaale-Busiki. In response to the health crisis brought on by the rapid spread of the HIV virus in this and many of the surrounding villages, women now use music to address other local women publicly and advise

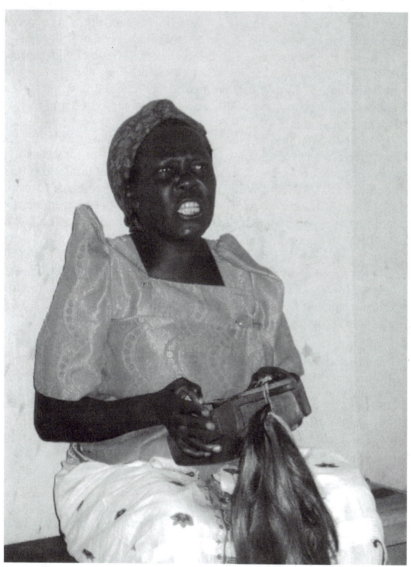

Figure 2.1 Vilimina Nakiranda.

the youth of the village—specifically girls—to adopt behavioral changes regarding sexual intercourse. Vilimina's closing sentiment is significant—she suggests that the women of the village have now begun to play *endongo* and *engalabe*, local musical instruments typically played only by men in this region of the country. That women in this region have now co-opted male performance traditions—and have done so in very public arenas—indicates both a significant departure from cultural norms and an assumption of power and authority regarding public health issues.

As she accompanied herself on the *akadongo*, Vilimina sang a powerful series of messages in her songs to all present—men and women—in which she outlined ways local women in the villages must fight back against AIDS, reclaim their health, and change their lives. Vilimina was in fact *singing for life.*

Since first encountering Vilimina Nakiranda, I have directly experienced music's ability to function as a powerful localized tool for addressing critical issues of public health in Uganda. The success of localized efforts to combat HIV/AIDS through medical interventions in the form of musical performances has, to a great extent, not yet been systematically quantified. I suspect that such efforts, if recognized and supported, could potentially strengthen, influence, and guide the initiatives of funding agencies, relief workers, educators, faith-based communities, and local non-governmental organizations administering programs in Uganda. As Noeleen Heyzer, director of the United Nations Development Fund for Women, suggests, the voices and sentiment of those living with HIV/AIDS are seldom recognized:

> Too often I have listened to women describe how their experiences are not part of the policy discussion. Whether talking about the unequal impact of globalization, the ravages of war and armed conflict, or the reality of living with HIV/AIDS, they feel marginalized and excluded from decision-making and resources that affect their lives. And yet, it is well known that the most effective policy approaches come from listening to those who have experienced such problems first hand, who can provide needed perspectives, improve understanding and offer creative solutions so that resources may be used creatively. (*UNAIDS Report on the Global AIDS Epidemic* 2004, 14)

Many women in Uganda who educate and counsel others about HIV/AIDS feel strongly that their efforts could be much more effective if only given the proper support, encouragement, and transportation that would allow greater exposure. Drama groups, dance ensembles, village music troupes—all are eager but hard-pressed to travel outside their local geographic areas. In addition, many participants in such groups are held back by their own progress through the HIV virus and AIDS, while others are discouraged by a perceived lack of commitment and support by local and regional governments. Time is critical for people actively engaged in health-care initiatives in Uganda—many are HIV positive themselves and lack access to ARV (anti-retroviral) drug therapies.

HIV/AIDS AND UGANDA—A PEACE IN THE BODY

My experiences in rural and urban communities in Uganda continue to challenge me to consider ways in which relationships exist between global peace and social justice. Varying degrees and types of peace exist in different parts of the world today, and just as social justice must be conceptualized as a socially determined construction so must peace also be understood as culturally determined. If peace is in fact an invention, an invented cultural phenomenon, then it is a highly determined social construction. Yet different ways of understanding and enacting peace occur in different regions of the world. There are active forms of peace that often occur as a direct result of conflict and aggression. There is also a peace that intervenes in order to resolve economic strife. And there is a peace of the mind—a peace that exists in our mental world as a partner to our spirit. The daily confrontation of issues involving condom shortages, exorbitant blood-testing fees, and the inability of life-saving anti-retroviral drugs to reach entire populations in sub-Saharan Africa suggests yet another understanding of peace that is located in the corporeal. Global populations have varying degrees of access to peace in the body; many are denied such peace, often with invented cultural, political, and economic justification. The physicalization of peace can in no way, however, be understood as a *natural* occurrence since peace is clearly globally determined, especially regarding the global AIDS health crisis.

AIDS is an English-language term that communicates fear to many, evokes sympathy from some, and causes confusion for others. Horrific images triggering highly emotional responses have historically accompanied the term in Europe and in the United States. Photographs of emaciated, dying Africans have companioned the history of the term since first entering the global imagination in the early 1980s. It was at that time that AIDS began a metaphoric transferal in awareness for many around the world from its position within the United States in a direct trajectory toward sub-Saharan Africa. AIDS, an acronym for Acquired Immunodeficiency Syndrome—SIDA (*syndrome immuno-déficitaire acquis*) in French, *Silimu* or *Slim* in many parts of Uganda—is a disease representing "the end-stage manifestation of an infection with a virus called the human immunodeficiency virus (HIV)" (Schoub 1999, 20). Although linked by an all-important virgule, HIV and AIDS are often conceptualized as separable, despite the close link between the virus and the disease within the silent infection process. The two—HIV and AIDS—are synonymous and in fact inseparable in the minds of many throughout the world. Referencing the virus as AIDS, however, can in some ways have damaging emotional and physical repercussions.

Uganda is at the center of the African HIV/AIDS pandemic in terms of global consciousness and regarding funding for research on the control and monitoring of fluctuations in infection rates. Testing, education, awareness, and treatment have become highly politicized as demonstrated in President Museveni's initiative to treat the virus and disease as a culturally "open secret," and the success of this embracive rhetoric has led some to label Uganda as the continent's AIDS Poster Child. In this and other ways, the country has dealt aggressively with HIV/AIDS to a much greater extent than other countries in sub-Saharan Africa. According to recent figures from the CDC (Centers for Disease Control), more than four hundred thousand people have died from the disease since first identified in the country in 1984; yet another two million people are now infected with the virus according to recent census information distributed by the WHO (World Health Organization). At one time, these figures represented approximately 30 percent of Uganda's total population; current infection rates are reported to be around 8.3 percent according to UNAIDS (Joint United Nations Program on HIV/AIDS), even lower according to unofficial Ugandan governmental reports. Yet, in the eastern and western regions of the country along Lake Victoria the HIV infection rate is estimated to be as high as 1 out of 4 individuals—roughly 25 percent—in villages where young women especially face phenomenal risks of HIV infection and ultimately death from AIDS.

HIV/AIDS is, as suggested in chapter 1, more than just a medical crisis in Uganda. Women, for example, are typically unable to spend as much time working in their fields when their husbands or other family members become seriously ill. In neighboring communities in Tanzania, statistical evidence demonstrates that women spend 60 percent less time engaging in farm-related work as a result of a spouse's HIV infection. (Statistical data in this section and throughout the book are drawn from recent UNAIDS and WHO materials, including the UNAIDS 2004 *Fact Sheet on Sub-Saharan Africa*.)

Even more troubling in Uganda is the issue of orphaned children. The WHO estimates that over 1.7 million children have been orphaned since the spread of the HIV virus began. The definition of "orphan" varies among governmental agencies and non-governmental organizations. Most frequently it is used to refer to the loss of only one parent. In addition, responses to the question "what is a child?" vary considerably in Ugandan research. In one study children were defined as persons under eighteen years of age (Muller and Abbas 1990). According to Elizabeth Preble, so-called "AIDS Orphans" are fast becoming a significant, and "tragic manifestation" of the scourge in Africa:

> They are joining those now referred to by the United Nations Children's Fund as "children in extremely difficult circumstances," including children endangered by armed conflict and other disasters, those exploited by child labor, street children, and children who are victims of abuse and neglect. (Preble 1990, 671–2)

It is helpful to note that Elizabeth Preble's definition of "orphan" is commonly held by many working in Ugandan contexts: "AIDS orphans are defined as children under age 15 whose mothers have died of HIV/AIDS. Because of the likelihood of heterosexual transmission between mother and father, many fathers will also die of AIDS, if they have not already predeceased the mother. The mother is the primary provider for children in African culture, however, and even if the father survives the mother's HIV/AIDS death, experience with child care in Africa suggests that children do not usually receive sufficient care from their fathers alone" (1990, 674). There are now approximately one million children living without one or both parents spread throughout Uganda, representing approximately 8 percent of the country's total population. And tragically, as mentioned earlier, gone are the "aunties" in many villages.

Several southern African countries now suffer rampant HIV prevalence rates[22] that exceed 30 percent (for example: Botswana—38.8 percent, Lesotho—31 percent, Swaziland—33.4 percent, and Zimbabwe, 33.7 percent). Such statistical data represent, however, more than HIV prevalence; these data indicate issues of potential instability related to present and future food supply, eventual decrease in or loss of labor forces, and imminent and ongoing medical needs and health-care personnel shortages. In Uganda, local and foreign agencies frequently celebrate a steady progress in the country's overall lowered HIV prevalence: "Uganda continues to provide evidence that the epidemic does yield to human intervention. HIV infection levels appear to be on the decline recently in several parts of the country—as shown by the steady drop in HIV prevalence among 15- to 19-year-old pregnant women. Trends in behavioral indicators are in line with this apparent decline in HIV incidence" (*Fact Sheet*, UNAIDS 2002). In a recent issue of *Science*, researchers Rand L. Stoneburner and Daniel Low-Beer suggest that Uganda's unique response is rooted in the country's localized responses at communicating the dangers of the disease that have caused the impressive decline within the country:

A better understanding of social elements that triggered the Ugandan response, and that may be hindering its evolution elsewhere, is important. The Ugandan approach to HIV control was practical but based on limited information, financial resources, and precedent for success. The government communicated a clear warning and prevention recommendation: AIDS, or "slim," was fatal and required an immediate population response based on "zero grazing," that is, faithfulness to one partner. Condoms were a minor component of the original strategy. AIDS reporting meant communities openly acknowledged morbidity... The Uganda approach clearly communicated the reality of the AIDS epidemic in terms of a rational fear of the risks of casual sex, which drew on and mobilized indigenous responses at the community level. (Stoneburner and Low-Beer 2004, 716–17)

It is this "human intervention" that lacks sufficient documentation and proper analysis to which this present study responds. In spite of the much touted success in lowering the national infection rate, the ongoing treatment, care, and counseling of PLWHAs (People Living with HIV/AIDS) continues to take its toll on Uganda, contributing to the already high medical, social, educational, political, and psychological burdens of this developing country.

Despite strong, localized efforts to control the spread of the virus, it is estimated that up to 27.9 million people in sub-Saharan Africa were living with HIV/AIDS at the end of 2002, representing exactly 70 percent of the total figure of adults and children living with HIV/AIDS throughout the world. Despite efforts to contain infection, approximately 3.5 million adults and children living in sub-Saharan Africa became infected with HIV in 2002, representing again 70 percent of the overall global newly infected rate, with nearly 80 percent of deaths worldwide due to HIV/AIDS during 2002 occurring in this region of the world.

In the 1980s the WHO established a schema that outlined specific ways in which AIDS could be interpreted and understood as a globalized disease. AIDS quickly became a trope, a specific brand of "We are the World" globalization. As Cindy Patton suggests, in order for the world to embrace AIDS as a pandemic, an "epidemiological mapping of the world" had to be proposed, and thus we were presented with specific geo-cultural patterns:

Patterns of AIDS incidence associated with North America and Europe, where identified cases were originally predominantly found among homosexually active men and injecting drug users of both sexes, [which] was called Pattern One. That of Africa, where cases were initially identified among heterosexually active but non-drug-injecting people, was called Pattern Two. Pattern Three was defined not by the demographics of its cases but by their location in a space-time framework: where "AIDS arrived late," that is, principally Asia. (Patton 2002, xi)

The development of these three conceptual patterns had the effect of defining and reinforcing a significant difference between "Western AIDS" and "African AIDS"—in other words, *AIDS in North American and Europe* versus *AIDS in Africa*, "us" versus "them"—with the latter naturally assigned a more pejorative connotation (Schoub 1999, 22).

> The history of HIV/AIDS to date reveals the desire by the west to read, once again, the map of the world in terms of a social imaginary which makes an imagined "other"—minimally a French-speaking Canadian, maximally the African continent—the source of an unstoppable contamination. (Griffin 2000, 109)

The establishment of the global epidemiology of HIV contributed to a definition of difference by labeling behavioral characteristics based largely on sexual transmission of the HIV virus—from largely male homosexual or bisexual contact in the West to almost exclusively heterosexual intercourse in Africa. In this schema, the ratio of men to women infected with the HIV virus is 20:1 in the Western model; this gender differentiation is nowhere near as pronounced in the African model. But the sex act and its role in transmission of the virus have long been at the heart of misunderstandings of the cultural indigenization of AIDS. Analyses offered by medical ethnomusicologists and medical anthropologists, however, offer opportunities to interpret epidemiological data within localized cultural contexts, thus, contributing to a grounded global discourse:

> Because of the importance of heterosexual transmission of HIV in Third World countries, medical and public health researchers have focused on patterns of sexual contact. Anthropological research and methods have been called upon to provide information about changing sexual behavior and expectations among different populations in Africa. While information concerning these issues may be essential for some epidemiological research, anthropologists and other social scientists have been wary of examining data concerning sexual behavior separately from the broader social context in which it was gathered. Research has consistently demonstrated that sexual behavior is conditioned and changed by changing social organization, economic expectations and historical events even by HIV itself. (Bond et al. 1997, 6)

African patterns of transmission lead to a large pediatric infection rate as a result of MTCT (mother-to-child-transmission), still a significant contributor to the overall global infection rate. A third aspect of the WHO schema projects the epidemiology on areas of the world where the virus has yet to be introduced or not yet significant—China, North Africa, Asia,

Eastern Europe, among others. Twenty years later, this schema perhaps needs reevaluation if not only for remapping a cultural understanding of the spread of HIV, but also for approaching an understanding of why the "West's" reaction to "African AIDS" has been problematic from the start and has limited an understanding of the "cultural" spread of the virus in other parts of the world.

By suggesting an alternate glance with a slight linguistic alteration—"Africa *and* AIDS"—I invoke an intentional binary construction that calls into question the all-too-frequent solitary social construction propagated by the WHO and others—"African AIDS"—by separating the continent (or culture area) from the epidemiology. Even "AIDS *in* Africa," a concept preferred by many, including writer Simon Watney, reveals too much of a monolithic understanding of what is, in fact, a multilayered cultural phenomena defined and determined country by country (if not culture by culture, ethnic group by ethnic group, or community by community) within sub-Saharan Africa (Watney 1994, 110). Each African country has unique and self-determined political, cultural, and localized responses to and understandings of AIDS. There is, therefore, no single way of understanding and interpreting AIDS "in" Africa, just as there is no single way of reflecting on how AIDS is uniquely "African."

PEOPLE LIVING POSITIVELY

By introducing these data in the previous section, I inevitably fall into a trap in which HIV/AIDS in Uganda is reduced to statistics, restatements of the rises and declines in infection rates, discussions of lack of funding initiatives, and charts and diagrams that illustrate fluctuations in mortality rates. In the film, *Coming to Say Goodbye*, Dr. Brigid Corrigan makes the poignant comment that "AIDS statistics are numbers with the tears washed off" (2000, and quoted in *Global AIDS: Facing the Crisis* 2003, 2). This strong statement is worth remembering by all of us who confront the humanity of the AIDS pandemic in our work. For those statistical fact checkers who inhabit and contribute to the maintenance of such numerical data, the mapping of such calculations onto human lives is a potentially dangerous exercise, especially when used as evidence for Uganda's internationally recognized success in lowering its overall seroprevalence rate, the prevalence of infection that can be detected in blood serum (see Figure 2.2).

Uganda has become a model for sub-Saharan Africa both internally and for many governments and external health organizations around world. It should come as no surprise that increased external funding initiatives are directly linked to Uganda's statistically provable "success" as the fol-

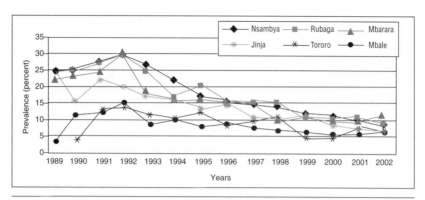

Figure 2.2 HIV infection prevalence rates among ANC (Antenatal Clinic) attendees in major towns. *Source*: "STD/HIV/AIDS Surveillance Report," 2003, 23.

lowing figures that outline the decline in Uganda's national prevalence of HIV suggest:

1995	18.5
1996	15.25
1997	14.7
1998	9.51
1999	8.3[23]
2000	5.2
2001	5.4
2002	5.0
2003	4.1

Numbers, statistics, figures, and data, however, vary from source to source, frequently varying according to perceived political agendas of reporting agencies. Even reports produced by UNAIDS and WHO openly admit the difficulties inherent in producing reliable surveys that accurately represent details about AIDS in Uganda today.

That said, the HIV-infection rate among Uganda's adult population has, in fact, quite dramatically decreased over 22 percent during the past fifteen years. Kyle Kauffman presents an alternate voice, questioning the ability of census figures to portray accurately Uganda's decline, yet qualifies this by suggesting that whatever the figures might be, they should be lauded: "Uganda often is viewed as the shining example of a country that was able to dramatically reverse the trend in HIV infection rates. There are those who believe that the reversal simply is an artifact of the data (or of bad data collection), but even if the numbers are off by an order of magnitude, which is doubtful, the underlying results and trends still are impressive" (2004, 27). One of the most convincing explanations for this very intentional intervention that I have encountered in both villages and in towns has been the use of music, dance, and drama to communicate, educate, and to persuade. If my field research has challenged me about anything, it has been the need to put a human face on what is all too often thought to be a medical issue—or at least a medical issue, as it is commonly understood—or merely an opportunity to develop statistical (and thus "fundable") health-care analyses and procedures. My own approach, however, to the individual agency of the many women and men working to provide indigenous and meaningful medical interventions in Uganda challenges me to avoid reducing human conditions to mere statistical measurements, for analyses grounded in lived experience, specifically within human relationships, lead to more compassionate levels of understandings and interpretations of individual and communal behavior.

The heading of this section suggests that a shift beyond numbers, statistics, figures, and data could be adopted when approaching human lives in Africa, although these terms remain clearly visible in the title, albeit *sur rasure*. The title—"People Living Positively"—references Uganda's public policy of openness regarding the HIV virus, often labeled as the country's "open secret," forcing a repositioning of overly statistical data. The open secret policy has supported (in theory) the lifestyle of people "living positively" in an attempt to move beyond living with the highly stigmatized label, "HIV positive."[24] When I asked Tony Kasule—music director of TASO's (The AIDS Support Organization) Drama Group at Mulago Hospital (see Figure 2.3)—about the Ugandan conceptualization of "positive living" and specifically how it could relate to music, he provided the following useful summary:

> **Kasule**—"Positive living" is a way of changing your attitude towards whatever has happened to you and going clockwise. You can't go anti-clockwise. Looking at your chances, looking at your opportunities, and looking at how best you can start from there—it is a very, very difficult step to take, but those who have taken it are fine in the sense that they've learned to live with themselves and can share with others. And that is very strong encouragement to others that are still wondering if they have the virus. But in counseling terms [positive living] is sharing your experiences, understanding yourself, making sure that you have enough rest, making sure that you tell those that would understand your situation. You share it out, suppressing the stigma, getting medical care, understanding more about the virus because the more you understand about the virus the more you can actually fight this virus.

Barz—So does "positive living" translate into music?

Kasule—Yes, it does translate into music. By first understanding what TASO is all about, by sharing myself, my ideas. Living positively is turning up and saying, "I can make it. I don't care what they say. What they say is theirs. But I'm going to live on." That gives you the will to live. What I've discovered during my years here is that the will to live is hope. Once the will to live is destroyed you will not live the next day. So in the spirit of positive living I create songs like, which one could I give you? "TASO is Going Forward." [He sings] "TASO's going forward, supporting with positive living, TASO's going forward supporting with positive living. It is a challenge, we all should come together. Love and guide all those with AIDS." So I create such songs and they keep on telling people about AIDS, selling the slogan of positive living, and this is a challenge. These songs are really a tribute to the TASO strength.

The musical efforts of the TASO Drama Group led by Kasule models the concept of positive living for many Ugandans as the group accompanies medical and health outreach efforts, touring with dramas, songs, and testimonies about the positive contributions many people are still able to make to their families, communities, and society as a whole. "TASO is Going Forward with Positive Living" is included as Track 5, and the song text provided below outlines the sense of community necessary if positive living is to be achieved.

Track 5 "TASO is going forward with positive living" Performed by TASO Mulago Drama Group

> *Chorus*—TASO is going forward, supporting with positive living
> *Solo*—We now without parents, we should all come together
> Now and all times, for those in need
> It is a challenge; we should all come together
> Encourage one another with positive living as the end
> We encourage everyone to never lose hope
> We are together in the struggle
> Everyone needs to know the facts about AIDS
> Abstaining is the sure way to stay safe
> Sponsors, counselors, medical staff, we want to thank you all
> And let the almighty Lord bless you all[25]

TASO's musical response encourages the adoption of positive living as a model for Ugandans not yet infected, as well as for those already diagnosed as being HIV positive who need the support and encouragement

Figure 2.3 TASO Drama Group in performance.

afforded by the model. Featured prominently in all TASO publicity materials is the following statement: "AIDS Education is provided to raise the level of HIV/AIDS awareness in communities. PHA (People living with HIV/AIDS) drama groups at all Centres, play a significant role in this regard, through their music, dance and drama" (*TASO Uganda Ltd,* general brochure). TASO's role as a CBO (Community-Based Organization) focused on AIDS care and prevention is legend throughout Africa and the world.[26] From the earliest stages of recognition of HIV/AIDS as both a global and local issue in Uganda, TASO was formed by a group of spouses and caregivers to provide care, education, and counseling for "clients"[27]:

> TASO represents one of the first organized responses to the AIDS epidemic in Uganda. Prior to 1987, AIDS care was provided in only a few places in Uganda. TASO came into existence in order to address the needs of people living with AIDS (PWAs) and their families through provision of counseling, medical and nursing care and material assistance, first in the capital city and, with time and experience, elsewhere, in response to requests from other towns to set up centres.... In contrast to 1987, there are now special AIDS clinics in many government and mission hospitals. Other organizations have also taken on AIDS care. TASO has acted as a model, for some of these initiatives, in the care of PWAs. TASO advocates and its work is guided by "positive living"; this has

come to be recognized as the philosophy of the TASO movement. The philosophy calls upon individuals, families and communities to uphold the rights and responsibilities of people affected by HIV/AIDS and their communities. These are:

- The rights of people infected or affected by HIV/AIDS to be supported emotionally, medically and socially.
- The responsibility of people infected or affected by HIV/AIDS to cultivate self-esteem, hope, respect for life, respect for and protection of their community, care for self, care and support for dependants.
- The rights of the community to protect itself and its responsibility to curb the spread of HIV.
- The responsibility of the community to support people infected or affected by HIV/AIDS so that hey have access to emotional, medical and social services and can live responsibly with HIV/AIDS. (*TASO Uganda: The Inside Story* 1995, 2–3)

While the distinction the TASO Drama Group describes between "positive living" and living as "HIV positive" relies heavily on societal abandonment of stigma, PHAs living today still confront what are often times extreme levels of discrimination and face potential job loss, rejection by families, and expulsion from homes when one's HIV status is made public.[28] The issues of the HIV virus quickly move beyond the medical toward what UNAIDS refers to as the "epidemic of stigma, discrimination, blame and collective denial" (*A Conceptual Framework and Basis for Action* 2002, 7). According to Rev. Gideon Byamugisha, the first Ugandan clergy member to openly disclose his HIV status, stigma is not only on par with presenting medical issues in Uganda, it sometimes surpasses physical conditions:

> It is not the condition itself that hurts most (because many other diseases and conditions lead to serious suffering and death), but the stigma and the possibility of rejection and discrimination that HIV-positive people have to deal with. (quoted in *Global AIDS: Facing the Crisis* 2002, 5)

Peter Piot, director of UNAIDS suggests that stigma is rooted in shame and fear and must be actively addressed in regards to HIV/AIDS:

> HIV/AIDS-related stigma comes from the powerful combination of shame and fear—shame because the sex or drug injecting that transmit HIV are surrounded by taboo and moral judgment, and fear because AIDS is relatively new, and considered deadly. Responding to AIDS with blame, or abuse towards people living with AIDS, simply forces the epidemic underground, creating the ideal conditions for HIV to spread. The only way of making progress against the epidemic is to replace shame with solidarity, and fear with hope. (quoted in *A Conceptual Framework and Basis for Action* 2002, 7)

Former South African President Nelson Mandela addressed the issue of stigma in a typical emotional tone, "AIDS is a war against humanity. We need to break the silence, banish stigma and discrimination and ensure total inclusiveness within the struggle against AIDS. If we discard the people living with HIV/AIDS, we can no longer call ourselves humans" (cited in *Fight Stigma!* 2002, 15). The theme for the World AIDS 2002/3 Campaign on Stigma and Discrimination, "Fight Stigma! Reach Out to Positive People," represents a very necessary and very real, ongoing battle that must still be fought in many areas of the world, even for those living positively in Uganda.[29]

WHAT IS "MUSIC"?

[M]usic and dance have a particular power to heal, especially in this age of AIDS, and they bring such comfort to the living, whether their makers are sick or well, participants or observers in the struggle with death. (Baker, *The Art of AIDS* 1994, 99)

In our African context, we realize that messages are portrayed better through music. It is like when you approach something like HIV/AIDS that has such a stigma. When you just walk up and say, "People have come to talk about AIDS," people are shy and they will not come. But if you say, "I'm going to a play," then you hear a song that has messages about HIV/AIDS and you're listening to the song, being entertained, then by the end of the visit you'll say, "What did he or she mean?" Then from there someone will get the message so much faster than just coming up to a board and saying, "AIDS is like this." That's why we sensitize through music, dance, and drama. People get the message very fast that way. (Anonymous youth, Kampala, Uganda)

I have already inserted the term "music" several times in this text, perhaps in a casual, rather broad manner, and in ways that might seem at first to reference multiple aspects of expressive culture in Uganda. The concept of music is wonderfully multi-referential in Uganda, as it is elsewhere in East Africa, if not in all of sub-Saharan Africa (I discuss this issue in detail, specifically regarding why such a broad understanding of music might be helpful in *Music in East Africa: Experiencing Music, Expressing Culture*, Oxford 2004). In addition, at various points in this text I adopt terms that at first glance may appear to be unique—terms such as dance and drama in addition to music—and I do so quite comfortably, as if they were distinct cultural phenomena with distinct meanings, belonging to distinct academic disciplines. But, they are often not in fact distinct in most Ugandan cultural contexts. As a concept and as a term, music is an artificial construct, often with no equivalence in local Ugandan languages.

I therefore use "music" in this text as a cover term to embrace a broad range of performativity that may at times include or be included within music, dance, and drama. I ask the reader to indulge this usage and to be assured that the separation of the arts that these terms afford is clearly noted when more specificity is needed.

There is another distinction that needs to be addressed regarding an understanding of music in Uganda. During initial interviews with individuals and groups in which issues related to HIV/AIDS were addressed, I began to question whether there was consensus on the use of the term, music, when specifically used in conversation, or whether in fact I just did not understand the broader cultural understanding of the meaning of music in Uganda. The term, for example, was often invoked in educational and medical ways in which I was not familiar. For many people in Uganda, music is directly associated with entertainment, as one might expect, but in regard to medical issues related to HIV/AIDS even entertainment is purposeful. As one youth from the Kashenyi Model Primary School in the western town of Ishaka suggested, "Music keeps people busy and stops or prevents them from being idle which could predispose them to HIV." The use of the term is typically more nuanced in everyday usage. I began all interviews by soliciting details that supported a group or individual's understanding of the term. I asked this *before* proceeding to a discussion of the ways in which that term might be related to HIV/AIDS outreach efforts. I point out this progression to demonstrate that no thoughts, remarks, or questions preceded the question, "what do you understand by the term music?" The responses remain intriguing, and in many ways reflect the HIV status or the relationship to HIV activism of the respondent(s). Broader understandings of music nevertheless reflect a relationship that exists between music and meaning in this area of the world.

The people with whom I work, more often than not define music as something quite a bit different than "organized sound," a typical definition found in Western music textbooks. For many peoples of East Africa, the concept of "music" does not exist, at least not in the sense you and I may be most familiar with. If the term "music" does exist, it is more often than not conceptualized within a greater and wider set of parameters. Frequently a foreign term has been introduced to local languages, such as *muziki* in KiSwahili, but such terms often refer specifically to Western musical performance, and not to localized music traditions. Responses clearly position music within a model that can best be approached from the study of medical ethnomusicology (which will be discussed later in this study). From the selected responses of the interviewees below to my simple[30] question—"what is music?"—the meanings of music are clearly situated within and integral to health educational outreach, specifically regarding HIV/AIDS:

> Music is a way of educating people about the dangers of AIDS.
> Music educates people on how to protect themselves from HIV.
> We understand music as a form of educating the masses about health issues, sanitation, and AIDS.
> Music is now the only way of communicating to people about AIDS because people are tired of sitting and learning about HIV—they are more interested in music and drama.

Each of the responses listed above directly couples music with community outreach, specifically regarding music's ability to attract audiences and communicate sentiment in a way that "interests" local audiences.

In a similar way, music is often conceptualized as inherently communicative, and it is not surprising that for many people that were interviewed music is a conduit through which information is expressed. As such, music is often understood as metalinguistic:

> Music is the transfer of a message in a dramatized way.
> Through music we teach—if we just used lessons they do not come, but if you start with music followed by lectures and testimonies people will be attracted to come and listen.
> Singing or even that kind of music that is a kind of talking [rap] accents well and communicates information.
> If songs are recorded, they can reach out to wider audiences and teach more people.
> Music educates people using messages carried in song texts.
> Music is centralized voices that are put together to carry a message through singing.
> Music is a way of teaching people mainly through messages carried in songs especially about how HIV is spread and how it can be prevented.
> Yes, music is just organized sound, but with the intention of delivering a specific message to a specified section of society.
> Music is a thing that you can do to help somebody without telling him or her in words, but you sing and somebody gets the message.
> Through music we can do things without acting—we can sing. If the song has news to tell people, they pay attention and hear what you are saying in that song.

In the responses detailed above, music is typically understood as an exchange, as a form of transactional communication—either direct or indirect—and as a significant act of approaching meaning. It is within the communicative act that the efforts of music clearly function as a medical intervention. By introducing this localized outline of the many layers of meaning attributed to "music" I anticipate the position of the term throughout this text.

TOWARD A MEDICAL ETHNOMUSICOLOGY— MUSIC AS MEDICAL INTERVENTION IN UGANDA

[Medical Anthropology's] rapid growth has not led to a unified theory, or even to agreement about what constitutes its appropriate subject of inquiry. In a recent polemic, Browner, Ortiz de Montellano, and Rubel (1988:681) bemoan medical anthropology's focus on meaning as one of the reasons why that subfield "still follows a particularistic, fragmented, disjointed, and largely conventional course." Other recent assessments of medical anthropology (for example, Greenwood et al. 1988) concur about the absence of authoritative paradigms, but argue that this ferment and division is a sign of the subfield's strength. Similar claims have been made for anthropology as a whole.... As no grand theory has supplanted functionalism, structuralism, or other totalizing frameworks, anthropology is, for the moment at least, postparadigm. In a review of these debates, Marcus and Fischer (1986:8) qualify this disarray as "the intellectual stimulus for the contemporary vitality of experimental writing in anthropology." (Farmer, *AIDS and Accusation* 1992, 12–13)

Music can be understood as a medical intervention when it both encourages medical analysis—"singing about HIV helps people learn about the need to go for testing"—and takes the form of medical treatment itself—"Music is taken as medicine. Even if one is in pain, they will get back some life if there is music. Even for the bereaved or those in shrines, even in the prison, music is there. So, *music is medicine for teaching*." Thus, expressive culture in Uganda functions as a significant contribution to health-care initiatives, as made clear in the definitions of music offered in the previous section.

Approaching performances of healing and localized understandings of spirituality has been central to many ethnographic studies over the past century. Ethnomusicological research that is informed by both biomedical and religious issues is of increasing relevance, and not only in the academy. Field research that takes into account the power of music to contribute to healing typically works within the realm of cultural context, meaning, and the everyday lives of cultural practitioners, especially concerning end-of-life issues. Spiritual concerns and awareness become heightened during illness and as one group of researchers suggest, AIDS affords PWAs (People Living with AIDS) opportunities to focus more directly on spiritual issues, post-testing:

Vatsyn [1986] notes that illness, especially life-threatening illness, offers persons one of the few ways in which contemporary society sanctions one's turning inward. Serious illness is considered adequate justification for surrender of one's active or busy side. Many do not seem able to experience this mode of life until illness strikes—thus, the often-reported observation that the PWAs focus on self, illness, and the meaning of life and death occurred after the diagnosis of AIDS. (Belcher, et al. 1989, 20)

Body and spirit are often afforded greater access during times of physical crisis. Biomedical research, on the other hand, has largely focused—some might say by necessity—on the decontextualized body and its physiological processes. The term "Medical Ethnomusicology" was first introduced in an article I published in a collected volume of essays in 2002 titled *The aWake Project: Uniting Against the African AIDS Crisis*. In the article, titled "No One Will Listen To Us Unless We Bring Our Drums!: AIDS and Women's Music Performance," the term was introduced to inspire the need for further ethnographic-based studies of the roles of music in the performance of health- and healing-related activities:

[T]here is a great (and urgent) need for documentation and further analysis and compassionate understanding of [women's] performance tradition.... The field research I engage with women's groups in Uganda is one of the first to focus on what might be termed "Medical Ethnomusicology," since it directly relates to issues of disease, suffering, bereavement, health care, and related topics. (Barz 2002, 172–73)

My own research (as well as earlier efforts of ethnomusicologists Ben Koen [2003], Marina Roseman [1991, 1996, 2000], Steve Friedson [1996, 2003], David Akombo, and others) contributes to an integrated methodology of ethnomusicological field research techniques based in ethnographic cultural investigation that takes into account physiological research and medical and religious understandings of faith, health, and healing.

As a closely related subdiscipline of ethnomusicology, medical ethnomusicology—specifically as Barz and Koen have practiced it thus far in field research—is a collaborative venture and purposefully transinstitutional, involving collaborative participation from medical and music schools. Just as its sister discipline, medical anthropology, highlights the performance of culture, so does medical ethnomusicology, while taking into account localized understandings of medicine, spirituality, healing, and general health care.

Music is often a bridge connecting the physical with the spiritual, two interconnected aspects that suggest to anthropologist Arthur Kleinman a "sacred clinical reality" (1980, 38–42, quoted in Koen 2003, 26). To explore music and healing in cultural contexts—to come to terms with localized expressions of this sacred clinical reality—ethnomusicology, religion, and medicine have the challenge of approaching health practices that are flexible, dynamic, and often based on sets of cultural theories, views, beliefs, and assumptions that are outside the Western scientific paradigm typically subscribed to by medical professionals.

Music is therapeutic for many, facilitating relaxation and thereby providing comfort and relief in tandem with medical facilitation. With the risk of overextending my allotment of ways one can look at a blackbird, I offer several more localized conceptualizations of music in Uganda. These responses from the interviewees, however, vary slightly from those presented earlier, and they form a theoretic core of my own approach, a more therapeutic understanding of musical performance:

> Music helps us learn how to deal with people and disease.
>
> Music helps sick people chase away bad thoughts and sadness.
>
> Music dispels fear, increasing confidence and openness about HIV/ AIDS.
>
> We have children suffering here, and in our group we sing songs that help those suffering children by asking the government to help us.
>
> I think that singing brings hope to live on even when you are weak with the AIDS disease.
>
> If you are bereaved, say you have lost your mum or a very dear person and the body is in the living room, once singing begins everything becomes calmer.
>
> Music dispels fear, sorrow, concerns, and worries.
>
> When we come together and sing we forget our problems. So it saves us too, it relaxes us.
>
> When you have a problem and that problem becomes a burden you can start singing, and you forget it. That problem can go away because of singing.

The conceptualization of health issues as they are communicated through performances confirms for many in Uganda tangible realities that would otherwise be inaccessible. Since medical ethnomusicology is still an emergent academic subdiscipline, it might be simplest to begin with the following definition that is adapted from a similar and closely related discipline, medical anthropology:

> Medical ethnomusicology can be briefly defined as a branch of research grafted onto ethnomusicological and biomedical studies that focuses on factors that cause, maintain, or contribute to disease, illness, or other health-related issues, and the complementary, alternative, or supportive musical strategies and performative practices that different communities have developed to respond to cultural conceptualizations of disease and illness, health and healing. (adapted from Baer et al., 1997)

As this definition suggests, the invocation of medical ethnomusicology takes into account cultural understandings and interpretations of disease and illness, while focusing on the performative nature of treatment and healing. Such a definition potentially leads us to a much deeper understanding of how disease is made meaningful. It is to the latter "strategies" and "practices" that take action with disease that this study of music and HIV/AIDS in Uganda responds, particularly regarding the application of a model for medical ethnomusicology.

COMPOSING SONGS THAT GIVE HOPE— LISTENING FOR LIFE

Ethnomusicology takes for granted a necessary focus on orality. By this I refer to the ability often ascribed to songs to circumvent literacy issues within a verbal art. Singers of "oral documents," according to historian Jan Vansina, frequently rely on the verbal art as a form of culturally determined verbal communication (1985). Positioned within this communicative act, singer-musicians function as "culture workers" who communicate specific information by performing and maintaining culturally appropriate texts. Oral performances of songs are, therefore, not necessarily distinct social products; there is a long history of relying on songs (however they are conceptualized) as a primary mode of communication in African contexts. Most groups with whom I have worked compose their own cultural texts—their own songs and dramas—drawing on *local* music and dance traditions to support and anchor their performances. That the didactic approaches of medical outreach initiatives are typically located within *traditional* performance contexts should then come as no surprise.

Performances of oral documents are still considered to be among the most culturally appropriate vehicles for communicating socially relevant messages—such as specific information pertaining to HIV/AIDS awareness and prevention—in many if not most parts of Uganda today. Faustus Baziri, the director of VOLSET (Voluntary Service Trust Team), an AIDS outreach center in the Luwero district, suggested to me that oral documents embedded within songs or dramas are not only the most appropriate tool in villages such as his, but often the *only* tool available for communicating vital information regarding HIV/AIDS in Nakaseke, his home village and center for VOLSET's outreach activities.[31]

> ***Baziri***—*Okay, here is a community, a real community, which does not have access to most methods of HIV dissemination. All they have is a radio. You know, they put out a lot on those radio announcements. But in this community they do not even have the batteries.*

So being a community which lacks some access to privileges which are found in cities, when we present this drama it is easier for them to get what we really want. It is easier to transfer our knowledge through drama to the community down in the village.

For Baziri, the function of oral documents in rural areas overrides other more mechanized modalities due to lack of economic access. The dramas he references are often the only means available for the transmission of information in the Luwero region, an area hard hit economically and socially during several aggressive political campaigns over the years.

The prominence of oral documents in the role of medical intervention is confirmed by recent statistics pertaining to health-care outreach programs. According to TASO, the primary source of internal information related to HIV/AIDS for most Ugandans is the outreach effort of social service agencies, organizations such as TASO itself and other NGOs. In a survey of its clients conducted in 1995, TASO attempted to track the various methods by which the population at large typically receives medical and general health-care information.[32] These informational methods are listed below:

TASO	68.1%
Radio	12.2%
Friends/colleagues/family	5.7%
TV/newspaper/magazine	3.7%
Health/extension workers	2.0%
Church/mosque	1.4%
Other	6.9%

As this breakdown indicates, the media—specifically efforts that are broadcast on the radio—have an expectable impact. The vast majority of the surveyed disparate population, however, does not regularly access information in this way. While available locally, batteries to power radios are often too expensive to purchase, and the cheaper national brand rarely lasts very long. It is frequently only through direct interpersonal contact with representatives of outreach agencies that an exchange of information concerning HIV/AIDS is approached. The public educational outreach efforts of TASO and other AIDS-related outreach organizations are often accompanied by musical and dramatic performances. As Baziri suggests above, dramas and songs are the *only* means of communication available, accessible, and appropriate for the residents of many villages.

The TASO Mulago organization tapped into localized forms of oral communication early in its development by creating a Drama Group[33] that typically accompanies medical outreach efforts in outlying areas as well as in schools and communities in the cities. Anne Kaddumukasa,

TASO's administrative director, suggested to me in an interview that the impact of oral performance traditions is significant.

> *Kaddumukasa—The TASO Drama Group composes the songs, all original, together with the clients. They have not been copied from anywhere, and all these songs carry messages—about AIDS prevention and AIDS care. Songs and plays depict the treatment that society inflicts on people who are HIV infected. Surely from those dramas people always gain a lot and realize how bad it is to mistreat a person who is HIV infected and that maybe one day you may find yourself the person being mistreated. And through the personal testimonies delivered by the Drama Group members—many of them look as healthy as the communities where they visit—some people have been inspired to take HIV tests and come to realize that they are positive. By looking at people who claim to be positive and who look healthy, society has come to know that it is not only the bed-ridden person or the person with the skin rash or the thin person who is HIV infected. But one could be positive and still remain healthy and be useful, like these Drama Group members. So, music and drama has an impact. Some people have even gone ahead to find out their HIV status by hearing what these clients have testified in song, in plays. It has had a better impact on some individuals who have also realized that if so-and-so claims to be positive and there is nothing to show, then maybe they also could be infected. So, some people take their blood tests because of the presentations. And so, we get many of our clients coming in and saying, "Oh, we had your group perform in our community some two months back, and it is from that performance that I thought seriously about taking the test, and I realized that I am HIV positive."*

Organizations such as the TASO Drama Group present songs and dramas that have been officially vetted by medical personnel and experienced administrators. Although the Drama Group presents materials composed by members of the group itself they nevertheless seek out the guidance and sanction of the TASO authority—counselors, administrators, and health educators. The directors of TASO have at times stepped in and redirected the efforts of the Drama Group.

> *Kaddumukasa—Yes, we listen and make recommendations. I have seen the training of TASO counselors. I've seen the improvements. I've seen the mistakes that we used to make. So, in the beginning many of the songs that they used to compose were songs calling for sympathy. We realized that they don't need people to sympathize with them. They need empowerment to live on. So, gradually they*

have started composing songs that give hope, that having HIV is not the end of their story. You can still live a positive life, even with HIV. So, after listening to these songs we make comments, sometimes we discourage them from singing some of them. Because the way the train of HIV is moving, people are hoping to live much longer. But before, they would only sing about death, death, death, and dying, dying, dying. It would be so stressful. And many people who would listen to their presentations would come out weeping and maybe this wasn't the best.

Kaddumukasa implies that a shift occurred in the mid-1990s as TASO counselors and the TASO Drama Group moved toward a perspective that emphasized "positive living" rather than singing only about the unpleasant but very real threat of being HIV positive. Yet, music and drama typically communicate more than messages of hope and sympathy as Kaddumukasa suggests. Essential and often specific information relevant to AIDS prevention is communicated through oral documents, as communicated to me by Ruth Namusaabi, a nurse in the AIDS clinic at the regional hospital in Iganga town.

Namusaabi—In music and drama the messages look at methods of prevention, the use of condoms, abstinence, and faithfulness, which is one of our primary factors. So, those have been topics. Also, in the music they focus on PWAs [People with AIDS]. They have looked at whether they are cared for or whether they are stigmatized and have to hide. When they hide they often spread the disease, because when she hides she is not able to open up and never comes, only goes. So in that way HIV spreads. So those have been some of the messages that have been delivered in music. People have been singing here at the Clinic, giving us support and helping the prevention of AIDS and the spread of HIV.

As Namusaabi suggests, highly specific information is intentionally inserted into the oral texts that accompany the musical-medical efforts of the Iganga Hospital's AIDS Clinic. Typical topics center on modes of prevention in the spread of the virus: condoms, abstinence, and faithfulness to one partner. Perhaps more importantly, musical and medical efforts are often in tandem in Namusaabi's outline; they are interdependent and support each other's efforts. The potential of songs and dramas to function as oral documents that communicate direct sentiment is understood by many as more efficient than products of the nonmusical, spoken art—lectures, seminars, and speeches.

Vincent Wandera (see Figure 2.4), director of GOSSACE (Good Shepherd Support Action Centre) in Kampala is comfortable with adopting

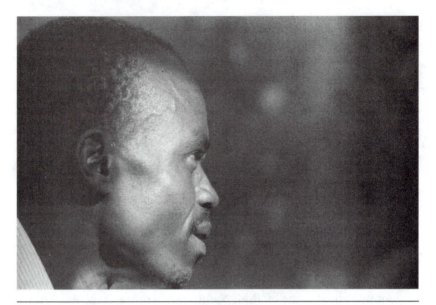

Figure 2.4 Vincent Wandera, director, GOSSACE.

aggressive, blatantly militant metaphors for describing how his drama group uses musical performance to interact with the communities they visit.

> *Wandera*—*Most of us discovered that we got HIV because we were ignorant of it. We did not have any information about it. So, having gotten the information we now try to warn others, like in the discos, about the factors that influence, like alcohol. So we use those factors and we convert it into music and dancing and drama. In most cases, when you talk about AIDS in Uganda, people say, "forget it. We are fed up of AIDS." Only if you use a drama venue, attack a meeting and blast out with the singing will they eventually say "Oh, Silimu" [AIDS]. Nobody will listen at you when you come to talk about AIDS. It is only through music that you will influence people. This is why I told you we attack meetings, say political meetings. They don't want to hear about Silimu. But just to blast out with a song, at least we've attracted them and they will go with a message. There was one time we went to a place where they first denied us access, they did not want to listen to us. But, by the time we left everybody was very quiet. The next day, very many of them were coming for testing. So far now I have registered 30 clients from there. It was because of the drama.*

Wandera's counselors—all HIV positive—"attack" listeners with songs, as if holding them hostage as they move, educate, and effect change in people with their musical and dramatic sensitization efforts. There is no doubt that Wandera (like others) has saved lives, and there is no doubt that his ongoing violent, "in-your-face," guerilla musical and dramatic interpretations of oral documents remain critically necessary.

Attempts to sensitize with music, dance, and drama are seldom peripheral among the overall efforts of AIDS outreach organizations (see Figure 2.5). According to Sarah Birabwa, early aggressive efforts to fight the disease were "combined efforts by government supplemented by those of churches, civil society organizations and different individuals. Many groups started coming up to fight the disease using various avenues such as *songs, drama, dialogues, sensitization seminars, etc.*" (2002, 41, emphasis added).

For the groups to which Birabwa refers, groups such as Meeting Point Kampala (MPK), music maintains a central position it has assumed from the start among many activities. According to the Meeting Point's 2002 Annual Report, the medium-size NGO uses music for the two purposes outlined above: to sensitize about the dangers of spreading and acquiring the virus and to demonstrate ways in which those already infected can continue to live positively in the time they have left. In addition, a special feature of the Meeting Point's outreach efforts is its advocacy for the rights of children:

> The Meeting Point drama group is one of the major activities carried out by MPK as a way of passing different massages and sensitizing the

Figure 2.5 Village sensitization session (Greg Barz and Dr. Peter Mudiope, seated left).

public about the dangers of AIDS and its related problems. Messages are carried in form of poems, songs, plays, and dances to the audience aimed at reducing the rate at which the virus is spread and at making the infected members live longer and more happily during the last days of their lives and to help those who are not yet infected to remain negative. Different messages to the youth and adolescents encouraging them to abstain until they are mature enough and get married and avoiding free gifts from sugar Daddies and sugar Mammies who can spoil their future. This drama group is divided into three major groups: the children's club, the Nankasa group and the Bendegere group. Due to the fact that members in this group come from different parts of Uganda, it has a variety of traditional songs and dances in different languages which makes it easy also to communicate to people of different tribes, educating by entertaining. It has also attracted the Government, Non Government officials, individuals and the community at large. The drama group has staged many shows in this year 2001 in different places and has also called upon to perform in different areas and on different occasions. On 6th Feb. 2001, Meeting Point organized a one-day Street Children's conference and was held at the Pride Theatre in Kampala. The guest of honor was the Mayor of Kampala John Ssebana Kizito. . . . The conference started with a welcoming song, which was presented by the children's club of Meeting Point with the message of the song called on the public to uplift the rights of children for them to live a better life especially by helping the disadvantaged people from different organizations. (*Annual Report, Meeting Point Kampala* 2002)

Discourse in medical ethnomusicology, while still in a developmental stage, nevertheless values the potentiality for research and reflection that can lead to both assessment and action. In order to approach the sacred clinical reality mentioned earlier from a holistic perspective, one that is inherently performative, preventative, curative, and grounded in both science and religion, it is perhaps time for new methods to emerge within ethnomusicology that combine the rich experiential and culturally rooted ethnographic research with objective scientific experimentation. Medical ethnomusicology demands such collaboration, levels of engagement that value an understanding of the difference between what it means to be HIV positive versus to "live one's life positively."

CONCLUSION

My ongoing field research with over 175 women's, youth, and community groups has afforded me opportunities to record, interview, document, and learn how music functions as a significant oral form of communication, contributing to the work of social indemnity groups that serve financial, educational, spiritual, and advisory roles for community members. That many of these groups draw on localized historical oral performance traditions—singing, dancing, and dramatizing their response to a nationwide health crisis—is not unusual and surprises no one within cultures in this area of the world. Close to the surface in my conversations with Faustus Baziri, Anne Kaddumukasa, and Vincent Wandera is the suggestion that the engagement of music is a timely and very necessary act of survival. None would question my title for this book *Singing for Life.* In fact, whenever I used this phrase during an interview to refer to my study, it was always received with affirmative nods of approval, encouraging me to adopt and maintain the profound desperation inherent in the simple phrase. If this study responds to anything, it is the successful efforts of many grassroots efforts in Uganda to combat the HIV virus and AIDS disease in very musical and thus very meaningful ways.

Interlude 2
"Our Problems Are Bigger than AIDS"
A Conversation with Dr. Alex Muganzi Muganga

DURING A RESEARCH TRIP IN 2001, I traveled extensively through Ugandan villages in the eastern Busoga and western Bushenyi regions with Alex Muganzi Muganga and Peter Mudiope, both young doctors recently graduated from the medical school affiliated with Mulago Hospital in Kampala (see Figure Interlude 2.1). Well trained in medical, psychological, pharmacological, and social issues regarding HIV/AIDS in Uganda, both participated in the clinical trial research at Mulago Hospital that led to the introduction of nevirapine, a one-time, inexpensive drug that greatly reduces the risk of MTCT (mother-to-child transmission) of the HIV virus during birth by HIV-positive women.[34] This drug was made available at no cost to all Ugandan women during 2001, a result of foreign aid.[35] Both doctors facilitated my research with drama and music groups when I traveled to remote villages, and we typically concluded our interviews and recording sessions with local villagers by engaging discussions on specific medical concerns regarding HIV/AIDS. More than remunerating the groups with whom we worked, these informational meetings were attempts to give something back to villagers who took time away from the fields to talk with us and perform for us.

Alex Muganzi Muganga is among the finest trained physicians of Uganda's young medical personnel, many of whom are affected by the brain drain occurring in the medical communities throughout sub-Saharan Africa; he is passionate, articulate, and outspoken on the need for more research and better trained medical and health personnel in

Figure Interlude 2.1 Aida Namulinda, Alex Muganzi Muganga, Greg Barz, and Peter Mudiope (left to right).

rural areas. Alex and I would often sit together at the end of a long day's work and process our day's experiences. On one such occasion Alex and I sat together on the second-floor balcony of the Mwaana Hotel located along the main road in Iganga town in Busoga, a stop on the truck and bus route to the east along the approach to the Kenyan border. It was early evening and we both stared down at the street as a waiter brought our order of cold Mirinda Fruitie soft drinks. As the sun began to set, I watched the overland truck drivers begin to stop along the road to rest and hire prostitutes for the evening.

The human drama unfolding before us on the street below has become a cliché for many, securely positioned within the genre of "AIDS Safari" narratives, as Simon Watney suggests (1994, 105), with the prostitute herself assuming a principal role in the "AIDS in Africa" drama unfolding before my eyes. Yet, as I witnessed the manifestation of this highly choreographed scene on the street below us Alex shook me out of reverie by clucking his tongue several times. I glanced over at what had caught Alex's attention and saw a young woman walking off, leading a man down the street. Alex's eyes glazed over as if he was looking through the scene, gazing behind the curtains. "You see, no amount of education can cure poverty," he muttered. "It's really not always about AIDS, professor. You know, our problems are much bigger than AIDS. They always have been.

Sometimes AIDS is third or even fourth on the list of an individual's social problems."

I pulled out my DAT recorder and we began reviewing the day's tapes, but I seized on Alex's reflective mood as an opportunity to address some very basic issues concerning the history of the culture of AIDS in Uganda. As an interlude, the transcription of this conversation below represents a clear articulation of the history and status of HIV/AIDS in Uganda from the perspective of a young Ugandan medical perspective.

Barz—Would you mind in your own words, since you are a medical doctor, sharing your understanding of the history of HIV/AIDS in Uganda?

Muganga—As far as I can remember, the first AIDS cases were identified here in 1982, in the west of the country in a small fishing village called Kasensero in the Rakai district. Of course, just as in the representation of the patients in the United States, these patients presented in quite a strange disease, with a type of pneumonia called pneumocytis [pneumocytis carinii pneumonia (PCP)]. It did not occur to people, being a strange disease, people perceived it, well, it was strange. The initial reactions were fear and denial, like an epidemic coming up in an area, and people reacted in different ways. This being a traditional African society, the main thing people thought was that it was a form of punishment. Others thought it was a curse from God. In the past, when a bad omen befell a village, people thought God was punishing the people in this way. By 1986, it became clear that this was an epidemic, which was identified in the US by 1986 as HIV and later called AIDS. The people at this time were referring to it as "Silimu" [Slim]. Slim[36] in the sense that it weakened the people who were affected became slim. So the people used the local term. Quite a few people died by 1986 and the government realized it needed to come up and do something. In 1986 we still had the war here when the current president [Yoweri Museveni] came into power, so not much was done. However, toward the end of 1986 the AIDS control program and the Minister of Health were sent to coordinate activities. Quite a number of people had died by then and the Kasensero fishing village was becoming deserted, and more people were dying. However, the reactions of stigma, denial, and people thinking it was witchcraft are still there. Because so many people did not know how this disease was caused, the government started control programs and awareness campaigns. Initially it was limited to messages over radio. The initial messages were to "Love Carefully," and they made lots of posters and put them around the country. Of course this wasn't enough of a message—to me it has very little meaning, "Love Carefully." So what? The other message was "Don't Point Fingers," because any one of us can be affected. We had problems right from the start in 1986. The adult infection rate was 30 percent. At that time, Uganda was the leading country in AIDS cases. The messages trickled down rather slowly. Of course, most of us don't easily part with our beliefs. Behavior change takes quite a lot of time. The other problem is that most of our people are illiterate, probably over 40 percent. Another problem is that most of our population is poor, and you know what poverty means to a society like this one. So, the rising levels of prostitution and poverty made the situation worse. By the time the government and the president thought they should come in, the figures were as high as that. Currently, it is estimated that 1.5–2 million Ugandans are infected with HIV/AIDS, with an estimated population of 23 million. That's about 1 in 10 people. In 1992, the government realized that AIDS—it took us quite a long time to realize—wasn't just a health problem, it was affecting all sectors of society—health, economy, production. So the president and the government started up the Uganda AIDS Commission. That was in 1992. They adopted what was called MACA [the Multi-Sectoral Approach to the Control of AIDS] after realizing that AIDS wasn't just a health issue. The Uganda AIDS Commission was pressed right into the president's office and it was created by an act of parliament to be right under the president's office. The AIDS Commission's MACA policy was both a policy and a strategy, and soon afterwards the prevalence rates started going down, and when studies checked their impact in 1998, the rates had come down to 15 percent, from 30 percent in 1986. And currently, in studies released in 2000, the prevalence rate is 8.3 percent. This is the praise that Uganda has received, but there is still a lot to do. We should not become complacent and keep praising the country over figures. The HIV infection rates continue to increase. AIDS orphans are on the rise. Child-headed homesteads are not uncommon, I think you have seen how when we are moving, many of the children are of the same age and most are AIDS orphans. When we move to the west of the country, you will see more orphaned.

Barz—Are many of the orphans infected themselves?

Muganga—By the end of 1998, the number of AIDS orphans, defined as someone who has lost one or both parents, was 1.9 million. This is a UN-AIDS figure of 1998. I don't have the Uganda figure. Perhaps I should have told you toward the end of the 1980s was when we had our first musician coming up, Philly Lutaaya, who was a Ugandan musician based in Sweden and he died of AIDS in December 1989. But he came up before that and openly declared he had AIDS. At that time that was still difficult. People still did not want to hear about anyone associated with AIDS. It was like a stigma. Many people thought he was trying to get sympathy and make money out of it. But, he came out, and by the time he died it had changed and it had become "Silimu," the word now adopted by most people. He died in 1989, but his music is still an influence. You know, when you are talking about Lutaaya you are talking about AIDS. A lot more people came out openly and now we have a number of people who have openly declared they have AIDS. Major Ruranga [Rubaramira Ruranga] has been living with AIDS for over ten years. Rev. Gideon [Gideon Byamugisha] is a priest living with AIDS in Kampala. Quite a number of organizations have come up. There is TASO, the AIDS Support Organization, which has done quite a bit of work helping people with AIDS "live positively." Others are coming up such as the AIC [AIDS Information Center] which provides counseling and HIV testing. Perhaps I should now bring up the role of music in HIV/AIDS prevention. The main preventive measure used at the start was awareness using the mass media. What was being done was using radio mainly. The messages they would give would start with the beating of the drum, just like in any traditional society in Uganda. When you sound the drum, it is a mode of communication and they sound them differently for different occasions. So the messages would start with the sounding of the drum, on the radio.

Barz—When did this start?

Muganga—When the AIDS Control Program started in 1986. They sounded the drums and said, "Do you know these things about AIDS?" And they would bring out the salient features, which they thought were important for the people. That has now continued and has been intensified. Everywhere you walk around you see posters for condom use, etc. Just last week I heard the government is starting up AIDS radio stations, FM stations around the country just for HIV/AIDS, to create more awareness about AIDS and other problems like malaria. AIDS is now the single biggest concern of the people.[37] Every family has been affected by AIDS in one way or another. But I should be happy to tell you that the awareness now is high. Almost everyone now knows how AIDS is spread and can identify at least two modes of prevention, though they might not be practicing what they know. But at least people know that AIDS is spread through sexual intercourse, you can get it from unsafe blood transfusions, needle pricks, other methods of transmission. At least people know. I think this is a step forward.

Barz—Has there been a change in the stigma attached to AIDS?

Muganga—Absolutely. There has been a change in the stigma of AIDS. At the start people thought it was due to bewitchment, that it was a curse from God. Which was of course untrue. But now that every family has lost at least one member, the reality is coming out. Every time the president goes somewhere he takes some time to talk about AIDS. So with increased awareness people have gotten out of denial, and they're getting to work and practicing different ways of prevention. The orphans are getting absorbed into our traditional families. So the stigma is coming down. More people are talking about helping people who are positive within the community. More are coming up openly. They no longer fear going to TASO, because it is providing them with a lot of support—spiritual, advice, counseling—which helps them live positively in their community. Yes, the stigma has gone down.

Barz—Could you talk a little bit about the religious institutions and their history with HIV/AIDS?

Muganga—The religious institutions, hmmm. At the start we had a lot of trouble, because, by virtue of the fact that AIDS is mainly spread through sexual intercourse, the religious institutions at first did not want to come out openly. It wasn't until the early 90s that the church started coming up. It has been more difficult for the Catholic Church, mainly because they don't believe in condom use, and the only way for AIDS prevention is abstinence and being faithful to your partner. Other religious denominations are coming up. We have a reverend priest who has openly admitted he has AIDS. He's living and still absorbed in the protestant church. We have an association of Muslims against AIDS. They have now changed their thinking and they believe they have a role. They bring together a lot of people. If they spread their message every Sunday, let's say if the priest talks to his congregation about AIDS every Sunday, the message goes deep down. But as I said, the church's main cures are faithfulness and abstinence, and many of them fear talking about condoms. Other than the priest, Rev. Gideon, who has talked openly about AIDS and has written a book about how the church can talk about AIDS and use of the condom. He has openly come out and said how he uses condoms so he won't infect his wife. The church is also helping by extending support to the AIDS orphans, of whom there are many in this country. The start was rough, but they are coming up and I am happy with their response.

Barz—So what do you think is going to happen in the next five years?

Muganga—Of course, AIDS is not ending today or tomorrow. I read a statement that said all of us will live with AIDS for the rest of our lives. That statement is sad but true, because most of us have been affected. Even those of us who have lost relatives, we live with this for the rest of our lives. There's hope in that progress is being made. What I want to emphasize is that we should not stop. The little hope that we have should help us aim higher, increase our awareness, and look out. Of course the vaccine is not anywhere in the near future. But in the next five years, if we have our efforts concerted, if we intensify the campaign further we are going to see the prevalence going down. It is all about openness, it is all about breaking the silence and letting the people know the modes of prevention and what options there are to help them prevent the infection. Of course, I see in the next five years a lot more Ugandans seeking treatment, because the drugs are more accessible. The outcry now has been on provision of treatment, now subsidizing the cost of drugs which are too high. In the next five years, I see more people accessing treatment and the prevalence going down. All the same, if we become complacent then the prevalence rates can still go up. I should add that the rates going down will depend on our efforts, our research. If more research is done to see what other methods are available and which are practical and if the efforts are intensified I see the prevalence going down. The area of music and AIDS is research that hasn't been done in this country as far as I know, according to the literature I have. I have all this literature from the AIDS Commission, which is coordinating these studies, and I don't see anything talking about music, using it to prevent HIV/AIDS, and I think this kind of study is commendable. I believe this kind of study will have a great deal to do in the prevention of HIV/AIDS. The struggle to defeat AIDS is going to be a long but worthy one.

Barz—What do you think can happen in the smaller villages today and in the next five years. How could they get more information, more testing? What mechanism could put that into place?

Muganga—Out of the many groups you have seen, you realize that most of the information hasn't gotten down to the grassroots. I could pull information from research I've done recently. One of the recommendations was that we use community health workers. These people live within the community and they have the potential of spreading the message right to the people at the grassroots. The advantage is, they live in the community and are more likely to be accepted. If we could support these community health workers and do our mobilization through them I believe they reach to the grassroots more than our radios and newspapers. Most of our people are illiterate, about 47 percent of the country. Not many of them read newspapers or have radios, since they are in poverty. To reach to the common people we have to use the people, the people in the community who understand the disease and reach out to them. We could also use the Local Council leaders because they are usually people who have gone to school at some level. So if we used council leaders along with the community health workers we could really reach the people. The problem is we need support, in terms of finances, transport, motivation, and most of these are not easily available. Unless they are willing to work with little motivation, the response is really going to be slow. If we go through them the response will change a bit. We found out on Friday, remember, that the only mode of communication, the only medical intervention in that village was music. So we need to have more people singing in groups about AIDS in their communities. They have done so, but they need support to sing and record. Through them they can have the messages spread. It is going to be a slow process due to logistical and financial issues.

3

"NO ONE WILL LISTEN TO US UNLESS WE BRING OUR DRUMS!"

AIDS and Women's Music Performance in Uganda

> The Kyamusa Obwongo Club (the women's group) carries out behavior change programmes through music, dance and drama. These educational messages have helped change the lifestyle of many people in this community most especially by encouraging and enabling people who are HIV negative to remain so.
>
> —*Annual Report 2002*, Meeting Point Kampala

PRELUDE

Following an interview with the women of the Kyamusa Obwongo Club of the Meeting Point, located in the Namuwongo area of Kampala (bordering the slum area frequently referred to as "Soweto"), several younger girls bring a set of drums into the small outer room in which we were meeting. The older women wrap *khangas* (colorful printed cotton fabric with aphorisms printed on the bottom, often in KiSwahili) over their dresses as a group of women introduce the repetitive rhythms associated with the highly athletic *Runyege* dance (also known as *Entogoro*) of the Banyoro people of the western region of the country (see Figure 3.1). I glance over at Noelina Namukisa, director of the women's group, and she covers her mouth with a hand and laughs as I raise my eyebrows. She comes over to join me, still laughing as she slaps my hand, shouting in my ear, "You think that just because we women are sick that we can no longer dance?"

Figure 3.1 Women Dance *Runyege* at Meeting Point Kampala.

The women take turns dancing the dual solo role of the ceremonial courtship dance once associated with weddings. As I continue to watch the performance of *Runyege,* an older woman who appears to be frail and quite ill comes into the room and sits in the far corner. The dancing women jump high in the air shaking their rattle-encased legs to maintain the rhythm. Mama Noelina explains, "These women come here for help, for community, and to dance. See. Look at them. It makes them feel better when they dance. They're *dancing their disease!*" As Mama Noelina and I continue to shout in each other's ears, the older woman, barely able to walk when she came in, stood up and took off the *khanga* that had been covering her head and wrapped it around her waist as she joined the line of dancing women encircling the solo dancers.

AIDS—A WOMEN'S DISEASE?

Within the focus of this chapter is an inherent assumption that women's responses, receptions, and reactions to HIV/AIDS are somehow different than those of men. Culturally this is true, certainly at a national scale, and throughout this chapter I propose ways of understanding the value placed by many women on coming to grips with their medical and social situations in unique and specifically gendered ways. Women in Uganda suffer not only the physical trials that accompany AIDS, but also the considerable social burdens of maintaining home, family, farm or job, and community in the wake of ongoing stigmatization. In an attempt to address the profound silencing of women's voices regarding HIV/AIDS, Peter Piot, executive director of UNAIDS, suggests that AIDS today is primarily a "woman's epidemic" (see Baylies 2004 for further discussion of this issue, especially her section titled "Factors of Vulnerability").

Yet, in addition to cultural ownership there is also a corporal way of understanding HIV/AIDS as a distinctly "women's disease." Sarah Birabwa provides a basic outline for understanding the physiological differences between transmission and reception of the virus among men and women, and I repeat it here to provide a springboard for further discussion on women's responses:

> AIDS has many dimensions, although it is a medical problem, since it deeply affects people as well as communities, it is closely intertwined with the relationships between women and men. *Females are more affected* by HIV/AIDS than their male counterparts due to a number of reasons:
>
> - Biologically, women face a higher risk of HIV infection considering that sexual transmission is several times more efficient from men to women than vice versa. During heterosexual intercourse, the seminal fluid of infected men comes into contact with the mucus membrane of a woman's sexual organs. Younger women are even more vulnerable as the tissue lining their genital tract is not fully developed, thus their mucous membranes are less protective.
> - Women suffer more asymptomatic sexually transmitted infections than men do. These infections often remain undiagnosed, which increases their risk of contracting HIV.
> - *Younger women and girls are culturally more vulnerable* to contracting HIV, as it is common for men to select significantly younger women as partners and wives. Many older men seek out young virgins for unprotected sex. However the men themselves usually have multiple sexual partners and may already be infected.
> - Due to economic, social and emotional *dependency on men*, it is difficult for some women to refuse unsafe sex or negotiate sex. When this is coupled with *cultural expectation of female submissiveness* and male dominance in sexual relations, it limits women's ability to exert control over their sexual and reproductive health. Females are often trapped between their wish to show love, care and trust and the necessity to protect themselves....
> - Females are often victims of rape and sexual assault. This predisposes them to higher risks of acquiring the disease more so if their abusers are already infected. (Birabwa 2002, 41–42, emphasis added)

Birabwa highlights the specific physio-cultural nature of exposure risk experienced by many African women in general, and Ugandan women in specific. These are the primary reasons why many doctors, researchers, and international health advocates feel that only when ongoing cultural education is set in place will the issue of women's empowerment be adequately addressed.

WOMEN'S SONGS, WOMEN'S LIVES

> No one will listen to us *unless we bring our drums!*
> No one will listen to us *talk* about *Silimu*—AIDS—*unless we dance!*
>
> —Aida Namulinda, Bute Village

The chance meeting with Vilimina Nakiranda outlined in chapter 2 was the first of many opportunities I had to record, interview, interact with, and learn from women who gather on a regular basis in order to educate other women and to discuss issues related to HIV/AIDS testing, care, treatment, and counseling. This is not an uncommon phenomenon in East Africa. Such social indemnity groups have historically formed on a frequent basis and function in many ways as extended families, serving financial, educational, spiritual, familial, and advisory roles; women in both villages and cities frequently form such groups. That many of these contemporary women's groups in Uganda, such as Vilimina's Bakuseka Majja Women's Group, turn to musical performance—songs, dances, and dramas—to increase the understanding of reproductive health and female sexuality and to promote the adoption of safer sex practices is not unusual in this area of the world. There has, however, been little discussion of this societal phenomenon in academic and health-care discourse. Further analysis and reflection, however, can potentially lead to a more compassionate understanding of the contexts of women's performance traditions.

By listening to women's voices and women's songs, opportunities are presented to move beyond charts and diagrams, figures and statistics, and to refocus attention on how grassroots efforts to educate and affect change are achieving significant effects. The musical performances of many women's groups now complement and in some cases are integrated into the efforts of local governments and private and multinational and bilateral non-governmental organizations to combat the disease.

Aida Namulinda, a farmer, musician, and community activist articulates clearer than anyone else the power of music to "speak" for women. The fieldnote that follows introduces my initial encounter with Aida Namulinda (see Figure 3.2). One of the strongest leaders and performers of music and dance I have encountered, Aida draws on traditional, local musical repertoires to a much greater extent than others with whom I have worked.

Figure 3.2 Aida Namulinda, Bute Village.

I sit in a small family compound in Bute Village in the Busoga region of eastern Uganda surrounded by banana trees, fields of cassava, and a dwindling and diseased coffee crop. A statement about drums made by Aida Namulinda on the previous day strikes me, "No one will listen to us unless we bring our drums! No one will listen to us talk about Silimu—AIDS—unless we dance!" Aida, a farmer and leader of the Bwoyidha Oyega Group—the local village women's music and dance ensemble with whom I have come to work—clearly positions herself within the medical inventions available to her community. Two medical doctors accompany me as usual—Alex Muganzi Muganga and Peter Mudiope—both of who are involved with HIV/AIDS medical research in Kampala, the nation's capital. While the doctors and I set up our recording equipment, Aida continues to mobilize her village's performing ensemble in order for our research team to document several of the group's songs, dramas, and dances.

As the afternoon's music-making began in Bute village, several men bring out a set of *kisoga*[38] xylophones, panpipes, tube fiddles, and drums from one of the huts in the family compound to accompany the women of Aida's group as they summon and engage the community of farmers returning from the fields. The women encourage everyone gathering—not only the women—to dance, sing, *and listen to the group's messages* concerning proper condom use, faithfulness to partners, and sexual abstinence. Aida sings directly to both men and women equally. During the break in the performances she responds to one of my queries about the gender focus of her songs by stating emphatically, "*Silimu* does not discriminate!"

After all the instruments are stored away and the villagers head off along various paths, Aida continues her thoughts about music. She asserts that whether by itself or incorporated within dance and drama, music is now embraced by village-based groups such as hers as the most effective and immediate means available for communicating, educating, and disseminating information pertaining to medical and health-care concerns. There are no other preventative measures to fight AIDS in her village. According to Aida, "Through our singing we are all making an impact—at least we are attempting. Singing is our only *Silimu* control."

When I returned to Bute Village I experienced Aida leading a group of women, dramatizing a powerful series of songs that outlined specific ways women could fight back against the *spread* of HIV/AIDS and how they must reclaim their health and change their lives... even though they are all HIV positive. Like Vilimina Nakiranda, Aida is in her own way also *singing for life* (see Figure 3.3). I provide a transcription below of a portion translated into English of one of Aida's songs, "Olumbe lwa Silimu" recorded on the first day I met her. This particular excerpt provides a detailed description according to Aida of the physical manifestation of the onset of AIDS, specifically the physical response to the HIV virus's weakening of the body.

Track 6 "Olumbe lwa Silimu" ("This disease of AIDS")
Aida Namulinda
Bute Village, Busoga, Uganda

Chorus—The disease of *Silimu*, the disease that has finished the village
Oh, we have got a problem
Aida—The disease of *Silimu*, the disease that has finished the village
Oh, the disease brought people many problems
Friends, the *Silimu* disease, the disease that makes people cry
Adults, oh, a problem came for us
My friends, adult friends, this disease, oh, brought problems to the people
Let me explain to you, friends
Silimu invades the body
It first makes you fat
It finishes the people
The sweeper
The problem came for all
First you slim
Then boils begin to sprout all over the skin
Then the skin becomes filled with patches

Figure 3.3 Aida Namulinda, Bute Village.

> Then the skin is covered with a rash
> The skin is covered with houseflies
> Then houseflies start to cover you
> The disease has finished us
> What shall we do to survive the disease?
> The disease of this kind is one of malice
> *Silimu* does not discriminate, even if you are elderly
> We must stop laughing
> Friends from Bute, yaa yee!
> We spend our days in mourning, woo wee!
> We spend our days in tears, woo wee!
> The disease has finished us all, woo wee!
> What shall we do to survive the disease?
> What shall we do; we are tired of the "broom"?
> The disease of that kind, the disease of malice
> My adult friends woo wee!
> My club is Bwoyidha Oyega
> My names are Aida Namulinda
> The club is from Bute
> Bute in the Kisiki zone
> We appreciate your work, thank you for recording
> Friends, visitors we thank you
> My adult friends, good-bye
> My friends, visitors, dears, good-bye

This brief excerpt from a much longer performance provides extremely direct and graphic medical details, in fact a rather specific description of the onset of the disease. Aida sings about ways in which the HIV virus weakens the body and of how *Silimu*/AIDS—often referred to as "the sweeper" or "the broom" in this and other areas of the country—finishes entire villages, "eating" its victims. Along with the didactic approach adopted in Aida's songs, the texts are clearly constructed in intentional ways to strike fear in listeners and thus affect changes in social behavior. When I asked Aida to reflect on the text of "Olumbe lwa Silimu," she told me that she really only has two goals regarding music and AIDS prevention. The first is to increase awareness among those who can understand issues related to AIDS. The second goal is to induce fear among those who do not yet fully understand these issues and thus affect behavioral changes (see Figure 3.4).

The adoption of extreme physical imagery in song texts is not unique to Aida Namulinda and her group. Similar efforts are embraced by women's groups throughout the country. In the far western village of Kitabi near Ishaka town in the Bushenyi region, another group of women, the Kanihiro Group, dramatizes the physicality of HIV in similar ways to instill fear. The Kanihiro Group performs dramas for other women into which are inserted songs such as "Nyine Obusaasi."

Figure 3.4 Aida Namulinda.

"Nyine Obusaasi"
Kanihiro Group
Kitabi Village

Solo—I am filled with sorrow
Even the sickness is getting worse
Please people, come and take me back home
I am dying
Chorus—He is filled with sorrow
His sickness is getting worse
Please come and take him home
He is dying
Solo—My dear friends, please let me tell you
I have a terrible disease that will soon kill me
There is a widow in Mubende
She insisted that we must have sexual relations
Now see what has come out of it!
I had really protected myself
But some people mislead me
I get very cold and feverish
Then I experience severe itching all over my body
The sorrow is overwhelming
I cough all the time
I vomit whatever I eat
What should I do people?
I spend over an hour when I visit the toilet
After I return, the abdominal pain gets worse
I have seen a number of doctors
I have sought several treatments without improvement
It is now time for me to die!
I have wounds, ulcers, and swellings all over my body
I can no longer manage to stand up
My dear friends, let me tell you from experience
Please, please avoid adultery!

Aida Namulinda—and many other women in Ugandan villages and towns—use music, dance, and drama now more than ever to engage *aggressively* the devastation the HIV virus has caused in their communities. She directs the musical efforts of her group from her village as home base, and she references death comfortably as it is an everyday occurrence in the village.

In her analysis of similar small-scale women's social indemnity groups in neighboring Tanzania, social anthropologist Janet Bujra also locates performances including both music and dance at the very center of the educational outreach efforts of *kidembwa* women's groups:

> Investigation of an institution called *kidembwa* had also taken place. Middle-aged and elderly village women organize the collection of goods in cash and kind to support their members on the occasion of life crises (marriage, childbirth). Collections are accompanied by dancing and singing at the houses of members and (subversively in a Muslim community) the brewing and consumption of beer. These are women-only occasions from which men are excluded. *Kidembwa* is more like a network than a corporate group. (2004, 120–1)

In Ugandan village communities, such as Bute Village, women often raise multiple generations of orphaned children and take care of sick or dying family members and neighbors, while simultaneously planning for the inevitable need for similar health-care and educational needs for themselves and for their offspring. With little—and often times no—support from governmental agencies and local and foreign non-governmental organizations, women's indemnity groups function as social networks, as Bujra suggests, now often turning to more traditional and demonstratively more effective means of communicating information and history in traditional Ugandan culture—music, dance, and drama—for purposes of healing, counseling, care, education, and introducing medical interventions regarding HIV/AIDS.

WOMEN, DRAMA, AND DEVELOPMENT

Localized forms of drama have long been used in sub-Saharan Africa for purposes of development and education. In Nigeria, for example, dramas are the principal tool used to educate about female genital mutilation (FGM) by the Performance Studio Workshop, detailing within their plots the risk of contracting infections, tetanus, and AIDS. These dramas also warn against the use of unsterilized blades and how such use potentially leads to the contraction of HIV. The use of drama by local theater troupes, such as those emerging in Uganda in the 1950s, drew on emergent "musical plays," a form of drama informed by traditional modes of music and dance to tell a story. As Margaret Macpherson states when commenting on this interrelationship of the arts in Uganda, "Music, dance and drama are perhaps as inextricably linked in East Africa as anywhere." That early forms of dramatized narratives were most often didactic in nature reveals the very roots of what is often termed "theatre for development" in this area of the world (2000, 31). In order to contextualize the emergence of new forms of urban and rural dramatic efforts in the 1980s I provide a brief political history of Uganda over the past thirty years in the following section.

UGANDAN POLITICAL HISTORY

Colonial rule of Uganda ended in 1962 when the British colonial authority handed over instruments of power. Up until that time, Uganda had been a protectorate of the British crown dating back to1894. Governing authority was originally selected by the British to rest with the Baganda *kabaka*, the hereditary king of the central Ugandan Buganda kingdom. As a result in part of political machinations and the increasingly central position afforded to the Baganda people in Uganda's new government, Milton Obote, the country's first post-independence prime minister, suspended the constitution and unseated the *kabaka*, assuming the presidency for himself. One of the first acts of the Obote I government—so labeled due to Obote's later return to power—was to put forward a new constitution that (among other acts) brought local kingdoms to an end. Obote's government was overthrown by a military coup in 1971 led by his chief of the army, Col. Idi Amin Dada Oumee, at which time Obote was offered refuge in neighboring Tanzania. Amin's military government expelled nearly all Asians (estimated at approximately fifty thousand) then living in the country, an act that quickly brought chaos to a majority of the nation's industries. In addition, Amin was responsible for ruling through an aggressive and brutal program that led to the deaths of hundreds of thousands of people, often ethnic-related deaths. The Obote II government reestablished control of the country in 1980 after the government of Tanzania helped oust Amin in 1978 and after two brief presidencies (Yusef Lule and Godfrey Binaisa). Ethnic difficulties within the army—particularly clashes between Acholi and Lango ethnic-based factions—led to the expulsion of Obote once again as Tito Okello an Acholi assumed power in 1985 until 1986 at which time Yoweri Museveni's National Resistance Army assumed control of the government.

Understanding the problematic shifts in regime from the Obote I through Obote II periods—from colonial independence to the current leadership of Museveni—helps position the lack of theatrical productions and activities in Uganda during that period of time. Any overt (or even slightly veiled) political sentiment within the context of dramatic performance was potentially an unsafe activity for theatrical performers for quite some time. As Marion Frank suggests, early attempts to address political matters during these "regimes of terror" led to quick censure:

> During that year [1968], the writer Wycliff Kyingi made a comment about Obote's usurpation of power in his Luganda radio serial, *Wokulira*. The transmission of the episode happened to coincide with the day Obote came into power. The show was banned immediately, and the cast was put into prison. After that Ugandan artists realized if they wanted to comment on the political situation in their country, they had to find

alternative forms which would camouflage the political messages of the play. (1995, 33)

According to Frank, dramatic efforts during this period drew heavily on local or "folk" traditions. Since the country is composed of a plurality of ethnic traditions, drawing on local expressive culture could often veil sentiment in just such a way as to "camouflage the political messages of the play" to nonlocals (1995, 33).

A primary theme emerging in the dramatic efforts of Theatre for Development—often referred to as TFD by its practitioners in Uganda—during the Obote I and Obote II periods was the seeming conflict between traditional cultures and modernity. This dichotomous relationship was dramatized in order to present the many ways modernity and traditional cultures in actuality "existed side by side in Uganda," according to theatre historian Margaret Macpherson (2000, 32). Eckhard Breitinger rightfully problematizes the representation of the relationship between traditional culture and modernity by suggesting that specific commercial urban theatrical troupes capitalized on localized traditions, but did so in localized ways according to specific indigenous traditions (1999, 19). This dramatic mode of communication continued in the post-1986 period.

Before introducing a theory specific to the relationship between Theatre for Development and AIDS community outreach, I present a transcription and translation of a drama performed by the women of Nawaikoke Village in the eastern Busoga region of Uganda. Recorded and documented in Kibaale–Busiki Village, the visiting women of nearby Nawaikoke came to present their dramatic efforts to educate residents of surrounding villages. In *Kamalire Abantu* ("The Virus has Killed Many People"), the women of Nawaikoke dramatize the need for everyone to participate in blood screening before entering into new relationships, particularly marriage. While the original drama was offered in the Lusoga language, I present the extended drama in English translation only. I recognize that much of the flavor and flow of the original text may very well be lost in this process of translation, but still feel that enough clarity in the group's messages emerges within the dramatization of Paul's dilemma. While the play can certainly be read as a text, the reader should keep in mind that the play was framed by local songs and dances, establishing an intentionally localized cultural site and allowing a specific and historically determined means of cultural access to the play for the local villagers. That the local dramatic form has been co-opted by the women of the community—both musically and in terms of gender identity—will be commented on later. It should be noted that the women of Nawaikoke village played all of the characters—both male and female.

Kamalire abantu ("The virus has killed many people")
Nawaikoke Village Women's Group

Characters: Paul, a young man
 Nabirye, Paul's mother
 Paul's father
 Girl, Paul's girlfriend
 Sadhaibi, messenger
 Girl's mother
 Kyambu, local witchdoctor
 Mukambwe, local medical doctor
 First person
 Second person
 Third person

Paul: Kodhi, kodhi! [He knocks at the door]

Nabirye: Welcome. You are most welcome.

Paul: Yes, please.

Nabirye: How are you doing?

Paul: We are fine.

Nabirye: Welcome back.

Paul: Yes, please.

Nabirye: How is your town?

Paul: It is fine there. Thank you for keeping this home.

Nabirye: Yes, please.

Paul: Where has my father gone?

Nabirye: Don't you know your father better? He has gone to drink local brew.

Paul: OK. Mother, I'm going to stop my schooling.

Nabirye: Why my son?

Paul: Because there is a girl I have been seeing.

Nabirye: My son, why do you make me cry?

Paul: I have failed in my studies and I cannot manage.

Nabirye: All that money we have spent on you? How can you stop your education?

Paul: If Ngobi's daughter also stopped her schooling then why can I not also stop?

Nabirye: In which class did this girl stop?

Paul: Senior four.

Nabirye: My son, you have killed me.

Paul: Tell him [the father].

Nabirye: I do not know. When your father comes back he will be upset.

Paul: Mother, you tell him so that I can marry this girl. I know my father will listen to you, and he takes your word seriously.

Nabirye: My son, you are creating problems for yourself, but I guess I do not really care.

Father: [Husband enters] My wife.

Nabirye: Yes, please.

Father: How are they?

Nabirye: They are fine. My husband, should I tell you?

Father: Yes, say it.

Nabirye: I have a lot of anger today.

Father: What is it Nabirye?

Nabirye: We have a problem.

Father: What?

Nabirye: I fail to understand our son Paul.

Father: What has Paul done?

Nabirye: This boy was here.

Father: Mmmmm.

Nabirye: He came and told me that he has stopped his education.

Father: He doesn't want to study?

Nabirye: I asked him what problems he could be having with schooling.

Father: Tell me.

Nabirye: This boy replied to me, saying that he wants to get married. Now, what can we do?

Father: Are you sure you are speaking the truth about this child? Paul no longer wants to study?

Nabirye: He said he is tired of studying.

Father: And you allowed him to stop?

Nabirye: I have decided to allow him to get married.

Father: I do not want him to get married with this AIDS scourge that is everywhere. I have just paid my money to this boy. He's completing his senior four year and would have continued with his studies so that he can eventually help his younger brothers and sisters. How can he stop schooling? The term is almost coming to an end? How can he stop schooling? Nabirye, you support this?

Nabirye: What can I do? Let me call him for you so that you can talk to him.

Father: Call him.

Nabirye: Paul . . .

Paul: Yes, madam.

Nabirye: First come. Your father is calling you. I told him about the words we had.

Father: What do you have to say?

Paul: Father, I have failed in my studies.

Father: And for what reason have you failed? Didn't I pay your school fees?

Paul: Yes, father you paid the school fees.

Father: Then what?

Paul: Father, where I have stopped will be enough for me. Maybe I will get a job.

Father: Friends, with this disease around surely you joke that you are getting married?

Paul: Father, no, allow me.

Father: Hello. You are joking about getting married, yes?

Paul: Where I have stopped will be enough. The girl also went to school and she stopped in senior four.

Father: Sure, she went to school, but you are both at the same level. This level will not take you anywhere.

Paul: There are jobs. What is difficult is if you never went to school.

Father: I do not agree. I refuse. [He calls for Nabirye]

Nabirye: Yes, please.

Father: What do you say? He asks . . .

Nabirye: Since the child has decided, let us leave him. Do we have the money for them to go for blood screening?

Father: Yes. I've got the money. Paul, I want you to go bring that girl, then go for blood screening.

Paul: I will bring her, father, if you allow it.

Father: Are we going to screen her blood? If not, then I do not want her here.

Paul: Are you also going to give her the money for blood screening?

Father: How much money do you have?

Paul: You know that when I was at school you were paying my school fees. Where do you expect me to get any money?

Father: Are we going to be buying everything for you, even paraffin?

Nabirye: Let him bring the girl first.

Father: Bring the girl here so that I can see her.

Paul: How can I lose my beautiful girl? [Paul goes to get the girl]

Girl: Khodhi, khodhi. [She knocks on the door]

Nabirye: Come in. You are welcome. How are you?

Girl: We are fine.

Nabirye: How are they? Has your father agreed? Did you tell our fellow elders about these things?

Girl: Mother, I told them.

Paul: Mother, it is our job to contribute this money because I am the one who needs this girl.

Nabirye: Both sides must contribute.

Paul: It is you who needs to overlook the demands. Let my mother give me the money with one heart.

Girl: Does this mean that every person must go for blood screening?

Paul: I will just take her at once. She agrees.

Girl: Mother, the money would really help us.

Nabirye: That is what it is all about? Money?

Paul: But *muzei* [term of respect, father] says that money is scarce. I will just take her like that.

Girl: The little money will help us with some other problems. Mother, it is God who keeps a person, even if we do not go for the blood screen.

Paul: She loves me and I love her too, although we are not screened, the girl is healthy, mother. Is this girl sick? Do you see any sign on her?

Girl: I abstained myself from sex, mother.

Nabirye: Since you have decided, let me accept your decision.

Paul: The girl is so beautiful, and as for myself, I have never had any problem in my body or disease. [The father re-enters. Knocks]

Father: Hello, Nabirye.

Nabirye: Come in. You are welcome.

Father: OK.

Nabirye: How are you?

Father: They are fine. What did Paul say? I would like to know his decision.

Nabirye: He brought the girl.

Father: Did you look at the girl?

Nabirye: The girl is very beautiful.

Father: You accepted this arrangement?

Nabirye: She is very tall and beautiful.

Father: She is beautiful and tall, but comes with a lot of problems.

Nabirye: Yes, but now what can I do?

Father: You have also agreed?

Nabirye: We better spend the money on them.

Father: What can we do? [He calls for Paul]

Paul: Yes, sir. [He calls from far away]

Nabirye: Let us just write a letter because there is nothing else.

Father: Hurry up, Paul. Now, you do not want to go for blood screening? Is this what you have decided? [Paul re-enters]

Paul: You said that you do not have any money.

Father: All you are worried about is the money?

Paul: You have yet to buy this wife for me. And her parents want some good money in the letter.

Father: She told me.

Paul: My girl is healthy. We are going to get married father.

Father: Listen. You'll see. Wife, let us write the letter and send it.

Nabirye: Let us give him the letter. That is all.

Father: The other money is under the pillow.

Paul: Father, put in some good money so that I am not ashamed of my family. Where I am getting the girl they are wealthy.

Father: Now, how much money do you want us to put in?

Paul: 300,000 shillings.

Father: I have 200,000. Nabirye, check under the pillow and bring 200,000 shillings.

Paul: Mother, tell him to add more on.

Father: Add on 50,000 shillings.

Nabirye: Now write and go yourself or tell your friend Sadhaibi to help you. [The father goes to Sadhaibi's home]

Father: Hello, my friend, hello, Sadhaibi.

Sadhaibi: Come in. You are welcome.

Father: How are you?

Sadhaibi: We are fine.

Father: Please, friend, I have come to request that you take this for me. You know, Paul has defeated me.

Sadhaibi: He has defeated you?

Father: He refuses to study.

Sadhaibi: People, children of these days are very difficult.

Father: What you have to do is to deliver this letter.

Sadhaibi: And to whom do I take it?

Father: Take it to the girl's home.

Sadhaibi: Where the girl comes from?

Father: Once they accept the remaining part is for them. Let them die of AIDS.

[Sadhaibi knocks on the door]

Girl's mother: Come in. You are welcome. [Sadhaibi introduces himself and hands over the letter]

Girl: Mother, they are the ones.

Girl's mother: These are the people you have been talking of?

Girl: They are the ones.

[Later, back at Paul's house]

Sadhaibi: Here is a letter from them.

Father: What do they say? [Father calls Nabirye and Paul]

Paul: Yes, sir.

Father: Have you heard? They said that they are happy with the letter you sent to them. You see, Paul? You were telling us that 250,000 was not good enough, that it would be refused. They said 250,000 is enough. The most important thing is to go for the introduction next, Mother.

[Later, back at Girl's house]

Girl's mother: But my daughter, will you manage married life?

Girl: Mother, that is our culture. I have decided and picked my lover. What can I do?

Sadhaibi: Have you accepted? If you have agreed, tell me and also give me a reply in the form of a letter to take back.

Girl: Take it for Muzei.

Sadhaibi: You have agreed. [Sadhaibi takes the agreement back to Paul's home]

Father: My friend, you are welcome.

Sadhaibi: I have come back. They agreed.

Paul: We'll go for the introduction the same day we come with the girl.

Father: The same day? [They prepare to go]

Father: Hurry up please.

Paul: Father.

Nabirye: You are welcome.

Paul: I have come with my girl. Mother, I stole her just from there.

Nabirye: I hope there is no problem [Girl greets her mother in-law]

Paul: Mother, I have brought my girlfriend.

Nabirye: My son, welcome back.

Father: Nabirye, Nabirye, Nabirye, Nabirye.

Nabirye: Sir.

Father: Who is that talking there?

Nabirye: The child has helped us.

Father: I hear someone making noise. Who is it?

Nabirye: What do I tell you? Paul has decided to steal the girl.

Father: Just stealing?

Nabirye: He brought her.

Father: Good thing we paid some money.

Nabirye: It is good we sent the letter.

Father: Do you know that Paul already has problems. The girl was not screened and Paul himself did not go for blood screen.

Nabirye: That is *their* problem.

Father: Maybe they have the virus or not. I'm wondering why they refused to go for a blood screen.

Nabirye: It is up to them. They know better.

Father: My daughter-in-law how are you?

Girl: We are fine. How is the work? [Paul starts coughing]

Father: Paul, what is it?

Paul: I haven't felt well since I got married.

Father: What?

Paul: I feel pain in my body. Coldness comes on and off.

Nabirye: My son. [She cries]

Father: Paul, I told you.

Girl: My lover, be firm. You will be all right.

Nabirye: Mukambwe is a medical doctor in Nabisoigi Trading Center. Go to Doctor Mukambwe, but tell your father. My husband, the boy is seriously sick. Please go and call the doctor. [Members of the community come in and advise them to take him to the witch doctor]

First person: Just go to the witch doctor.

Second person: Go to Kyambu, the witch doctor. [The two start singing about the Walugono, the ancestors]

Third person: Are these not spirits?

Father: They are spirits.

Nabirye: Cover him. Put some local herbs on a broken piece of a pot and put burnt charcoal on it so that he feels the smoke.

Girl: The spirits. Please come slowly, slowly.

Nabirye: We want you to tell us what is in this home.

Father: Bring the chicken. Bring the chicken. People, the one with a chicken should hurry up.

Kyambu: *Lubale* [spirit], if you are the one or *wintu* [spirit], all of you stand up and come and tell us what is in this home.

Nabirye: My son has never been with AIDS unless you are the one who came with it.

Girl: Please leave me. This is a big problem I now have.

Nabirye: Bring the doctor so that he can check him. People, my child is dying. My fellow ladies, help me. The boy is dying. My child is dying. [Community starts crying]

Nabirye: People, the boy is dead.

Girl: People, he is dead.

Nabirye: My son, I told you to leave the girl.

Father: This is what you wanted. The community is dead. It is dead.

Theatre for Development is a dramatic effort that has continued to grow in influence and importance in several countries in sub-Saharan Africa since the 1970s. TFD is a well-recognized phenomenon in East Africa—elsewhere in Africa such efforts are often labeled as "popular theatre"—yet the two framing terms in this cultural phenomenon of TFD need qualification. First, the term "theatre"—as a dramatic genre, theatre for development is unique, and in many ways different from other cultural dramatic activities, such as performances by local community theatre, European plays performed in local language translations, and local-languages theatrical productions, such as those offered by the Luganda Language Theatre in Uganda. In Uganda, this difference is clearly marked. There are often differences, for example, in the intent, language, and entertainment value of TFD. Second, the term "development"—Theatre for Development does not attempt to address "figures and infrastructures, gross national product, the growth of industries, and suchlike," as Rose Mbowa suggests (1998, 261). This is perhaps, as Mbowa points out, a traditional and mistaken understanding of development in the so-called third world. Rather, as Mbowa and others underscore, the "development" in TFD frequently attempts to ignite and inform the consciousness of people, communities, and the nation in order for meaningful change to occur.

TFD is especially of significance in rural areas where literacy is lowest. While figures for rural literacy rates cannot be accurately measured or represented, the overall rate for women is significantly lower than is the rate among men. According to the International Red Cross, the overall literacy rate is 62 percent of the entire population, but only 54 percent of women are able to read and write. That the women in Nawaikoke village have access to neither television nor radio coupled with the fact that the

54 percent literacy rate is most likely much lower in this village helps to explain the importance of TFD in the women's outreach efforts of this village and those of many other villages. "How could we do otherwise," one woman explained to me during my visit with this group of women after the death of Paul in Nabirye's arms in their dramatic presentation.

THEATRE FOR DEVELOPMENT POST-OBOTE II

Tanzanian theatre historian Penina Mlama outlines several ways in which TFD and other popular theatre movements in East Africa since the 1960s have brought about significant social changes (1991). In her study of the important Kamiriithu Project, a theatrical educational effort in Kenya in the 1970s, Marion Frank confirms that in the group's initial play (drafted by Ngugi wa Thiong'o and Ngugi wa Mirii), music and dance were inextricable to the efforts of the drama in such a way as to allow, according to Mlama, "the peasants to unleash their rich artistic talents in an expression of their suffering" (Mlama 1991, 93).

TFD efforts began in earnest in Uganda in the mid 1980s when The National Resistance Movement (NRM) of President Yoweri Museveni came into power in 1986. At that time there were significant opportunities to support the use of music, dance, and drama in the efforts to rebuild the spirit, culture, and political and economic infrastructures of the country following the devastation incurred during the regime of Idi Amin (1971–1979). The late Rose Mbowa's efforts to document and analyze the power of TFD can be understood as an excellent example of how such community-based social phenomena can provide the roots for many of the dramatic and musical traditions discussed in this study, such as the Nawaikoke women's drama presented earlier in this chapter:

> [L]ocal people were attracted to the grounds of the village's Catholic Church by drumming and dancing. The drum is a powerful emitter of messages in Uganda. It is also a great source of entertainment throughout the country. When a sufficiently large group of people had assembled, Muganga started a discussion. By the end of the first day six women had committed themselves to the project with the full support of their husbands. . . . Already the first stages of articulating more effective development strategies had been reached. At subsequent meetings in Natyole parish on Saturday afternoons—all meetings took place on Saturday afternoons—each problem was discussed in turn, and a start was made at composing songs relating to them. Then, with Muganga's assistance, these songs were elaborated further and incorporated with other creative material into plays. These plays dealt with local people's problems and possible solutions. When ready, the plays were performed in the local church grounds for the whole village; this was after forth-

coming plays had been advertised through the resistance committee, at church services and via the mosque. Through plays, the community was enabled to debate its problems publicly and to arrive at collectively agreed solutions. (1998, 264–65)

Music, dance, and the drum are highlighted in Mbowa's description of the culturally organic approach to engaging TFD in a village setting. It is interesting to note in Mbowa's overview that the symbolic importance of the drum is further situated within the communicative arts. The specific "event" to which Mbowa refers took place over several weeks, as the village was encouraged to draw on the powers of music, dance, and drama to address socioeconomic challenges facing the community. The central mission of TFD, as Mbowa suggests, is to transform

> . . . peasants into planners, [TFD] has within it the capability of enlarging the popular constituency for change. It can reduce the burdens on an overstretched, limited national budget by encouraging and empowering ordinary people to make many local but strategic decisions for themselves. In sum, it provides a powerful facility for the development of the country, attractive to the central government as well as to local people. (1998, 269–70)

Today, many villages in Uganda adopt the strategic tools of TFD for addressing HIV/AIDS in local areas. The women of Nawaikoke village, for example, directly address much needed local changes by introducing music and drama as very necessary medical interventions in their village.

SONG TEXTS AND BLOOD TESTING

Most women's groups with whom I have worked compose their own songs and dramas, drawing on *local* musical and dance traditions to support and anchor their performances. None claim to have "borrowed" their materials, although several groups have songs in their repertoire that originate with music and drama groups such as TASO, the AIDS Support Organization in Kampala—songs such as "When We Lose One Member" are common to several groups. The didactic efforts of women's group are typically located within traditional performance contexts. Several village groups draw on traditional forms of dance, drama, and music to demonstrate, for example, the problems that can arise if one turns solely to the traditional, local medical model—the witch doctor—rather than embracing the so-called Western medical model. My encounters with women's indemnity groups confirm that musical or dramatic performances are often the principle sources for the production of knowledge and the development of behavior change regarding HIV/AIDS. For many women, music and, in particular, songs are powerful tools not only for education, but also for patient care and bereavement counseling.

Embedded within the texts of many songs I have recorded in various areas of Uganda are direct accounts of the medical issues women confront on a daily basis. One theme that is centrally located in local performances concerns the efforts of women to encourage villagers to travel to larger towns to have their blood tested, especially those who are considering marriage or entering into new physical relationships. According to Aida Namulinda of Bute Village, "you know, these men that we live with, they cannot do without sex. For men sex is a *natural biological act*. They feel it is something *God given*." By singing about the need for blood tests, Aida and other women feel that they can fight the spread of the virus head on, especially regarding male-to-female transmission. Performance for many women is their only weapon, and communicating to others that knowledge of one's sero blood status translates to power is a primary reason for singing.

There are many commonly held beliefs associated with the HIV virus detailed in village women's songs, such as the suggestion that AIDS selects the body it wants to infect, deliberately choosing its victims. Another view that emerges in song texts is that if an HIV-positive man sleeps with six women, only the sixth woman will become infected with HIV: the other five are thought to remain safe. Recurring themes include warnings about men purposely piercing their condoms and that alcohol should be avoided due to the potential for one to lose their sense of direction. Songs also warn of the problems associated with women who attend discos or social clubs frequented by so-called "disco boys." A more troubling theme found in several of the song texts I have recorded in disparate contexts is the belief that the HIV virus was introduced to Africa as a biological weapon by American and European governments.

The following series of excerpts of song texts underscores the issue of blood testing as a means for social empowerment of women. In the first song, "Luno Olumbe Lwatwhidhira," Florence Kumunhyu (see Figure 3.5), the leader of the Buwolomera Development Association (BUDEA) in Buwolomera Village, concludes the first section of an extended performance with the suggestion that blood testing be undertaken *together* by couples. Having one's blood tested and determining one's sero blood status should, therefore, lead to knowledge and power, thus putting an end to secrecy.

"Luno olumbe lwatwidhira"
BUDEA

Chorus—If you have knowledge of the disease, please tell us

Solo—Do not say that we are no longer scared
Though talking about it brings more sorrow
But since you have asked me to tell you properly
Then sit comfortably and I will tell you
This disease has sincerely come to finish us
When you first catch the virus, it is fearful
But now that we have all caught it, we are no longer ashamed
When we first came to know, we felt sorrow
But now we are used to it, we have no problem
Even you people here today
We tell you that when you catch it, you need to know
When you get to know you find something to do
Then you take care of yourself and continue your life for some days
This disease came for us
Sincerely Ugandans, friends, we are in sorrow
It has combined the adults with the young
Furthermore, it has been a shameful disease to talk about
It is still a problem
Furthermore, there is no treatment
But, those of you who are unmarried should take an HIV test with your lovers
Also, those of you who are planning to marry should take the HIV test along
with your partner

Figure 3.5 Florence Kumunhyu.

The women of the Tulamuke Group in Bugwe Village take Florence Kumunhyu's proposal one step further. In the chorus of "Twelile Bene," the women's group suggests a specific site in nearby Iganga town where blood can be tested and where patients and clients can be treated and counseled. IDAAC—the Integrated Development Association and AIDS Concern in Iganga—runs a weekly testing clinic at the Iganga Hospital, and through songs and dances—often inserted into dramas—local villagers acquire information about testing dates and times, and even specifics about medical procedures.

"Twelile bene"
Tulamuke Group, Bugwe Village, Busiki County (Iganga)

Let us mourn, let us mourn, let us mourn for ourselves, wooo
Now that we are in hell
Let us mourn, let us mourn, let us mourn for ourselves, wooo
Now that we all have AIDS
Clap and drum
The AIDS disease came to finish us
Let us go to IDAAC
Friends, we need to go for HIV testing

As with the women in Bugwe Village in their performance of "Twelile Bene," the women in Bukona Village also encourage fellow villagers to visit IDAAC in Iganga town within the context of clapping and drumming in "Silimu Okutumala!" In addition to sexual partners, the excerpted text from a performance by the Bukona Women's Group encourages family members—specifically the singer's mother—to accompany their children in order to provide support as well as access to testing and counseling for themselves. In "Silimu Okutumala!" women of the village are encouraged to don banana leaves—symbols of death and mourning—and adopt a position of openness regarding HIV in order to live longer and healthier lives.

"Silimu okutumala!"
Bukona Group

Fellow women, put on a banana leaf if you see your friend, go to IDAAC
Women, put on a banana leaf if you see a friend
AIDS has finished us
Clap and drum
My mom, Nabirye, let us go to IDAAC for HIV counseling and testing
So we can raise our children for a longer period of time

In the remote village of Kitabi near Ishaka town in western Uganda, the Kanihiro group of women perform among the surrounding rural communities when they have available funds for transportation. In the summary of a drama performed by the Kanihiro Group, a young girl refuses to accept the proposal of marriage to a young man due to her fears of contracting HIV.

Omwishiki yayangire omurekye
("The girl doesn't want to get married to you, leave her alone")
Kanihiro Group, Kitabi (Ishaka, western Uganda)

Summary: A young man wants to get married to a certain young woman. The woman refuses at first due in part to bad experiences she has had with her family and HIV/AIDS. All of her sisters and brothers have died from complications resulting from AIDS. The woman's parents ask the woman and her suitor to take an HIV test first if they wish to get married. They visit a doctor, have the test taken, and rejoice when they find that both of them are negative! A large ceremony is then performed where the woman is "given away" in a colorful traditional Kinyankole ceremony with dancing, drumming, and singing.

Boy: This girl is very beautiful, eee.
   I really must take her.
Chorus: The girl is really beautiful, and you must take her.
   You really must take her now that you are sworn to each other.
Boy: I swear by my mother, by my father.
   The girl has a very nice and long neck.
   Very white teeth.
   Very good buttocks.
   Her legs are like banana plants!
Chorus: Now that you really love that lady, eee.
   You really must take her.
Boy: Gentlemen, you have said those words.
   But I am worried about the killer disease AIDS.
   Please come to my home.
Girl: I cannot come.
Boy: Please come to my home.
Girl: I cannot come.
Boy: I will buy you beer.
   I will give you one hundred Uganda shillings.
Girl: I do not want that.
Boy: I will buy you a watch.
Girl: I do not want that.
Boy: I will buy you a nice dress.
Girl: I do not want that.
Boy: I will buy you beer.
Girl: I do not want that.

Boy: I will take you to a dance.
Girl: I do not want that.
Boy: I will take you to watch a video.
Girl: I do not want that.
Chorus: The girl has refused, please leave her alone.
　　She is worried about the deadly AIDS.
　　The girl has refused.
　　Please leave her alone.
　　She is worried of the deadly AIDS.
Girl: I am a girl from the famous clan
　　Even if I am poor,
　　Even if I have not paid my school fees.
　　You can say whatever you want to,
　　Even if you bring the most expensive item
　　You may kill me from here, but I will not come to your home,
　　I swear by my father.
Chorus: She's taken an "oath," ahh.
　　The girl has refused, please leave her alone.
　　She is worried about the deadly AIDS.
　　The girl has refused, please leave her alone.
　　She is worried about the deadly AIDS.
Boy: You are the girl I love.
　　But I have asked you to marry me and you have refused.
　　Now that I have gone, I will return.
　　I will come back with my car.
　　If you refuse to enter it, I will bribe a policeman.
Chorus: AIDS has killed all her relatives.
　　She is the only one remaining.
　　The person she really wants to get married to is the one she will not
　　go with.
　　She listens to her parent's advice.
　　She responds to the calls for the need for protection against HIV.
Boy: Please come to my home.
Girl: I cannot come.
Boy: Please come to my home.
Girl: I cannot come.
Boy: I will buy you beer.
　　I will give you one hundred Uganda shillings.
Girl: I do not want that.
Boy: I will buy you a watch.
Girl: I do not want that.
Boy: I will buy you a nice dress.
Girl: I do not want that.
Boy: I will buy you beer.
Girl: I do not want that.

Boy: I will take you to a dance.
Girl: I do not want that.
Boy: I will take you to watch a video.
Girl: I do not want that.
Chorus: The girl has refused.
  Please leave her alone.
  She is worried about the deadly AIDS.
Boy: You are the girl I love.
  But I have asked to marry you and you have refused.
  Now I have gone.
  When I come back, I will come with my car.
  If you refuse to enter it, I will bribe a policeman.
Chorus: Whose car is that? Whose car is that?
Girl's Mother: Who is this man visiting us?
  He might be HIV positive.
  He is disturbing my daughter.
  Please call the LCs [Local Council members] and they will arrest
  him.
  They should take him to prison.
Chorus: The girl has refused, please leave her alone.
  She is worried of the deadly AIDS.
Girl's Mother: Gentleman, if you really want to marry my daughter,
  Go to the doctor and have your sero statistics checked.
  If both of you are safe, then you can come back and take my
  daughter.
  Come back and you can take her.
  We are on our knees praying for you my children.
  We are on our knees praying for you.
  Go to the doctor.
Boy: Mzee[39] we are back, Mzee we are back.
  We have been declared HIV negative.
  Here are the results!
  I must marry this girl
Girl's Mother: You must really take the girl.
  Please join us in the celebration as we officially give her away
  She is free of HIV.

The text of the song that closes the drama illustrates the young woman's reluctance to engage her suitor's offers of marriage. Only after the young man agrees to have his blood tested along with the young woman, and when the results are demonstrated to be negative for both, does the celebration of the union finally occur.

Encouraging blood testing before entering into new sexual relationships is just one of many interventions communicated in musical performance that can be isolated for analysis. In other songs community consciousness concerning presumed immorality of and danger associated with prostitution is raised, as are the effectiveness of total sexual abstinence and the practice of zero grazing (that is, faithfulness to one partner). Other song and drama texts inform communities of local and regional government initiatives regarding medical interventions, as well as possibilities for developing income-generating activities (IGAs). The most prominent intervention introduced in song texts, however, points to the need for empowerment by women grounded in the knowledge of behavioral patterns regarding sexual activity.

WOMEN TAKING CARE OF THEMSELVES: "WE DO NOT LOOK SICK"

The main office of The Good Shepherd Support Action Center (GOS-SACE) is located along the Jinja Road leading to Mukono Town. In a one-room office, the counselors of GOSSACE gather for ongoing training, to collect medical supplies, and for their own continuing medical care and counseling. All are HIV positive themselves. During my first encounter with the GOSSACE counselors, several of the women offered their personal testimonies. The testimony offered by Hadija Namutebi on that day is particularly poignant and clearly representative of so many women who find themselves in her situation—HIV positive and left alone to raise multiple children.

> *Namutebi—My names are Hadija Namutebi. I am thirty-five years old. I have eight children. Their father died in 1990 and left me with those children when they were young. The eldest child stopped school and got a boy and married because of lack of money. The next child is in S3 [Secondary 3], the next in S2, the next in P7 [Primary 7], the next in P6, and last is in P3. One of them is sick. I say I am living today only because I came to GOSSACE. I had friends who said they had a big clinic here. I thought it might be like home care, so I went to get treatment. When I first found out that I had this disease, after I had just buried my husband, I immediately thought that I was going to die in just two days. But due to my internal strength and by obtaining good counseling, I have been kept alive to this date. Now, I joined this organization and together we move around singing, sensitizing people who have been hiding. Even me, when I joined [GOSSACE] I was very thin. I knew that I could die at any time. But when I joined here I became stronger, and now I eat, I drink, and I go out in order to counsel others. I tell them, "Come out, do not spread the disease." This association helps us to*

live for much longer periods of time as you can see. We do not look sick, and I pray that I will have more years, like twenty more years. Those are my words.

Women's indemnity groups in eastern Uganda fight an uphill battle on a daily basis against a fast-spreading virus and disease. Many such groups sing and dance for themselves and for others to introduce interventions that focus on gender-specific issues for women and female youth, and their songs and dramas warn against participating in risky environments or engaging in unprotected sexual behavior. These village performances also outline support networks available from the greater community (the availability of condoms and testing), as well as disseminating information, mobilizing resources, and raising consciousness concerning issues related to HIV/AIDS, and to counsel and support women in individual groups.

As the following excerpt from the Annual Report of Noelina Namukisa's social service agency, Meeting Point Kampala (MPK) outlines, a holistic approach to servicing a clientele of HIV-positive women and their children is essential for the success any of educational outreach. That music, dance, and drama are highlighted in the outline of MPK's functions in the community is not unusual; women place tremendous value on the ability of performance to achieve many of the very necessary goals of community health outreach and care:

Purposes of the Organization
- To create general awareness of problems related to HIV/AIDS among PLWHAs [People Living with HIV/AIDS] and the affected persons.
- To provide social, spiritual psychological support to people with AIDS and their relatives.
- To help the most vulnerable groups to meet their day to day needs.
- Promote social reintegration and rehabilitation for youth in difficult conditions in Kampala city.
- To increase the literacy levels in the area.
- To educate and disseminate information through Music, Dance and Drama.
- To support Income Generating Activities [IGAs] in these vulnerable communities.

(*Annual Report 2002*, Meeting Point Kampala)

CONCLUSION

Not everyone is at risk. Some couples have followed Christian tenets to the letter, married without prior sexual experience, and remained faithful to one another. Some men are polygamous but do not seek women other than

> *their wives. Moreover, even among the most sexually active people, access to formally and informally transmitted information can lead to rational reflection and risk reduction. Nevertheless, numerous constraints related to sex, gender, and power impede HIV prevention.*
>
> *The rapid spread of AIDS in Africa results from the deep, multistranded crisis in political economy and health. Transmitted via sex and blood, AIDS is surrounded by dense meanings to which cultural constructions of gender roles are central. Women are especially at risk because of their poverty, their relative powerlessness in the overall organization of African societies, and their subordinate position with respect to men. These conditions circum-scribe their options so that few are able to practice safer sex. Those who have reduced their risk are women with decision-making autonomy based on their capacity to support themselves without resorting to sex within or outside of marriage. (Grundfest Schoepf 1997, 16 and 329)*

Problems faced today by women and women's indemnity groups in Uganda are legion. Cultural expectations for engagement in polygynous relationships create perhaps one of the most harmful pathways toward infection:

> In Africa, 30 to 50 percent of married women are currently in polyganous marriages and nearly all wives must be emotionally and economically adjusted to the possibility of finding themselves in a polygynous marriage at any time. This means that African women are aware that the greatest danger comes from their spouses, and it is most likely that the majority of female AIDS victims have been infected by their husbands. (Hope 1999, 6)

Other issues confronting women in Uganda today include inadequate sources of medical supplies and drugs for even the most basic care and treatment; some hospitals have no drugs whatsoever available to them, no painkillers or antimalarial treatments or other basic essential drugs and medicines. Most women's groups do not have viable, ongoing income generating activities to sustain their collective efforts. The increasing availability of HIV/AIDS diagnosis, follow-up care, and treatment, how-ever, *is* a source of hope and a powerful incentive for many to continue encouraging others, for example, to go to testing centers to determine their sero blood status.

Women's drama and music groups contribute significant medical interventions at the grassroots in Uganda. The reflections in this chapter underscore at a basic level the efforts of many women and women's in-demnity groups throughout Uganda to combat the HIV virus and AIDS disease in ways in which local governments and private multinational and multilateral non-governmental organizations have been largely chal-lenged. Local and external funds have enormous difficulty finding their way to any social and medical networks that exist in remote villages.

The songs, dances, and dramatic performances of the women's groups documented in this chapter (and countless others) challenge us, therefore, to situate women's efforts in the ongoing decline in Uganda's HIV infection rate. The implementation of external initiatives based solely or in part on the Western medical model have proven largely inaccessible and expensive in rural Ugandan contexts, and only when contextualized within performances drawing on local music, dance, and dramatic traditions do medical initiatives offer a chance of hope and change in local health-care systems.

Interlude 3
"Stick to One Person"
Nawaikoke Village Women's Ensemble

THE WOMEN OF NAWAIKOKE VILLAGE whose drama about Nabirye's son's reluctance to be tested before getting married (referenced in this chapter) also rely on musical performances not associated with dramas to tell their stories. This interlude offers the text of one such song performed by the Nawaikoke women on the need for zero grazing, that is, sticking to one partner.

Figure Interlude 3.1 Women of the Nawaikoke Village Drama Group perform.

"Ogumire kumuntumoyiza"
("Stick to one person")

Solo—Marriages are no longer stable
AIDS has stopped the seduction by introducing funerals
Chorus—Marriages are no longer stable
AIDS has stopped the seduction by introducing funerals
Solo—Seduction is no longer sweet
AIDS stops the seduction at the funeral rites
Be firm, my child, stick to one person, my child
Be firm and stick to one person, my daughter, Edithy, be firm
Stick to one person, my daughter, be firm
It has finished killing people, the disease of AIDS
Have you seen that thing, the virus, the AIDS disease?
Have you seen that thing, the virus?
When that thing comes you get malaria
Things start to swell, you do not go out into the sunshine
You get body itches, women, you begin slimming, you always feel worried
Cultural things will come in
They ask for a goat, we bring a goat
We go to a witch doctor called "Kyambu," that is the name of that witch doctor
We bring the sheet, we bring the basket
He asks for a chicken, we bring a chicken
Have you seen that thing, the virus?
Then the big one, the really serious virus comes
You get malaria. diarrhea comes
Puss will flow, then flies will swarm
Then you can no longer drink water from such place
It will be difficult to eat food from that place
Have you seen the earthly things, have you seen that thing, the virus?
That virus killed my father, it killed my aunt, it killed my uncle
It killed very many people in the village, the rich and the poor, the disabled
The virus is dangerous and deadly
I have even stopped the singing
Bye, I have finished

4

"TODAY WE HAVE NAMING OF PARTS"[40]
Languaging AIDS Through Music

"Baasi ya sirimu efuuse ntanda ya walumbe"
The bus of *Slim* has become the carrier of the killer
It parks at TASO[41] as it embarks on its journey through the valley
From there it goes to the killer
Where you have bought citizenship
Woe to us who are orphaned when we are still babies
The widowers are nowhere to be seen while
Many widows have remarried
Rape cases are numerous
Lord help us, we are tired of the bus

—Ambassadors of Hope

BEFORE HIV/AIDS WAS "INVENTED"—that is, before it was (re-)named with contemporary, scientific nomenclature—the virus was known at far-reaching levels in Uganda as *Slim* (or *Silimu*). Today, musical performances continue to draw on historical linguistic localizations, such as with the term *Slim*. The first scientific study disclosing the presence and manifestation of HIV in Uganda was authored by David Serwadda (along with others), a clinician at Mulago Hospital in Kampala. The title of the study published in *Lancet*, "Slim Disease: A New Disease in Uganda and its Association with HTLV-III/LAV Infection" (1985), reveals that in the early 1980s a deep, localized enculturation of the disease existed, even within African medical communities.

Figure 4.1 Robinah, Ambassadors of Hope.

In his documentation of individual stories of people living with HIV—*Growing Up Positive: Stories from a Generation of Young People Affected by AIDS*—Ian Lucas underscores this very issue by including a story of a young Ugandan mother, Hope. In her narrative, Hope locates memory of the disease in a time before it was "named" and after it was known to be sexually transmitted:

> When I came to know about AIDS, I didn't even know the name AIDS. We used to call is *Slim*, because the people used to die thin. So they used to say, that illness, it slims you down. You become very thin. We didn't even know that it was a sexually transmitted disease. We used to think that Slim was a disease that was traditional, like charms. In this tradition of medicines that they use on people, if they don't pay their debts, or if they steal things from people, the bewitch them and they become slim and they die. So we used to hear "Slim, Slim, Slim." (1995, 96)

Terms such as *Slim* continue, however, to communicate more than mere colloquialisms for the disease. For many in Uganda, this term—and many others—references the history and the cultural rootedness of the AIDS pandemic, specifically in Uganda. Positioning the localization of AIDS in African contexts within social and medical discourse becomes increasingly important for mapping the spread of the disease, as anthropologists George Bond and Joan Vincent suggest, "if it follows the moving frontier of AIDS to the newly pacified north and northeast, knowledge of 'local knowledge' will become critical to AIDS intervention and control" (1997b, 89). The use of the term *Ukimwi* in neighboring Tanzania and in bordering Kenya indicates a similar, local nonmedical "naming." In Kenya, for example, every *kabila* (ethnic tribe) has a term for HIV/AIDS. *Ukimwi* is the more generic for the majority of the country's Kiswahili speakers. Other Bantu language speakers embrace differing local terms, often in addition to *Ukimwi*. Such linguistic localization confirms that the HIV/AIDS is culturally determined in many parts of East Africa. In a conversation with David Akombo, Kenyan ethnomusicologist, he suggested that "some tribes believe sexual promiscuity to be the cause while others believe that bad spirits are responsible. The Luo of Nyanza call it *Chira*, which means a curse." Thus, a "naming of parts," as the title of this chapter suggests, potentially opens doors not only to cultural analyses, but perhaps more importantly to culturally sensitive medical interventions.

As critical as the localization of HIV/AIDS within many African communities is the concomitant linguistic effort by other communities to assign the virus and disease a nameless, unlabeled status, what author Greg Behrman calls an invisible status (2004). Linguistic stigmatization and social isolation, for example, often create social spaces within which accepted cultural responses to AIDS intentionally reference the disease as unnamed or at times even unmarked or (re-)marked, as Yegan Pillay suggests:

> In Uganda, Zimbabwe, and Tanzania AIDS is such a taboo subject that people refer to it as "the disease" and children whose parents have suc-cumbed to the disease would rather attribute their deaths to poisoning, tuberculosis, or diarrhea. (2003, 110)

One of the most common ways of referencing the HIV virus in the Lu-ganda language is *akawuka obulwadde bwobukaba*, meaning "disease through sexual contact," a reference that circumfuses the manifestation of the virus with the most common means of transference of the virus in Uganda. Another popular reference to the disease, *nawukera wa Silimu AIDS*, ("the *Slim* disease of AIDS for which there is no cure") interestingly links the local—*Silimu*—directly with the global—AIDS. *Mukenenya*—to slim or to waste away—is another frequent Luganda term attached to HIV/ AIDS. The languaging of the disease—the active linguistic engagement of naming of parts—occurs frequently and perhaps most significantly and creatively within the performance of songs and other musically infused dramas, and in this chapter several unique musico-linguistic responses are documented.

The term *wolilawofula*, for example, was first introduced in the song "Wolilala wofula" performed by popular Ugandan musician Mathiasi Walukaga. The term evokes an image of HIV/AIDS leading to social abandonment since, as Walukaga suggests, there is little chance for surviv-ing in a place where "you have just eaten." Such strong images continue to emerge within songs texts and are not anomalous; they are increas-ingly expected and anticipated. Such localization of HIV/AIDS in song texts—whether marked or unmarked—confirms what Sarah Birabwa suggests as mirroring the "shock" experienced by many Ugandans even to this day:

> HIV/AIDS has shocked the Ugandan population. The different names the dreadful disease is known by include, *current affairs, slow leak, slimming diet, slower puncture, silent killer, wailing for all, the modern disease* and many others exemplify the extent of fear. (2002, 41)

LOCALIZATION OF AIDS

I open this section, a more detailed "naming of parts" if you will, drawing on a conversation with Mzee Mutebi Musa, a highly respected traditional healer in Uganda. In response to a general question concerning the ways in which AIDS is referenced in the songs with which he was familiar, he immediately drew on three distinct categories of localization—physical (*Silimu),* social (*Obulwadde bwaffe*), and objectification (*Akavera*)—as is clear in his response given below:

Barz—*Do you know any terms that people use in songs that refer to AIDS?*

Musa—*Yes! Because AIDS came through sexual intercourse some people see it as Silimu, or as a result of sexual immorality, Obul- wadde bwaffe (Our disease). They use many metaphors nowadays in songs and in dramas, just as in real life. We do give them condoms to protect themselves against HIV/AIDS. Other terms we sing about include Akavera (polythene bag). You know, a cow cannot survive for a day after eating a polythene bag. The bag gets in their stomach and destroys them.... We also have Mubandha mpola (slow pain). You see, one can live with this disease for a long time until death.*

For Mzee Musa—and others—AIDS was initially a social phenomenon outside of Western medical discourse for a long enough period to allow local conceptualizations to take root and flourish. Musa interjects a fourth category at the end of his response, almost as an afterthought—*Mubandha mpola*—one that references a very human, physicalized manifestation of pain and suffering that accompanies the onset of AIDS.

Musical performances such as the song texts that Mzee Musa draw on in his reflection can be understood as tools for positioning historic localizations of AIDS within older referential experiences of the disease. For example, in the text of "Olumbe lwamalo abanta" performed by a local *embaire* xylophone group in the remote village of Kibaale in the eastern Busiki region, a solo male singer outlines how local villagers first became aware of AIDS through local councils and various media. The singer continues by suggesting that AIDS does not have the ability to discriminate based on race, physical strength or stature, social status, or religious affiliation. Only at the end of the song is AIDS referenced directly with the Western term. It is interesting to note that the older, lo- calized term, *Silimu,* is used first before quickly juxtaposed with the more Western medical term *Ayidisi,* i.e., AIDS, a localized pronunciation (and spelling) adopted by many, at least in eastern regions of Uganda.

"Olumbe lwamala abantu"
("Death killed all the people")
Kibaale *Embaire* Ensemble

My grands [parents and elders], I am happy to see you
Death killed all the people

My fellow deaf people, let me sing about how death has finished us
My grands, death has finished us
Whenever I think about death I sit and mourn
God is great and has power
Death, my friends, came to finish us
My fellows, death came to finish us
Youth, the virus has reached you
And my mothers also where you are seated
I am happy to see you
My fellows, Happy New Year
And I am happy to see that you have made it through your problems
And also that the sun is shining
And to have made it through that famine
When I was listening to the radio
I picked the news
Kasujja [the electoral commission] announced it
And in the *New Vision* [English language newspaper], they also wrote about it
When you bring the *Bukedde* [local language newspaper],
they also wrote about it
That in Mukono District they have this disease
My friends, it has come with force
Death has come to finish us
Even this side of Seeta town has got the disease
My friends, it comes with coldness
Death comes from Mukono
Father, it has entered in us
It also entered Bbombo
Listen, when it reached there
All who were there were killed
Diseases reached in large numbers
Death led to graves and to the soil
Father, even if you are brown, friend, it takes you the same way
Even if you are small, friend, it takes you the same way
However black you are, friend, it takes you the same way
The rich and the poor follow the same path
However red you are, I tell you this my mothers
This soil will never be satisfied
It would have been satisfied with Sheika
This soil will never be satisfied
It would have been satisfied with Muzeyita
When I think of the death of youths I sit and pray
There are those who are saved and those who are Muslim
Even if you are a Muslim you also pray to Allah, to God
It takes you out of the world without any opportunity to respond

Listen, *Silimu* has killed us
Look, it has also killed the children
Like this *Ayidisi* [AIDS]—that is *Silimu*—has also finished people
All the brown people, *Silimu* has finished them
It has killed all the ladies
Whenever I sit down I mourn
Thinking about death and how it will force me to leave this world

Sheika, a famous sheik and leader of the local Muslim community, lived in Namakoko Village in Busiki County, Busoga, the area in which this performing group lives. This sheik had the largest and most beautiful house in the entire Iganga District before dying of AIDS in 1998. The reference to the soil not being satisfied, suggests that even the death of a powerful man will not satisfy the earth. Muzeyita is the name of the boy who first sang for me when I recorded in this village in 1999. On reflection, this was an indirect musical way for the group to inform me of the boy's death.

Local terms for HIV/AIDS as well as for condoms appear in many of the songs, dances, and dramas that I have recorded in Uganda over the years. As will quickly become evident in the song translations included in this chapter, references to the disease are often spontaneously contextualized in performance. So, one might ask, in a world where HIV and AIDS are everyday terms for the majority of Ugandans, why are localized terms still maintained? I asked individuals on several different occasions if the use of HIV/AIDS as a blanket cover term was avoided as a way of purposefully remembering older conceptualizations, or if in fact this avoidance represented a lack of penetration of technical knowledge of the disease. I often found the answer to my questions directly in front of me within musical performances. Medical professionals have confirmed my observations that audience members at musical performances appear to be much less threatened, much less anxious when highly technical, scientific, or medical "AIDS talk" is abandoned in favor of "un-translated" localized terminologies.

In the sections that follow, I outline a series of translations—surely not all-inclusive by any means—an unpacking of many localized terms for HIV/AIDS. Each of these terms was verified and crosschecked with language educators at the City Language Center in Bwaise, outside of Kampala. In addition, I ran a focus group with a group of high school students attending Makerere College School in Kampala with the goal of confirming the accuracy of my observations, transcriptions, and translations.[42] For each example in this exercise of "naming of parts" I note the original musical source of the localization and offer a brief cultural and linguistic translation. The intent of these sections is to demonstrate the overwhelming wealth of linguistic referential modes that are adopted and maintained in songs, dramas, testimonies, and everyday discourse within communities throughout the country, from the Bushenyi region to the West, to the Busoga region to the East. It is beyond the scope of this study to cover the phenomenon of localization of HIV/AIDS throughout the country of Uganda. Rather, I offer my reflections on experiences in eastern, central, and some areas of the western part of the country.

During the process of transcribing and translating song texts that I have recorded or documented over the years, I began to see patterns that led me to organize a particular schema for positioning local knowledge of HIVAIDS through musical performance. The schema suggested below positions individual textual references into eleven categories. Each category collects similar thematic references to the virus and disease. As the breakdown of these categories illustrates, musical performances throughout the country not only reinforce local processes of knowing and understanding the disease, but they also preserve historical ways of remembering the disease (as will be discussed in greater detail in chapter 6).[43] The illustrations support an understanding of the wide variety of cultural experiences available to the musical performance of HIV/AIDS within the following eleven categories:

1. Disease and Virus
2. Medical and Physical Issues
3. Slimming, Wasting Away, and Physical Diminution
4. Death
5. Insects, Animals, and Nature
6. Transportation
7. Objects
8. Cautionary
9. Clearing Away, Destruction, and Disaster
10. Personification and Embodiment
11. Cause and Effect

DISEASE AND VIRUS

The first category documents internal references to local understandings of HIV/AIDS as a specific virus or disease in songs and dramas. As discussed, *Silimu* is perhaps the most common local conceptualization adopted in songs, as the following song text, "Silimu yatumaraho," performed by the Kashenyi Model Primary School (see Figure 4.2) in the western Bushenyi region, demonstrates.

"Silimu yatumaraho"
("*Silimu* is finishing us")
Kashenyi Model Primary School

Chorus—Please, all Ugandans, listen to us
Listen to our sorrowful and depressing message
Life these days seems useless
The deadline disease, *Silimu*, is wiping us out
Solo—To show that *Silimu* is very deadly
You become severely wasted, losing all energy
At the end of it all you get severe diarrhea
Your relatives run away from you
Our president and other people have been trying to fight the deadly evil
There are messages over the radio every day
But Ugandans have refused to listen and take heed
These are the ways HIV is transmitted
Unprotected sexual intercourse
The use of unsterilized needles and instruments
Unsafe blood transfusions
Ladies and gentlemen, this is how you are supposed to protect yourselves
from *Silimu*
Avoid unprotected sexual intercourse
Avoid using unsterilized needles
Ensure proper use of condoms
Avoid coming into contact with sharp instruments

Figure 4.2 Children in the Kashenyi Model Primary School, Ishaka.

As with the performance by the Kashenyi Model Primary School, the Meeting Point drama group in Kampala (see Figure 4.3) also frequently includes elaborate details illustrating the manifestation of AIDS by localizing its messages within the traditional understanding of the disease as *Sirimu*. (Substitutions of "r" and "l" are frequent labial exchanges in Luganda as in other African languages, thus *Sirimu* is spoken and understood as the same word as *Silimu*). The disease, *Sirimu* is often also located within specific theological contexts. *Sirimu* in some song texts, for example, "shames" the population and ultimately reveals to them their "nakedness." This connection is made clear in text of Meeting Point's "Abange a'eno" given below. Meeting Point's intentional theologizing links the diseased body with the biblical revelation of original sin when Adam and Eve were first made to realize their humanity after consuming fruit from the forbidden tree in the Garden of Eden.

"Abange a'eno"
("Is someone there?")
Meeting Point Kampala

Is someone there?
My audience, I will not greet you because my nights are terrible
I do not know who you are
This tyrant is going everywhere itching
Friends, we have been invaded
It fells the healthy, the mass killer
Which has carried many away
one by one to where there are no words
I am telling you, its victims are babies and the youth
Plus the beautiful and the ugly all in a mixture
Even the gray-haired ones are not spared
You are merciless
Oh! You are ruthless!
I can really hear
You fatten your prospective victim, and they do not know it
Then slowly you gnaw at them in the quiet of their ignorance
At times they consult the witch doctors calling it a spell
All the money goes there and they become poor
Then they hate their friends that they think put a spell on them
Until the patient dies with no answers
Dying in a traditional shrine, once a religious person
It is a grim picture
It is shaming us and has showed us our nakedness
Sirimu, what did we eat that was yours?
We would vomit it back
To bring it back to you, Oh!

Sirimu is merciless
What do we owe you?
Have mercy on us and stop
We have left our families on you account
What do we owe you, have mercy on us and stop
Babies among them
What do we owe you, have mercy on us and stop
He has eaten all the professors
What do we owe you, have mercy on us and stop
How does *Sirimu* infect, and what brings it?
Sirimu has many traps through which he gets people
Like razor blades, needles, and others
Like transfusion of infected blood or contact with it in an accident
You get *Sirimu* immediately, then it is the grave
Lastly *Sirimu* is transmitted through the garden that everybody likes
The owner of the garden has laid traps that cannot be missed
We all know it but we ignore it
It is sexual sin among the elites and the non-elites
Sexual perversion is ruling nations
It is terrible
Until God overlooks the situation none of us will survive
Among students (Look, maybe God will overlook them, otherwise it is bad)
Among the youths (Look, maybe God will overlook them, otherwise it is bad)
Among the habitual drunkards (Look, maybe God will overlook them,
otherwise it is bad)
Those with gray hair (Look, maybe God will overlook them, otherwise it is bad)
Look, look (Look, maybe God will overlook us, otherwise it is bad)
I hear someone asking themselves about the signs of a *Sirimu* victim
Sirimu is merciful when you have just acquired it
You scorn those whose signs show they have it
But, after some time things change
You begin to get fever and skin rash
Your security cells weaken and many things hurry into your body
Diseases come to your body, like diarrhea, hepatitis, and vomiting
Then you *slim up*, and your body size runs away
Bones appear in the skin like a shirt on a hanger
Your color changes to be black like charcoal
Then friends run and you remain alone
You are sick and confused
That is the reason why some take their lives
Therefore, you who do not yet have this disease, this advice is free for giving
You who are infected with this disease and those who will be infected
My request is for us to unite so that we can save the one
who has not been infected

Figure 4.3 The Learning Center for youth at the Meeting Point Kampala

That Meeting Point Kampala is a NGO closely associated with funding sources from Catholic associations in Italy comes as no surprise, especially at the point in the song text where *Sirimu* and "original sin" become conflated. Human sexuality, however, is problematized to a degree in the Meeting Point's song, specifically in regard to the transmission of disease in the area of the world—"What did we eat that was yours? / We would vomit it back." Consuming the forbidden fruit and immortality are mapped onto human sexuality and in this conflation historic and traditional ways of understanding the disease—*Silimu*—are somewhat confused with newer, more informed understandings of the disease—HIV/AIDS.

Another frequent trope used in musical performances (as in everyday life) is the conceptualization of HIV/AIDS as a disease or virus so small that it cannot be seen by the human eye. Thus, by introducing a term such as *Akawuka* in many songs, for example, a powerful means of referencing local ways of understanding the virus is reflected back to the communities from which such terms originally came. The women of the eastern Iganga branch of the National Community of Women Living with AIDS (NACWOLA; see Figure 4.4) frequently reference the disease in this way as *Akawuka,* which is literally a tiny virus or insect, one that eats the body. The group's "Kava wa?" is one such musical example.

"Kava wa?"
("Where did it come from?")
NACWOLA, Iganga Branch

Where did it come from?
Akawuka came from where?
Where did it come from?
Sincerely we do not know
What can we do to warn the people who remain?
They have tried, singers have tried to use radios
In schools they have tried so much
We, NACWOLA, have tried so much
All of us have tried so much, but this is beyond our control
The parents?
We have suffered, sincerely we have suffered
Ah, *Mukenenya* [to slim, to deteriorate]
The children have died
Their generation is being phased out
We have suffered too much
Akawuka came from where?
Sincerely we do not know, my fellows
Akawuka came from where?
Sincerely we do not know
Ah, *Mukenenya*

Figure 4.4 Members of NACWOLA Iganga. Director Apofia Naikoba is shown kneeling, front left.

In each of the examples given in this section, it would be all too easy to focus on ways in which contemporary performance avoids or circumscribes readily available medical information by rejecting Western medical terminologies. It would also be overly facile to note the ways in which such song texts potentially misinform the general public on issues of accuracy regarding a life-threatening disease. To the contrary, as the women of NACWOLA in Iganga and Kampala have told me on several occasions, the specific and intentional localization of AIDS—such as demonstrated in these songs—attracts listeners by evoking the natural world and traditional culture that resonates with many of their audiences and home communities.

What follows is a selection of other such terms used in the expressive culture of songs, dances, and dramas that clearly fit in this initial category, Disease and Virus. Brief translations in English are provided for each term. In addition, references are provided to the group or groups whose song texts provided the terms.

Akaakoko   A tiny virus, an insect that eats up somebody's body
   Kitabi, Kanihiro Group; Kashenyi Model Primary School
Akahangire   The current epidemic
   Kashenyi Model Primary School
Akawuka   A virus or insect so small that it cannot be seen (from
   ekiwuka, an insect) Meeting Point; Baligeya Club, Kityerera Village;
   TASGA; VOLCET; Igunda Village; BUDEA, Buwolomera Village;
   Ambassadors of Hope; BAPET; Tulamuke Group
Akawuka katira   A killer virus
   GOSSACE
Buno'bwaffe   This disease of ours
   Makerere College School
Endwadde   A sickness or disease
   Makerere College School
Kawumpuli   An outbreak of a disease
   Bukato Youth Fellowship, Bukato, Kampala
Kookolo   Cancer
   Bukato Youth Fellowship, Bukato, Kampala
Lumala banby   Disease that will finish people
   Negro Angels
Lun'olubungeta   This meandering or wandering disease (from *olumbe*
   [disease] and *okubungeet a* [to wander]) (also *Lun'olubungeta*)
   Makerere College School
Lwaggya-lwaggya   The disease came once and for all
   MUDINET
Lumalabantu   Pestilence
   BAPET
Obuliwo   The disease that it is of major concern nowadays
   PADA

Olumbe lwa Silimu   The disease of *Silimu*
   Bute Village: Bwoyidha Oyega Club
SIDA   From the French abbreviation for AIDS ("*Syndrome immuno-
déficitaire acquis*")
   Bukato Youth Fellowship, Bukato

MEDICAL AND PHYSICAL ISSUES

Local terms included in the second category of Medical and Physical Issues highlight ways in which HIV/AIDS is referenced through symptomatic manifestation. Common to many song texts, for example, are internal references to AIDS as a fever. In the excerpt from the TASGA Drama Group's song "Abanje abe yo" transcribed below, reference is made both directly as "AIDS" and indirectly as "the fever," that is, "*Omussujja okutawono.*"

"Abanje abe yo"
"Friends, let me tell you the problems"
TASGA Drama Group

Solo—Friends let me tell you the problems
Chorus—Okay
Solo—Friends I have come with burning issues
Chorus—Yes, yes
Solo—Friends let me tell you the problems
Chorus—Okay
Solo—What did we do, disease, yes, sincerely what did we do to disease, sincerely, disease?
Chorus—Maama ["mother," cried in a mournful voice]
Solo—*Omussujja okutawono* [the fever] is bewitching, you feel stomachache, you get a cough and backache
Chorus—Your legs are like as if you are crippled, you wish you were not born
Solo—*Omussujja okutawono* is bewitching, you feel stomachache, you get a cough and backache
Chorus—For what I have seen here, there is no peace now
Solo—Peace, peace, there is no peace in the world, there has been no peace for many years
Far back, since the time of Adam and Eve, we are cursed to die
Chorus—Ordinary people from here are really in bad conditions nowadays
Solo—This issue of our disease no longer allows us to think of other diseases
Chorus—Maama!
Solo—Everywhere you go people are preoccupied with rumors about our disease
And you cannot blame them because it is too much
Chorus—Those who survive this are very lucky

Solo—They will narrate a lot to their sons and daughters when the cure is invented
Chorus—Maama!
Solo—We used to hear about world war and famine which struck in the older days
But now the problem of our disease which struck as the end of the world in near
Chorus—But let me ask who will survive?
Omussujja okutawono of the past decades used to go for many years
Solo—Me, I got *Omussujja okutawono* when I was born
Now I am 60 years, my wife and I divorced and I have never married because of AIDS
But there are many funny habits
Chorus—Which ones are they?
Solo—Ee ee when they use unsterilized instruments
Chorus—You can get AIDS
Solo—Fall in love with your friend's wife
Chorus—You can get AIDS
Solo—When a friend sustains a cut and you do suturing
Chorus—You can get AIDS
Solo—Traditional birth attendants
Chorus—You can get AIDS
Solo—Dentists
Chorus—You can get AIDS
Solo—Lastly prostitution
Chorus—You can get AIDS
Solo—Now for me what I have seen, we are in danger
Chorus—We are to die, we are to die, the end of the world has struck

Other musical references given below draw on the physical manifestation of fever and other skin ailments.

Akaswija akatakukira   Fever which does not resolve
Kitabi, Kanihiro Group
Lukusense   Measles among adults
NACWOLA, Iganga branch
Olutentezi   A skin allergy
MUDINET
Omussujja okutawono   The fever that never heals
Meeting Point
Omusudha gwe mpemo   Unresolved fever
BUDEA(also *Omusudha ogwe mpewo*)

SLIMMING, WASTING AWAY,
AND PHYSICAL DIMINUTION

I have grouped those terms that reference the corporal progress of AIDS that slowly emaciates those infected with the HIV virus into this third category. As suggested in the first category, while *Silimu* is perhaps the most recognizable term used throughout the country to refer to the perceptible wasting of the body, *Mukenenya* is also frequently substituted. For many, *Mukenenya* evokes the very real physical deterioration of the body that affects carriers of the virus and is found in many songs that both reference the disease and evoke the physical manifestation of the disease. In the song text that follows, *Mukenenya* does not appear on the surface to reference the slimming process, but rather it seems to function merely as a cover term for AIDS. The power of the term to evoke its deep, localized context, however, cannot be underestimated.

"Guno gwe mulembe gwe tulimu kati"
("This period we are in")
NACWOLA, Iganga Branch

This period we are in is the one infested with **Mukenenya**
The adults and the youth, **Mukenenya** does not discriminate
Let us pray for God to forgive us
This disease is difficult to describe
It has very bad symptoms
Fever and headache plus vomiting, shivering plus cough
This period we are in is the one infested with **Mukenenya**
Let us pray for God to forgive us
Let me start with young children who move around with many men
And you do not pay attention to the present diseases
Now we know that you are in the wrong

Even though for a large segment of the population *Mukenenya* and other such linguistic expressions are cover terms for AIDS, the original linguistic references such as physical wasting are unpacked for many in songs such as NACWOLA's "Guno gwe mulembe gwe tulimu kati." In the performance by BAPET transcribed below, *Mukenenya* is quickly mapped on to *Siriimu* (*Silimu*), a simple linguistic transposition since the two terms reference the same aspect of physical wasting. In the second example a song performed by Bright Women Actresses of Bwaise, *Mukenenya* is suggested to invade homes and communities causing destruction and grief as "it eats us without skinning us first."

"Siriimu, mukenenya a-ffe atumalawo"
("*Siriimu, mukenenya* are finishing us")
BAPET

My neighbors, Westerners and Easterners
You all should know that **Siriimu, Mukenenya** is finishing us
We have to avoid it
You see me here but I have bad nights
This word gives me bad nights
It is **Mukenenya**, my friend, that causes suffering
Because wherever you go they shun you
Saying the virus scooped him
Then they abuse and shun you
I want to warn you my friends
This **Mukenenya** causes suffering

"Bannange twajjiowo"
("We have been invaded")
Bright Women Actresses (Bwaise)

Eee, ee, we have been invaded, we are struggling, we are wailing
Where shall we turn today?
Hey, you there listening to this lamentation sounding the warning
Many are asleep and others are on beds
They are not guilty of anything, they are just the victims of *nawokeera*
Oh, *zzisa byaal* [mass murderer] over there, what do you see?
This word has a dangerous origin
All diseases are hidden there
This *nawokeera* [disaster] destroyed the man I struggled together with
If it is a spell, you can look for a doctor
See, your friend has become death and you cannot trust each other
We no longer trust our God, there is nothing to do
You are the almighty Creator of all
The one gone out to work cannot trust the one at home
While the wife waits at home for the disease
The hearts of children are afraid, it threatens to leave them as orphans
at any moment
If you still have children, your Creator is still covering you
It the disease begins in your womb, then you bury them continuously
When it begins in a family, it is like an ambush
Oh, it is a skilled lumberjack
Mealtimes used to be firm with everyone seated
They are all now in mounds of soil
It is a grim picture, it arouses fear
It eats us without skinning us first
You will not know who will get it today

It begins slowly, gnawing away and shows up only after three years
It can cook even him with good looks
Then one by one they come late, it does not wait
It begins right away to grip
Those who test using machines have tried, but it always shows after time
It alludes and hides
You cannot know those infected after a day, a week, or a month
When it takes your lover your heart melts, you expect your life to end
Many diseases come, worry is the first
Everywhere you go you picture yourself leaving your family
Poverty is number two, you need to eat well
Body weaknesses come one by one, then slimming immediately
It has shamed us, my friends, to look around and wonder when you will die
The one lying on the bed considers lucky the one it has taken
Wondering why it still spares him
We are invaded, **Mukenenya** is a deadly disease
There is no solution for us all, let us weep
Let us pull up our socks, "nobody will be spared from the crying"[44]
The barren, those without siblings, they all leave you looking
See the doctors, it causes even them to decay helplessly
The professors, ha! It does not trusts them
Oh, this is terrible, why does it take the babies?
Sure, we are at a loss, it has attacked from a deadly point
The creator is the medicine
Let us pray, let us beseech him for our sins
We are guilty of "thou shalt not commit murder"
Sexual sins are prohibited, but we rebelled
Oh, Creator, owner of creation and forgiveness
Authority and praise are yours, your will always happens
You hand can prevent it
We implore you to change your wrath and lift this invader
We beseech you, Amen, we have all known it
The sickness came and there is nothing to do
Let us be firm, for how long shall we cry for the cut and dried
While it eats us to the last person, we have come out today with medicine
Listen, hope that we will be able to take it in better situations
Abstinence is the first medicine, listen, youths
Never give away your life to those who encourage you to make love
with someone
Do not let friends and relatives cause you to do deadly things
Make a personal decision you who are still children, know that life
is more important
Be patient as you look for a trustworthy marital partner
Before you decide, go for the test, if you are both healthy do not waste time

In your home be faithful to each other
Never do anything alone that you would not do if your friend was present
You will preserve your life for a long time
And people will wonder if that is the provision for your journey
To survive *Sirimu*, stop love-making, do not try it at all
You who have not tried it yet, do not try it at all
If you decide to have the pleasure, then condoms are available
Use them, use condoms like shoes
They are very helpful in the prevention of *Mukenenya* infection
Try very hard to pray, for your Creator is your doctor

As with other localized terms for AIDS, *Mukenenya* is often used in song texts to evoke fear among listeners. "This word gives me bad nights," the soloist with BAPET declares. *Mukenenya* is a "deadly disease" for Bright Women Actresses. Such linguistic localizations directly reference HIV/AIDS while simultaneously conjuring images of physical diminution that are both horrific and very real for most citizens of Uganda today.

Other general terms for AIDS that are used to reference the "slimming" nature of the disease include the following:

Kantono   Emaciated person
BUDEA, Buwolomera Village; Bukona Integrated Group; Bute Village: Bwoyidha Oyega Club; NACWOLA, Iganga branch; Igunda Village; Tulamuke Group

Mukenenya   To slim, to deteriorate (from *okukenena*)
(BUDEA, Buwolomera Village; TASGA; Bukona Integrated Group; GOSSACE; Namirembe Post Test Club; BAPET; Giant's Group; Meeting Point; VOLCET; Ambassadors of Hope; Bukato Youth Fellowship, Bukato, Kampala; Negro Angels

Muniafu   *Slim* in the Lugisu language
Bukato Youth Fellowship, Bukato, Kampala

Nabutono   A small, emaciated person
Baligeya Club, Kityerera Village (see also *Kantono*)

Nasimu   A small person
Baligeya Club, Kityerera Village

Silimu   To slim (also *Slim*, *Sirimu*, and *Siriimu*)

DEATH

Another distinct way that language communicates the cultural depth of understanding of AIDS in Uganda is through the evocation of death. Such terms are frequently used to instill fear in listeners as well as to locate the disease within a continuum of physical decline. In "*Baasi ya sirimu efuuse ntanda ya walumbe*" ("The bus of *Slim* has become the carrier of the killer"), the song text performed by the Ambassadors of Hope that opened this chapter, the children directly reference AIDS as *walumbe*, the killer, in the song's first line. In the following song performed by the counselors at MUDINET (Mukono District Network of People Living with HIV/AIDS), this same term, *Walumbe*, is used to reference AIDS as a "killer" disease.

"Zino endwadde ezitakyawona kusaasira"
("These merciless incurable diseases")
MUDINET

These merciless incurable diseases have confused us all with the way
they have come
They are painful to humans, no joke
Now there is no inferior disease
We used to joke about diseases
Flu used to be for kids, and we would ridicule them
But now this advent is excessive
I do not know what our ancestors used to eat
Walumbe has left people hollow
Every new disease causes a lot of pain
Even a pimple causes a throbbing headache
The veins stand out and tears roll
People used to suffer from boils
But today's disease is beyond this
Every new disease is so painful
For fever we had our medicine
Herbs used to heal
But today's fever kills people
In fact it can find those who are hidden
People used to have hydrocells with excitement
Because whoever had it was said to be wealthy
He would send for a special chair to see the world
He would sit relaxed and the world would be peaceful
Now, patients have a lot of pain
We have been ambushed

In many of the songs performed by Prince Juuko, the late popular singer who died of complications resulting from AIDS, the issue of death looms close to the surface of his texts. In "Silimu alina amanyi," one of the many direct songs Juuko recorded about AIDS at the end of his career, the character of Satan emerges as the harbinger of death. After some rational reflections on the distress felt by the singer, AIDS and Satan become interchangeable toward the end of the song in such a way as to confuse the listener as to who is in fact killing thousands of people throughout Uganda—AIDS or Satan. Even my English translation falls short as the use of the pronoun "he" fails to clarify the actual bearer of death.

"Silimu alina amanyi"
("AIDS has the power to kill")
The Late Juuko

Solo—Hurry up, God's people, our father is listening
Let us ask for forgiveness because this world is worsening with each day that
passes
All of you should get on your knees and pray
The word of God is there and it is still working and it is sharp like
a razor blade
It is sharp and has a lot of power
I had a vision when I was sleeping one night
I was told that I have a lot of information about HIV/AIDS, that was
the vision that I had
Many people cry because they have lost contact with me, and this is because I
am so silent
They are so depressed and they have lost hope
They are all scared about my death at this tender age
I fear to reveal a lot about myself, mainly because people will not believe me
They may think am telling lies
Oh my dear friends, I am still alive and I spend most of my time at my home
Be assured, your prayers really work for me
I just cannot understand why people love me that much
And who am I that I should be loved by many people
Your knees are now in pain due to constant praying to God
Asking, "how can Prince James die like that, God?"
It is God who brought all this and why Prince who cannot die
Since I contracted AIDS I cannot care for the many people praying for me
I decided to ask for forgiveness from God and I do not know how long I am
going to live
When God is in heaven where he stays he listens attentively when we pray
He asks his angels, "Who is that person that makes many people cry for him?"
They answer him quickly that "it's your servant Juuko and he is a very good
singer"
"He sings good music that is not obscene and he has educated the world"
"That is why many people are crying for him," "They really have a lot of hope
in him"
God then sends his angels to give him more time so that he can tell this world
"I have not let you live longer to sin again," "No that is not the reason"
"I have appointed you now because many people like you"
"So you can persuade them to do what I want them to do"
"This is because he is now saved in his heart and he proclaimed that he has
AIDS"
Yet there are very many people that aim to kill as many as possible when they
get AIDS

When you contract AIDS you are finished, this is because AIDS has the power
to kill

Even if you are taken to America where there are many experts, you are just
wasting time

That is where Satan bases himself and he gives them wisdom to invent nonsense

Here he demonstrates his power and works hard to try to convince people that
God has no power

God will punish all those involved in the spread of AIDS

Even the computers that make you feel nice, you will leave them there

When Satan leaves the United States and comes to Africa where he has
another headquarters

You see the shrines around, that is where he hides and those are
his headquarters

They pretend to be so kind during daytime

But when darkness comes he instructs them to kill

Satan gives them guns to go out and kill people

They even kill innocent people who protect the nation

They get out their guns at night to steal money, but the people you kill are not
dying for free

You will pay, I am anointed with the Holy Spirit and he makes me say all this

I am not alone, all God's eagles come to the home where I stay to protect me
at night

Even when you send me evil spirits they will always come back to you and tell
you that I am protected

People behave as if they are blind or as if they are God

Satan makes him so annoyed, when God takes the time to live and testify

Satan gets so annoyed, when you pray he fears to come closer to you

I am going to travel around this world and take this message around and
many will become saved

I have to save God's children because AIDS has claimed very many

Chorus—God's servants, come quickly to pray, God our father is
now listening

Let us plead so much for forgiveness because this world has become a bad
situation

Everyone fall to your knees and pray to God our Lord

Solo—There is darkness in the shrines and Satan is there and he finds the
blood of humans

He is smeared with blood on his body and he has his walking stick, a snake of
a cobra type

Yet God's walking stick is the medicine to all your problems

**Satan gives people AIDS, his work is to offer a dose of AIDS and
then spread it**

**He (AIDS/Satan?) is a killer, he has no mercy, he traps people in his death
traps and takes them to hell**

Repent while you still can, it is only God who offers life
Even when you contract AIDS it is only God who can really help
He can cure you and He always follows through
We are the people who ask for this power from him
What I am talking about are not my words
They are His, so I have no case that I have committed
One day these people are going to stone me to death, calling me a mad person
And they will be religious people, they will think that I am there to divide
people
Yet that is not true, do not take me as a bad person
Because I am just God's prophet and I do not have any problem with anyone
I cannot divide religions saying, "this is the true one or not this one
and that one"
If I did I would be making a deal with religious leaders who would have
bribed me to have a side
I have AIDS and the virus has made me suffer so much every day

Other terms used in songs and dramas to refer to HIV/AIDS as somehow related to death include the following:

Ddekabusa   Something deadly (from *okuleka* [to leave] and *obusa* [left with nothing])
Makerere College School
Kattira   The skilled killer
TASGA; VOLCET
Namutta   Something that kills at a high rate
VOLCET
Ntaanathe   A grave
VOLCET
Zisabusa   Deadly
Makerere College School

INSECTS, ANIMALS, AND NATURE

It is common for HIV/AIDS to be masked behind the metaphor of an insect, an animal, or some other aspect of the natural world. This linguistic technique often presents an opportunity for a singer to talk openly—albeit behind a transparent linguistic veil—about health-related issues. In addition, the specific natural metaphors are frequently intended to evoke fear among listeners. The best-known example of this phenomenon is a song text originally inserted in the drama, *Gampisi*, made famous by the drama group Negro Angels Balamaika in Kampala. Gampisi was a character in the drama that took the form of a greedy hyena, a metaphor for AIDS that comes from *ammadu g'empisi* in Luganda, referencing the excessive greed of the hyena.

"Bulamu ki buno"
("What kind of life is this?")
Negro Angels Balamaika

Solo—What is this life we are longing for? What is this life?
Chorus—In the 90s
Solo —Since 1980s we have been fearing "Julu julu"
Chorus—Yaye, yaye
Solo —Wo, we, wo, we, what is this life we are longing for? What is this life?
Chorus—In the period of the 90s
Solo —We would have stayed in the 80s, but we did not know
AIDS, AIDS, AIDS you catch it through sex
AIDS, AIDS, AIDS you catch it through the struggles of grown-ups
AIDS, AIDS, AIDS you catch it through unsterilized needles
AIDS, AIDS, AIDS you catch it through unscreened blood
But you see, see, see *Gampisi* [hyena] has set traps
He is full of jealousy
Chorus—In the 90s
Solo —The period of the 90s, the 90s, everywhere you go
Chorus—The period of the 90s, how will it be? This period!
Solo—I am always in fear
Chorus—The period of the 90s, how will it be? This period!
Solo—Tighten our belts
Chorus—The period of the 90s, how will it be? This period!
Solo—Construct graves
Chorus—The period of the 90s, how will it be? This period!
Solo—Oooh
Chorus—The period of the 90s, how will it be? This period!
Solo—Read your will
Chorus—The period of the 90s, how will it be? This period!
Solo—Do not get drunk
Chorus—The period of the 90s, how will it be? This period!
Solo—Gampisi? Gampisi? Why do you [*Gampisi*] kill us?
Why do you make us miss Millenium 2000?
And yet the government policy does not allow us to discriminate for exams
Or hate our friends because of their religion
Chorus—Or hate our friends
Solo—Because of their tribes
Chorus—Or hate our friends
Solo—Because of the way they were brought up, but now see, sir, you have
disorganized us
Sincerely, *Gampisi*, you have disorganized us, people who used to love each
other
Chorus—Sincerely *Gampisi* you have disorganized us

Solo—In this world of the 90s
Chorus—Sincerely *Gampisi* you have disorganized us
Solo—Because of his several traps
Chorus—Sincerely *Gampisi* you have disorganized us
Solo—As we die out, as we fade out
Chorus—Sincerely *Gampisi* you have disorganized us
Solo—My friends
Chorus—Sincerely *Gampisi* you have disorganized us
Solo—I am not lying
Chorus—Sincerely *Gampisi* you have disorganized us
Solo—Let us open our eyes, open our ears, and shave our heads in order to get
to Millenium 2000
Now you people what do you say about this?

Perhaps the most interesting example of an insect personifying HIV/AIDS in the context of a song occurs in the late Herman Basudde's recording of "Ekiwuka ekyaga muntamu." Basudde, himself HIV positive, recorded this song to educate his audiences as well as to tell his own story, to disclose his HIV status publicly. The title of the song sets the stage well for the story of the song told through the tool of a dream as a rhetorical device. Basudde's song title tells the entire story—*Ekiwuka* is an insect or lizard, but in the context of this song it also refers to HIV. *Ekyagwa* means "it failed" in the *Muntamu* (form of *Entamu*), a term for a cooking saucepan, but also slang for a woman's vagina. The title of the song, therefore refers to the failure of the virus/lizard when caught in the cooking pot/vagina, or "do not eat that poisoned food, it is dangerous." I include a translation of the first stanza only below.

"Ekiwuka ekyagwa muntamu"
("The insect caught in the saucepot")
Herman Basudde

Solo—I had a dream during the night that passed and I was so scared
I could not get back to sleep so I remained awake until daybreak
When daylight came I did not waste any time
I went directly to my mother to interpret the dream and tell me the meaning
behind it
I dreamed there was an insect in the saucepan at home
The insect looked like a lizard, it was big as a kitten with a tail like
a poisonous insect
We converged to look at it critically, no one had the guts to kill it or
beat it to death
The bad thing was that when you hit the insect you could also break the
saucepan

We could not get anything to eat because the insect was in the saucepan
used to cook food

When we saw that the insect had taken over our saucepan one of us picked up
a piece of wood

He hit it so hard on the head that the insect died, but the saucepan was badly
destroyed

Then we looked at each other because we had lost the saucepan

When I asked my mother to explain to me the meaning of the dream, this is
what she said:

God made a fence [woman] and he put in only one path [vagina] which is
very small

And it is the only one that leads you inside the fence

Once to get through the fence, you can eat anything you like

When you have sex with a woman the enjoyment is tremendous

But getting back out of the fence is difficult because you cannot always find
your way

Yet, the fruits that God put in the fence were tested long ago when the trees
were still free

The trees where we used to pick the fruits are now dry and very aged

The young trees were all fenced off by God, so it is difficult to get fruit

We remain with an appetite, which is too large

If you try to see through the fence, you can see much that is ripe
and ready to be eaten

When you force yourself into that small path that goes into
the entrance to the fence

You'll find that God put it in a very hidden place

But if you enter, you can pick any fruit you want,
chewing and swallowing easily

When you lose your appetite then you can stop eating

Then you have to pass back through the narrow path again because it is the
only way out

People who try to give up on women are very few

Even those who give up do so for only a little time until they again continue

The tree that bears fruit has much ripe fruit, and even young flowers that are
just opening

Even you who said that we should abstain and thus escape AIDS

You will soon feel the need to go back through the fence

The taste of the fruit is too sweet and nice

That no one who has ever eaten the fruit decides to stop

The day you say no to sex is when you will see one who enjoys sex and has not
contracted AIDS

The next day you wake up early and take out your stick [penis] to pick as
many fruits as possible

Then go back home to pick fruit but when you go back the owner of the fence
will release her trap
You will never come back, that means you are dead
Sometimes you come back with wounds all over your body
Just because you ate a fruit which was rotten and full of maggots
I have interpreted my dream, AIDS will kill us all, you cannot imagine!

Other terms used to evoke the natural world, insects, or animals in musical performances include the following:

Amasanda   Sticky sap
Ambassadors of Hope
Akakala   Blackjack, a type of thistle that sticks on cloth and doesn't
fall off easily, i.e., you can walk with it for a long time not knowing
that you have it
Bukona Integrated Group
Akanyoni   A small bird or airplane
Makerere College School
Bisimizi   Insects
Igunda Village
Enkuyege   Strong brown ants that cut through big plants and live in
anthills, i.e., termites
Negro Angels
Emungwe   A type of weevil or beetle that attacks bean seeds, destroy-
ing the entire bean
Kitabi, Kanihiro Group
Ffene   Jackfruit
Ambassadors of Hope
Kamununa   The sucker of blood (referencing an insect or the virus)
GOSSACE
Kayovu   Tiny black insect with a proboscis like the trunk of an el-
ephant that infects grain and eats banana; banana weevil
Giant's Group; MUDINET; VOLCET; BAPET; GOSSACE; Negro
Angels; Meeting Point
Kombola   Type of fish that causes diarrhea when ingested
Baligeya Club, Kityerera Village
Namujinja   A worm that eats sugar and eventually causes sugar cane
disease
Makerere College School

TRANSPORTATION

I readily grant that the category is somewhat limited, yet the imagery of
AIDS as a vehicle, specifically a large vehicle that holds many people, is
common. The song text performed by the orphans of The Ambassadors
of Hope that opened this chapter is a clear example of the use of such a
transportational reference.

"Baasi ya sirimu efuuse ntanda ya walumbe"
("The bus of *Slim* has become the carrier of the killer")
The Ambassadors of Hope

The bus of *Slim* has become the carrier of the killer
It parks at TASO as they embark on their journey in the valley
From there it goes to the killer where you have bought citizenship
Lord help, we are tired of the bus

In another excerpt from Basudde's extended recording, "Ekiwuka ekyagwa muntamu," quoted in the category above, the singer warns listeners to practice zero grazing, suggesting that the "Bus of AIDS" transports more than one person if one is engaged with someone who might be suspected of having multiple sexual partners.

"Ekiwuka ekyagwa muntamu"
("The insect caught in the saucepot")
Herman Basudde

Those who abstain and also those who still plays sex with many women
Stop that habit of pointing at your friends saying
"Oh it is sad that man has AIDS"
When you in fact bypassed each other when you were both
with the same woman
The Bus of AIDS dropped one over there
And another one returned on that very same *Bus*

Terms for HIV/AIDS related to transportation include the following:

Bus   The bus
    Ambassadors of Hope
Baasi ya sirimu   The bus of *Silimu* (AIDS)
    Ambassadors of Hope
Kayola   A term first used for buses (from *okuyola*, to pick up)
    Makerere College School

OBJECTIFICATION

One of the most common ways of communicating HIV/AIDS indirectly in songs texts (as in everyday conversation) is to objectify it, and there is no more common term today in Uganda used for objectifying AIDS than *Akavera*. Literally, *Akavera* refers to a polythene bag. AIDS becomes an *Akavera* in the metaphor of what happens when a cow eats a stray *akavera*. It is well known that cows cannot digest polythene bags and therefore they die shortly after consuming a random *akavera*. Another means of objectification is the reference to AIDS as *Akawulura*, literally a stick with a hook at the end of it commonly used to strip beans from a coffee branch during coffee harvesting.

Akavera   Polythene bag
  Bukato Youth Fellowship, Bukato, Kampala; Baligeya Club, Kityerera
  Village; Ambassadors of Hope; BAPET; Giant's Group; VOLCET;
  Buwolomera Development Association, BUDEA; Negro Angels;
  NACWOLA, Iganga branch; PADA; TASGA; Tulamuke Group,
  Makerere College School
  (see also *Kavera*, *Kaveera*, and *Akaveera*)
Akawulula   See *Akawulura*
Akawulura   From *okuwulula*, coffee branch (see also *Akawulula*)
  Buwolomera Development Association, BUDEA; PADA

CAUTIONARY

This category is quite broad and is meant to include terms used for
HIV/AIDS that are cautionary in intent, whether it is the use of *Awooza*
to caution young people that they will have to defend their lives in the
court of disease, or the term *Akatachenshora* (among others) that attempt
to caution that HIV does not discriminate. The women of the Bakuseka
Majja Group in Mayuge Village use the term *Mulamuzi* as do other groups
in this area to caution listeners of the ability of AIDS to judge between
the living and the dead.

"Visitors, we are happy to see you"
Bakuseka Majja, Mayuge

Solo—Visitors, we are happy to see you
Chorus—But *Mulamuzi* [something that judges between the living and the
dead] came to judge us
Solo—Girls, I do not hear you clapping [elder starts playing the drums]
Chorus—I tell you even if we are happy to see you
Solo—God, Father, this disease can separate us
AIDS came to our mothers, some come from Nairobi schools
Doctors coming from Mulago hear these words
Mzee, I am happy to see you, God Father the disease separates
Then listen here how he [AIDS] is calling me
The disease ate the grandparents, the disease ate my mom
The disease ate my aunt, the disease ate my father
Elders, hear me calling, AIDS has become a disease you call for yourself
It first ate the elites, now it is eating the illiterates
It first ate the rich, now it is eating the poor
AIDS, even if you have money, I tell you even if you have riches
A person who was obese becomes emaciated
Those who used to cry because of obesity, those who used to laugh
have stop laughing
Those who used to have extra marital affairs no longer have them
I tell you the storms of selfishness come, Lady, I do not want coldness

I tell you I do not want mosquitoes, I do not want people to see me
Father, it is a dangerous disease, today even if you suffer from any fever
I tell you even if your foot becomes diseased, doctor what shall we do
Doctor here is the outcry, come out and help us
Father, bring for us sensitization seminars, father, we want teachers
Doctor, what has brought the disease?
Today our drinking water, she just fetches from a ditch
Father, AIDS is painful

Other cautionary terms include the following:

Akatachenshora   HIV does not discriminate
Kashenyi Model Primary School
Awooza   Defending yourself in the court of disease
Negro Angels
Endwoala y'abashaya   Something that affects mainly those who are
as strong as men
Kashenyi Model Primary School
Ndiwulira   I will listen (from *okuwilira*, to listen, also from the title
of a play originally performed by Bakayimbira Dramactors Pride
Theatre in Namirembe, Kampala)
Makerere College School
Mulamuzi   Something that judges between the living and the dead
PADA

CLEARING AWAY, DESTRUCTION, AND DISASTER

Terms are often used to locate HIV/AIDS within the experiences of destruction and disaster in the natural world. *Nalurima*, for example, is a term for something that clears away the whole family. Other common terms include "the sweeper" or "the broom" that refer to the ability of AIDS to clear away all in its path. In the following excerpt from a song by Bright Women Actresses, the term *Nawookera*—a disastrous disease— is used to evoke the image of a natural disaster.

"Bannange twajjiowo"
("We have been invaded")
Bright Women Actresses

Where shall we turn today?
Hey, you there listening to this lamentation sounding the warning
Many are asleep and others are on beds
They are not guilty of anything, they are just the victims of **nawookera**
Oh, mass murderer over there, what do you see?
This word has a dangerous origin
All diseases are hidden there
This **nawokeera** destroyed the man I struggled together with

Another common term for HIV/AIDS in this category is *Mubandha mpola* which refers to the slow pace at which AIDS destroys one's life, family, and community.

> *Nalurima*   Something that clears away the whole family
>   Bute Village: Bwoyidha Oyega Club
> *Namuzisa*   When a home or family compound has been "cleared," i.e., the place has become bush again
>   VOLCET; NACWOLA, Iganga Branch; Tulamuke Group; Baligeya Club, Kityerera Village
> *Kitiiyo nankumbi*   The spade and the hoe
>   TASGA
> *Mubandha mpola*   Slowly destroyed or slow pain
>   BUDEA, Buwolmera Development Association, Buwolomera Village; Bukona Integrated Group; see also *Mubandha mpora*
> *Mubandha mpora*   See *Mubandha mpola*
> *Nawokeera*   See *Nawookeera*
> *Nawookeera*   A disasterous, incurable or deadly disease
>   Giant's Group; Bukato Youth Fellowship, Bukato, Kampala; TASGA; see also *Nawokera*
> *Nawookera*   A disaster
>   Meeting Point
> *Zisabusolo*   Something that is destructive
>   Makerere College School

PERSONIFICATION AND EMBODIMENT

In many song texts, AIDS is either directly embodied (such as "Someone who has inhaled bad air" or "The one who came") or referenced as owned by an individual or group ("Ours" or "Our disease"). AIDS is also directly personified, such as with the label of "Philly" commonly used to evoke the memory of Philly Bongoley Lutaaya, the first popular musician to declare his HIV status publicly. In the song "Friends, let me tell you the problems," the TASGA Drama Group does not use the term AIDS until the end of their performance. In the excerpt below, AIDS becomes *Obwaffe*—Our disease—a medical issue that emerges from within the group, from within the community itself.

"Friends, let me tell you the problems"
TASGA Drama Group

Solo—Peace, peace, there is no peace in the world
There has been no peace for many years
Far back, since the time of Adam and Eve, we were cursed to die
Chorus—Ordinary people from here are really in bad conditions nowadays
Solo—This issue of **Obwaffe** (Our disease) no longer allows us to think of
other diseases

Chorus—Maama!
Solo—Everywhere you go people are preoccupied with rumors about **Obwaffe**
And you cannot blame them because it is too much
Chorus—Those who survive this are very lucky
Solo—They will narrate a lot to their sons and daughters when the cure is
invented
Chorus—Maama!
Solo—We used to hear about world war and famine that struck
in the older days
But now the problem of **Obwaffe** which struck as the end of the world is near
Chorus—But let me ask who will survive?
Omussujja okutawono [the fever] of the past decades used to go for many years

In the following song performed by Bright Women Actresses already quoted several times, a unique phrase *Mpawo atalikaba* is used to evoke AIDS as a person who cannot or will not mourn or cry. This phrase used by several performing groups is perhaps the most complex and poetic personification of AIDS.

"Bannange twajjiowo"
("We have been invaded")
Bright Women Actresses (Bwaise)

We are invaded, *Mukenenya* is a deadly disease
There is no solution for us all, let us weep
Let us pull up our socks, **Mpawo atalikaba** ["Not even a single person will
mourn, cry"]
The barren, those without siblings, they all leave you looking
See the doctors, it causes even them to decay helplessly
The professors, ha! It does not trusts them
Oh, this is terrible, why does it take the babies?

Other terms frequently used to refer to the embodiment or personification of HIV/AIDS include the following:

Akaffe/Obwaffe   Ours
Namirembe Post Test Club (see also *Obulwadde bwaffe)*
Amaze abalungi   The finisher of the beautiful
TASGA
A yasika empewo   Someone who has inhaled bad air
Negro Angels
Bamuzze eka   Bring him/her home (refers to people who are brought home to rural villages when they are in the end stages of from the disease)
TASGA
Kamuwunga   It caught him
PADA

Lumala bamboo/bambu   The disease that fill finish people
   Negro Angels
Mpawo atalikaba   Not even a single person will mourn or cry
   Negro Angels
Obulwadde bwaffe   Our disease (see also *Obwaffe* and *Olwaffe*)
   Meeting Point; Bukato Youth Fellowship, Bukato, Kampala; BAPET,
   GOSSACE
Obwaffe   See *Obulwadde bwaffe*
Obwaggathe   The one who came
   GOSSACE
Olumbe lwaffee   Our killer, *our* disease
   MUDINET
Olwaffe   See *Obulwadde bwaffe*
Philly   Refers to musician Philly Bongoley Lutaaya
   Negro Angels

CAUSE AND EFFECT

In this final category, I include a list of several terms used in songs and dramas as ways of referencing the cause and effect of HIV/AIDS evoked when a person undergoes change or is "disorganized" due to the virus. These terms are oblique and indirect and are often used to avoid mentioning AIDS directly by name. There is another way, however, that cause and effect can be understood within performance. In many songs older myths and historical understandings of the transmission of HIV are outlined and called into question, while medically sound methods of transmission are suggested. In the following excerpted text transcribed from a cassette recorded by the famous Eschatos Brides group (known throughout Africa for their earlier evangelical recordings, including "Utukufu Bwana Yesu," popular throughout East Africa), a soloist details older, localized misunderstandings concerning the transmission of HIV (mosquitoes, bedbugs, saliva, etc.), while providing actual modes of transmission (sharing needles, etc.).

"Obulwadde bwa sirimu butabubui"
("AIDS kills badly")
Eschatos Brides
Abbey Kibalama, composer

Solo—How does this disease reach people and then kill them?
Chorus—It is all caused by bad behavior, by loving many women
Solo—They tell us that AIDS loves nightclubs with discos
Chorus—That is very true, it comes from the hopeless behavior of adultery
Solo—Those married men who maintain homes apart from their wives
Those who spread AIDS have decided to use a lot of money
It is not money that brings AIDS

It cannot come like that
It is not mosquitoes that transmit AIDS
It is not bedbugs that spread AIDS
That is a lie
It is not saliva and sweat as others say
Wololo, sir [sad expression used when someone is troubled]
Chorus—AIDS kills so miserably and terribly
Chorus—It is murder and in the daylight many innocent people who die of
AIDS are murdered too
Solo—The dirty injections that doctors use also spread AIDS
Even blood if not tested properly by a doctor
If one of the married couple is not well behaved
Even the children they produce do not survive, sir
That is the sin which is known and it is sinful
Be prepared to help the AIDS patients your friends
Chorus—That is love and love should never fear an AIDS patient when you
know one
Solo—Do not be harsh to a friend who has contracted AIDS
Help him wash the clothes
AIDS is not transmitted that way
Treat them well when they go into a coma
Do not be harsh
Sing to him songs that can encourage and let the sick rest a bit

Below are several more indirect terms used to refer to the cause and effect nature of HIV/AIDS within the general population in Uganda. I should note, however, that in the Eschatos Brides song quoted above the solo singer suggests that we need to move beyond a mere "naming of parts" and that we need to focus on more than mere details concerning how not to catch AIDS. The singer seizes the opportunity to plea for compassion in everyday interactions with PLWHAs as well as in the care of patients. The power of such songs occurs within performance (either live or through recordings), when local knowledge of HIV/AIDS is coupled with newer, medical ways of conceptualizing the virus and disease.

Akihanga   Something that affects the whole world
Kashenyi Model Primary School
Ekizunga   Something that does not settle down, something that keeps
roaming around (from *okuzunga*, an object that turns around)
Makerere College School
Munywenje   Something that disorganizes a whole person's status
Kitabi, Kanihiro Group; Kashenyi Model Primary School
Kanera   Everyone will cry
Bukona Integrated Group; Namirembe Post Test Club (see also
Kanera mpawo atalikaba)
Kanera mpawo atalikaba   See *Kanera*

CONCLUSION—
LOCAL TERMS FOR CONDOMS IN LUGANDA

I conclude this chapter with a brief diversion, albeit directly related to the issue of the localization of medical issues within song and drama texts. The localization of terms related to condoms and condom usage within musical performances and dramas is just as highly nuanced as those terms and expressions already documented in this chapter for HIV/AIDS. Local terms for condoms communicate not only an immediate referential object—the condom itself—but they also position condoms within cultures in which condoms are a foreign concept. One local term for a condom, *Obukwata ensenene*, for example, literally means a grasshopper catcher and suggests that condoms catch semen, much the same way as the traps catch grasshoppers for eating. Another term, *Kabulabutugiro*, literally means "something that will fail to strangle"—from *obutugiro*, a place where someone can be strangled, i.e., the neck, and *okubula*, meaning to get lost, to fail—is used to educate potential users that even though condoms should have a tight, secure fit, they nevertheless will not strangle the penis.[45] Other terms frequently used include references to gloves, gum boots, socks, bullet, and coats.

In the final section from the TASGA Drama Group's "Abanje abe yo" offered below, the first reference that is made to condoms is with the local term *Galimpita*, a variation on *Kalimpitawa*, before the English variant, *Kondom* is introduced. Inherent in the meaning of *Galimpita* is an explanation of the purpose of condoms—"how will the virus pass through," meaning that condoms block the transmission of the virus from one person to the next.

"Abanje abe yo"
("Friends, let me tell you the problems")
TASGA Drama Group

Solo—Yesterday I had a sick toe and I used Tom's safety pin to operate on it
But I had forgotten that Tom has AIDS
Now even me I have HIV, even me
I went with Viola to the dentist, but the instruments used on Viola are the same used on me
I am dead
Chorus—We are dying, we are dying, this is the end of the world, we are dying
Solo—I have been asked by the leader of this home
Chorus—We are dying, we are dying, this is the end of the world, we are dying
Solo—They are thankful for coming on this burial
Chorus—We are dying, we are dying, this is the end of the world, we are dying
Solo—This is the seventh child to die in this home

Chorus—We are dying, we are dying, this is the end of the world,
we are dying.
Solo—They have all died the same way
Chorus—We are dying, we are dying, this is the end of the world,
we are dying.
Solo—Because they refused to obey the commandments
Chorus—We are dying, we are dying, this is the end of the world,
we are dying.
Solo— If they had used *Galimpita* [condoms, literally "How will the virus
pass through me?"]
Chorus—We are dying, we are dying, this is the end of the world,
we are dying.
Solo—I say *Kondom* [condoms]
Chorus—We are dying, we are dying, this is the end of the world,
we are dying.
Solo—Friends we are all in danger
Chorus—We are dying, we are dying, this is the end of the world,
we are dying.
Solo—This is a problem, AIDS has finished the world
Our great grandparents had peace
Even if they could die and were buried, but their diseases were curable
Chorus—This is a problem, AIDS has finished the world
Our great grandparents had peace
Even if they could die and were buried, but their diseases were curable
Solo—I am standing, but when I went to TASO Mulago the AIDS disease has
progressed far
One patient was dying while others convulsed
Not only youth but even the elderly
Chorus—This is a problem, AIDS has finished the world
Our great grandparents had peace
Even if they could die and were buried, but their diseases were curable
Solo—But if we went wrong God should forgive us
We are in danger
AIDS is cleaning us
See how he is exploiting us
There is even no cure
Forgive me God
We are getting finished
What shall we do?
Chorus—This is a problem, AIDS has finished the world
Our great grandparents had peace
Even if they could die and were buried, but their diseases were curable
Solo—It is dangerous

> **Chorus**—This is a problem, AIDS has finished the world
>   Our great grandparents had peace
> Even if they could die and were buried, but their diseases were curable

Other localized terms for condoms that appear in song texts and dramas include the following:

Akapira   A ball
Engabo   Bullets
Galimpita   See *Kalimpitawa*
Gamubutusi   Gum boots
Giravuzi   Gloves
Kabulabutugiro   Something that will fail to strangle
Kakuumabutamu   That which protects or preserves life (*okukuuma* meaning to protect and *obulamu* meaning life)
Kalimpitawa   How will the virus pass through me? (*Ka-li-mpita-wa*, meaning "It will pass me where?")
Kondom   Local spelling of condom
Koot   Coat
Obukwata ensenene   A grasshopper catcher
Sokisi   Socks

As demonstrated throughout this chapter, the localization of medical and health-related topics within musical performances creates a very different site within which knowledge about HIV/AIDS—and condoms—is not only transmitted but, perhaps more importantly, made meaningful in the lives of Uganda's citizens. The creation of a scaffolding of categories within which to locate local terminology for HIV/AIDS was by no means scientific, nor was it an attempt at complete and all-encompassing coverage of such linguistic localizations. Rather, my goal was to provide the schema that began to develop as I listened more intently to the voices of Ugandan singers, dancers, and actors, and learned. All performed the medical conditions of HIV/AIDS with unique, local responses. And the more I listen, transcribe, and translate, the more I suspect that any attempt on my part to represent such responses can only open up opportunities for others to analyze, reevaluate, revise and even rethink my hypotheses.

Interlude 4
Excerpts from an Interview with the Bukato Youth Fellowship

GROUPS OF YOUTH from the Bukato Youth Fellowship of Kampala gather several times each week. This interlude is an excerpt of an interview conducted by Vincent Wandera and Gregory Barz. In this transcription, the anonymity of the participants has been protected by assigning false names.

Figure Interlude 4.1 Bukato youth.

Wandera—Can you tell us some of the objectives as to why music and dance is in some sort of relation with HIV?

Rogers—The music that we usually compose, or the dramas, these are related to the society and our way of living because we know that society is part of the Christian way of life. So to carry the message across to the people what we usually do is we have to sing messages related to the people. For example, you have the epidemic of AIDS which is seriously taking our lives. So what we do is we usually get musical themes which are related to AIDS, and at the same point we ask the people, "come on, don't do this or else you will be in the times of Sodoms and Gomorrahs." So we sing our music of AIDS into the society in which it earlier began.

Wandera—Do you think by so doing that you have achieved these objectives and aims of yours?

Scovia—Well it is hard to realize the tangible impact of something, but as we deliver the message to the people, usually we pick something, on some tangible occasions; we find that when once you sing, you will find members from the outside who will join the association due to the comfort that has been delivered. In some circumstances you may find that someone has a problem, for example he has lost his friends to AIDS or a brother to AIDS, but getting comfort, when they listen to this music they usually get comfort and go to the organization. Life is more fulfilling from within the organization. Not only that, but as we sing these songs people usually take the words, or go on making these words. So in the end, we assume that as they go on singing these words there is a message that has transferred into their minds. So, we believe that a message has been carried on. At least a part of our aims has been achieved.

Shira—When we go to any chapel or any organization some of the people we have touched, they come out and say "that song has really touched me," and maybe the plays we also take out, they will say that has also meant something to them.

Wandera—Do you think that music has played a role in the prevention and control of spread of HIV in your community?

Sarah—Well you know, music has a very big impact on people that listen to it. For example, if you sing about the danger of AIDS and you illustrate in the music, you sing about how slim you will be, how you suffer, if you include all the symptoms in the music, someone will be touched. They will think, "oh, I cannot suffer, I cannot be like that." So they will always try not to be like that, because we want people to really get the point and realize the danger of AIDS. So I think that it can really touch the people's hearts. It has a bigger impact than just using radio talk shows because most people like to listen to music. So once you pass through that channel it gets better.

Winnie—*If I want to guess the magnitude of how we have reached out to the people you could try to measure how deep people feel our songs. Some people are nationally known and have come to hear us, and you could actually measure the reactions of people and how they actually feel. People bring with them the kind of experiences that they are going through. So, I think through music and talking we reach quite far out to the people, nationally and further.*

Evans—*In addition to that, AIDS not only tells people not to get involved in sexual malpractices, but more importantly, music can also bring comfort to people who have AIDS. So music helps people not to feel isolated. It gives them comfort to stay among us and helps keep them in a positive state. I believe the music also gives awareness to society. If someone is told that you can get AIDS through such and such a way, then he knows that yes, this is the wrong way, and he is made aware of whatever he will be doing.*

Barz—*So what kinds of problems are facing your group?*

Youth—*There are many problems with this, as far as the music is concerned. That's why we are trying to get our message to people on the outside. So, a problem we have is, let me say, the musical instruments in the public system. If you go out, you cannot sing out with your voice unless you have a microphone, then you cannot be heard if you sing.*

Eliod—*So as he put it, the financial bit of it is a big hindrance. Especially since most of us here are students, money stands out as a very big obstacle. The other is that there are times when we have music instructors here. We accept them and we really need them. But still at other times we find that we are running short of them, due to commitments elsewhere. So at times we feel we lack someone who is going to create a song, someone who is going to compose something that can be disseminated to the people.*

Charity—*All in all, our major problem here is funds, money. Because you can find that sometimes we will have that master tape, but we haven't yet produced it in order to sell it to reach the people. And as we are talking we are preparing to produce another one, but how can do it? We are handicapped.*

Gordan—*And there is the problem of transport, in that to produce things for other people in villages instead of only producing them to people here there is the problem of transport so that we can transport ourselves to those people in far away places.*

Wandera—*What is your feeling, as youth, when you think up a song about AIDS? What do you feel when you sing about AIDS?*

Proscovia—*As a youth? I think of helping someone out there. Maybe through praying I could help that person from doing away with themselves because of AIDS or be happy as a positive AIDS patient and have hope.*

Rogers—First of all, the message is "come to me." Yes, I am telling people, "come on, don't do this," but am I myself getting into what I am doing? So, in the end I am also a receiver of the information that is communicated to the people through music.

Evans—Maybe as you act some things out, you are required to begin to feel what you are acting out. If you have to act as someone who is in pain then you might be more open to someone in real pain.

Shira—These songs about AIDS, in most cases are encouraging. So they tend to encourage people who are living positively, and if you can affect one person, sometimes these people who are affected write other songs. When we take our songs people feel that we care about them and so we are strong.

Wandera—So, as youth, how do you fight back against AIDS using music?

Winnie—I think many people really are idle and do nothing. You know, an idle mind is the devil's workshop, so it can lead you to sexual immorality. Once you, as a youth decide to engage music, well you are doing something constructive, because maybe you are creating songs about AIDS which you are going to give to the people, and at the same time you are busy and the chances of being immoral are very few. So you prevent AIDS by creating songs about AIDS which again you are going to use to make the people aware.

Evans—I think that most songs are spiritual in nature, If you have AIDS, or if someone has it and you are singing to them, when you sing these words they think, "surely this is not the end." It is not the worse they can face or the end of their lives. It seems to give them hope so they don't feel down, you are suffering from something so bad that no one is suffering more than you are. If you see someone with AIDS you can tell them that this is not the end of your life. You have an eternal life, you live an everlasting life.

Wandera—Now let me see, what is mostly your audience, what do you attract.

Rogers—Mostly we target the youth, because the youth are the future, the people of tomorrow.

Scovia—Not only that, but we believe that being youth, we offer the best medium for youth. As we sing, the youth get in with us because we fall into the same age bracket and the same status, so we try to extend to the group that we sing to. Usually the youth come and check out the youth fellowship that they hope to join in the future. So they come and give us attention.

5

"SINGING IN A LANGUAGE AIDS CAN HEAR"
Music, AIDS, and Religion

We usually compose songs that aim at specific tasks, and OK we do in fact all come from a Christian background. Our dramas are particularly geared toward changing people's attitudes towards *Slim* [AIDS]. The dramas are related to everyday societal living, so to carry the messages to people we have to sing messages that relate to the people. For example, you have the AIDS epidemic taking over our lives and sometimes all we can do is sing. So we sing our music to ourselves and to others. *You know we sing our religion for the rest of society.*

—Member, Bukato Youth Fellowship

A Ugandan Catholic official recently said, "We as a church cannot offer condoms, except, of course, in the case of a couple in which one partner is seropositive." "And how would you know that he or she is?", a doctor inquired. "Here it's better to proceed as if all couples were discordant regarding HIV-serology," replied the Father. An ethic of responsibility, in other words, which tempers the ethic of conviction. Too often, those who make decisions in the fight against AIDS feel they must obtain the agreement of the most eminent religious leaders of their hierarchy, forgetting that it is precisely the duty and function of the latter to reaffirm the traditional positions of their faith. Nevertheless, at the heart of each denomination, real spiritual work is underway and there are multiple voices.

—Daniel Defert 1996, 449–50

AT THE WORLD AIDS DAY CELEBRATION held in December 2003 in Kampala, Uganda, President Yoweri Museveni publicly criticized local African religious institutions for conflating issues of religious morality with public health, and consequently further contributing to the spread of AIDS in Uganda. Like many other countries in sub-Saharan Africa,

Uganda is home to a plurality of religious communities—a variety of forms of Christianity, Islam, and traditional spiritual practices. Yet, in their efforts to educate and care for those already HIV positive and those not yet infected, many faith-based institutions and religiously oriented NGOs purposely or unconsciously mix "morals and safety," as Museveni suggests (2003). This is a common dilemma not only in Africa, but also in the Caribbean as well as in other parts of the world.

In regard to HIV/AIDS, religion has in many ways determined the expressive responses surrounding the disease in many areas of everyday Ugandan culture. Perhaps more importantly, religion often guides a variety of direct cultural interventions specific to AIDS. In their study of the cultural demographics of AIDS in the Rungwe area of neighboring Tanzania, researchers Marjorie Mbilinyi and Naomi Kahula introduce one of the principle issues with which religious institutions continue to struggle—that is the mapping of morality directly onto sexuality:

> [R]eligion, namely Protestant Christianity, has framed the discourses within which morality and sexuality are debated and acted out in Rungwe, with often *contradictory responses* to the epidemic. Strong religious principles and doctrine govern people's overt moral, sexual and cultural behaviour. (2004, 77, emphasis added)

"Contradictory responses" continue to confuse and manipulate local responses to HIV/AIDS not only in Rungwe, but throughout East Africa. While it might seem overly simplistic to reflect on broader issues related to religion and sexuality, there are nevertheless certain issues that are worth exploring, particularly regarding the expressive culture of religions. As Mbilinyi and Kaihula state elsewhere, music—songs in particular—often functions as a means of mediating and stabilizing cultural and religious conflict. This is clearly demonstrated in Rungwe among youth who use songs to separate themselves morally from the mainstream culture of youth in neighboring Tanzania:

> In Rungwe, AIDS discourse is also permeated by Christian views of morality, especially amongst adherents of the more fundamentalist sects. *Religious songs* of the Galilaya Youth (Assemblies of God) condemn "the evil of AIDS" as the product of an "adulterous life". Youthful members of their congregations often take the lead in these denunciations, as if to distance themselves from generally negative views of youth. Church members and leaders in Rungwe not only blamed the youth and unfaithful for their sinning ways, but also parents for being lax in moral education of their children. Mothers, especially, were said to be preoccupied with economic endeavours. (2004, 87, emphasis added)

To problematize the coupling of religion and AIDS from the start, I suggest that the borders surrounding typical conceptualizations of religion in this part of the world are fluid, as they are elsewhere (if not everywhere). It is not a profound observation on my part, however, to suggest that faith-based institutions and NGOs do not always practice what they preach. On more than one occasion in Uganda I witnessed condom distribution, for example, occurring in one part of a building—typically a *back* entrance—while no evidence or advertisement of such health services was noted elsewhere, such as in the building's *front* entrance. It no longer surprises me that such phenomena occur in Catholic-sponsored organizations. Again, Mbilinyi and Kaihula share similar observations:

> In Rungwe, a counselor at a Roman Catholic facility confided that he surreptitiously gave condoms as well as advice on how to use them to his clients, in spite of the official church position. Joinet (1994) has openly accused the church of being unfaithful to the call of Christ, in its casting out as devils or sinners those who have AIDS. Stigmatisation is "anti-Christian" according to this outlook. (2004, 95 4n)

What is still needed in academic studies of disease and health care are field-based research studies, such as on the culture of AIDS—specific transinstitutional efforts to study religion, medicine, and music with a focus on the interaction between faith, expressive culture, and healing within local conceptualizations of disease and healing in sub-Saharan Africa. Supporting such studies should be the premise that there are many localized patterns adopted by religions or faith-based organizations that inform the reception of medical interventions in various parts of the world, just as there are cases in which localized medical approaches conversely reflect and reinforce traditional religious beliefs and values.

Performances of religion and medicine occupy social spheres of influence that are as often complementary as they are conflicting in many parts of contemporary Africa. This is true in Uganda. As in other formerly colonized areas, foreign faith-based institutions were often introduced to African cultures accompanied by external conceptualizations of health care and medicine. Today, in addition to embracing mainstream religions, as I previously suggested, many East Africans openly deny the need for traditional spiritual healers and traditional health-care practitioners. Urban dwellers and those affiliated with churches and faith communities publicly disavow the efforts of traditional healers. Privately, however, many avail themselves of a variety of healing systems, drawing on multiple faith traditions. Understanding the epidemiology of AIDS in East African contexts will only be enhanced when such deep cultural and religious layers that contribute to diagnosis and care are identified and acknowledged.

One historic stumbling block for many religious institutions in their approach to HIV/AIDS is the deeply embedded cultural reaction to AIDS as a form of divine punishment. Given the presence of such underlying cultural sentiment, it is not much of a stretch to imagine the difficulties experienced in the early reactions to AIDS in Uganda's churches and mosques. Dr. Alex Muganzi Muganga—a research colleague, Ugandan medical doctor, and friend—made the direct, historical connection between AIDS and God clear to me during a recorded interview:

> It did not occur to people, *Slim* being such a strange disease, that something or someone was not to blame...it was strange to everyone. Initial reactions were fear and denial. The epidemic would come up in an area and people reacted in different ways. This being a traditional African society, the main thing people thought about was that it was a form of punishment; others thought that it was a *curse from God*. In the past, when a bad omen befell a village, *people thought God was punishing people*, or that it was bewitchment or a curse. (emphasis added)

For Muganzi Muganga and others, religion—whether organized or as a marker of identity—has been inextricably linked in the historical cause-and-effect of HIV/AIDS in Uganda from the start, and as such has been an enormous hurdle to overcome. Rev. Jackson Muteeba, director of the Integrated Development and AIDS Concern (IDAAC) in Iganga, maps the early reluctance of many Christian churches to embrace issues related to AIDS onto those churches' rejection or isolation of church members who were found to be identified as HIV positive. In a conversation with Rev. Jackson, he outlined for me the initial reactions of many churches, while also suggesting that churches—and people in general—should learn to *sing in a language that AIDS can hear*. I draw on this sentiment for the title of this chapter to reflect a suggestion that is more prophetic than prescriptive:

> As far as AIDS is concerned, *the church initially took a very small role in HIV prevention because many different churches in Uganda taught that it was a punishment for sinners*. So, churches started losing members to evangelical or gospel churches. Some of my own friends wanted to disown me, my own church too. I felt like I was being tossed aside. But when members from the church, very influential people, people very supportive of the church, started dying one after the other, churches eventually began waking up. *In a sense churches are now coming up and opening up*. There is a former archbishop that said we should open up and *sing in a language that AIDS can hear*. I hope—no, I pray—that we may all someday learn that language.

For Rev. Jackson—as is true for many others—learning to sing in a language that AIDS can hear and understand and learning to come to terms with the realities of the disease—both cultural and medical—can only take place within the context of metaphoric "languaging" that occurs in singing. By extension, Muteeba suggests that meaning concerning HIV/AIDS needs to be *performed* in order for cultural re-translation to occur.

Several major world religions—Christianity, Islam, Bahai, and Judaism—are actively practiced in Uganda, but there are also numerous breakaway, independent churches and religious groups, and indigenous religions particular to specific regions and communities. Within organized religions, a large number of denominations flourish—often misunderstood and mislabeled as sects and cults—each with their own interpretations, beliefs and practices. Religious, faith-based, and spiritual efforts address and combat AIDS within the contexts of localized musical performances that government and private organizations often find inaccessible. Attempts to educate and heal based on Western medical models have proven largely expensive and, as I suggested at the onset of this book, frequently culturally inappropriate. When situated within the performance traditions of religious, faith, and spiritual communities—and supported by localized understandings of cultural traditions—medical initiatives regarding HIV/AIDS have achieved their greatest successes.

Women (rather than men) in Ugandan communities—particularly sex workers—are often conceptualized as the carriers of and primary cultural agents for spreading the HIV virus. Many facets of the culture of AIDS in Uganda respond to religious traditions and beliefs by positioning women in weak socioeconomic positions where they are unable to demand the use of condoms or to insist on monogamy from marital or sexual partners. Throughout this chapter, my observations on women's roles in religion and in culture in general are supported by the invaluable work of Catherine Campbell (2003). Many Ugandan communities also situate women in economically dependent relationships, whereas men often experience significant societal pressures to demonstrate acceptable displays of masculinity, and these expectations coupled together culturally compel many women and men into relationships with multiple sexual partners, as well as support engagement in risky sexual behavior.

Deep religious and spiritual beliefs concerning HIV/AIDS also impact the spread of the virus and contribute to ongoing physical violence against women in many parts of the country. For example, the belief that HIV is caused by witchcraft or that it is a direct punishment from God continues to contribute to the ongoing stigma experienced in general by women in many Ugandan communities. In addition, local healing traditions have confused many as to the distinction between diagnosis and cure. This was (and is perhaps still) problematic in the claims by a select group of traditional healers to cure AIDS in ways that actually infect (or re-infect) women, or when cultural myths suggest that having sex with a virgin (usually a younger girl, involving either rape or consensual sex) can cure a man, thus contributing to the further spread of HIV among women.

A paradox exists among contemporary practitioners of traditional medicine and religion (both healers and herbalists). Many continue to exploit the HIV/AIDS pandemic in the country by selling what are largely ineffective traditional cures to people, while others have significantly altered their approach to HIV through retraining initiatives in collaboration with medical doctors, such as with the educational outreach programs instituted by THETA (Traditional and Modern Health Practitioners Together Against AIDS and Other Diseases) in Uganda. THETA was initiated as a partnership between TASO (The AIDS Support Organization) of Uganda and the international humanitarian organization *Médecins Sans Frontières* (Doctors Without Borders). Begun in 1992, THETA was instituted as a collaborative clinical outreach effort in Kampala, Uganda, that attempted to evaluate the efforts of traditional healers and the effectiveness of local herbal treatments for select AIDS-related diseases and related opportunistic infections. The success of THETA (and other similar initiatives in sub-Saharan Africa) has transformed the work of many traditional healers in regard to rural HIV/AIDS education, counseling, and care and treatment.

While medicine and religion were once conceptualized as distinct cultural institutions, more frequently today they are acknowledged as interdependent and perhaps coextensive. In a 2002 address to the African Religious Leaders' Assembly on Children and HIV/AIDS held in Nairobi, Kenya, Carol Bellamy, head of the United Nations Children's Fund (UNICEF), suggested:

> You can spread the word about what it takes to confront and beat this terrible disease *through mosques, temples and churches*, through your lay people and women's groups and youth organizations. The bottom line is that you have a unique power within your organisations which, if mobalised, could change the face of this epidemic. The challenge is to realize it. (2002, emphasis added)

Today, Bellamy and others frequently underscore the need for medical doctors and religious leaders to be approached as the most relevant local institutions and local leaders in HIV/AIDS education and outreach. Many feel that only with the support and leadership of such faith-based initiatives will the facilitation of effective ways of dealing with the HIV/AIDS pandemic occur, ways that are imperative for the future of the health and well-being of countless communities in Uganda. It must be stated, however, that for many People Living with HIV/AIDS (PLWHAs), deeply held religious convictions can also inhibit or discourage active engagement in diagnosis, treatment, and care. According to Rupert Francis:

[r]eligiously based moral beliefs about AIDS can have dangerous implications for the treatment of its victims by society and its care providers.
Many see AIDS as more of a solution than a problem, drawing support
for this conviction from religious or biblical tenets. (1989, 1146)

According to a 1988 survey directed by Francis in and around Nashville,
Tennessee, conducted among physicians, freshmen medical students,
liberal clergy, conservative clergy, rural whites, and urban blacks, up to
70 percent of those surveyed responded that they believed AIDS to be
a result of "divine intervention" among patients. (While I acknowledge
that Nashville is geographically and culturally distant from Uganda, the
comparisons nevertheless underscore the need for further study and
ongoing educational outreach with religious leaders in both locations.)
Such statistical data stagger the imagination when considering the processes of early, initial acceptance and (mis)understanding HIV/AIDS
experienced in the United States almost twenty years ago. How could it
not be expected that in other cultural contexts—such as Uganda—that
there would be other spiritual and religious conceptualizations of the
disease present that problematize care and treatment?

Central in many historical religious debates in Uganda concerning AIDS
is the issue of condoms. As Dean Shuey and Henry Bagarukayo suggest,
"condom talk" is a featured element of Uganda's openness to HIV/AIDS,
especially among churches:

> In Uganda, religious leaders, although many are still opposed to condoms,
> debate the issue openly, and condom use in general and the instruction of
> adolescents about how to use condoms is an accepted national strategy.
> (1996, 124)

Yet, condoms are rejected by many religious groups as a tool of active
sexualization of HIV/AIDS. In addition, condoms are also conceptualized by many as a form of contraception, an interference with a presumed
natural order of procreation. In addition, Daniel Defery further suggests
that condoms have long been linked to unwanted physical responses:

> [T]he promotion of condoms is more than a problem of contraception.
> It incorporates the acknowledgment that sexuality is neither uniquely
> nor essentially inscribed within the perspective of the transmission of life
> but is pleasure. Second, it acknowledges sexuality as a physical exercise, a
> learning process, and as a play, and not essentially as a spiritual openness
> toward the Other (which every religion emphasizes) or as a relation to
> the self, that is to say, asceticism, continence, and chastity. (1996, 419)

Many leaders of churches, mosques, and synagogues root their personal
responses to the issue of condoms and to the disease within the context

of their initial or early exposure to HIV. Most leaders were trained and educated at a time when the disease was not known, and most admit to having had little or no training in issues regarding HIV/AIDS during the time of their pastoral education. It is critical, however, that church ministers, priests, imams, rabbis, and traditional healers—doctors, nurses, and health-care professionals—as well as singers, musicians, and composers—be understood as working and training in a post-HIV/AIDS era, an era that brings with it many challenges, such as those outlined below in the action plan issuing from the 2001 "Ecumenical Response to HIV/AIDS in Africa":

> But the challenge to the churches is felt at a deeper level than this. As the pandemic has unfolded, it has exposed fault lines that reach to the heart of our theology, our ethics, our liturgy and our practice of ministry. Today, churches are being obliged to acknowledge that we have—however unwittingly—contributed both actively and passively to the spread of the virus. Our difficulty in addressing issues of sex and sexuality has often made it painful for us to engage, in any honest and realistic way, with issues of sex education and HIV prevention. Our tendency to exclude others, our interpretation of the scriptures and our theology of sin have all combined to promote the stigmatization, exclusion and suffering of people with HIV or AIDS. This has undermined the effectiveness of care, education and prevention efforts and inflicted additional suffering on those already affected by the HIV. Given the extreme urgency of the situation, and the conviction that the churches do have a distinctive role to play in the response to the epidemic, what is needed is a rethinking of our mission, and the transformation of our structures and ways of working. (2001, 2; also quoted in *Global AIDS: Facing the Crisis* 2003, 4)

This report, produced for a meeting held in Nairobi for African church leaders, articulates a shift in the responsibility and understanding of historical accountability. That church leaders have begun to acknowledge openly the role of religious institutions while simultaneously addressing degrees of culpability is a significant redirection of the efforts of African church leaders to address stigmatization. This will surely only occur when the "transformation of our [religious] structures" occurs.

INDIVIDUALS MOTIVATED BY FAITH

Many of the issues raised in this chapter are typically ignored by the WHO, USAID, and UNAIDS, and, if broached at all, they are more often than not relegated to appendices or footnotes. This position within the margins tells us more about the true missions of multilateral organizations than about the efforts of individuals and communities in faith-based or spiritually rooted cultural institutions at the grassroots who dance and sing medical interventions on a daily basis.

My observations in this chapter do not attempt to be concerned, in general, with the institutional responses of African faith-based NGOs such as the Catholic-sponsored Meeting Point Kampala or Muslim medical associations in Africa, such as PADA (People with AIDS Development Association) in Iganga or the Islamic Medical Association of Uganda (IMAU), or the ongoing medical outreach undertaken by traditional healers such as those affiliated with THETA in Uganda. Rather, the focus of my field research has been on the role of the individual as interpreter within faith-based institutions.

Leaders of such religious NGOs and institutions mentioned above are rarely mentioned, let alone their individual agency detailed to any degree. In fact, discourse on religion and AIDS in Africa seldom departs from the realm of religion as cultural institution. Seldom does dialogue occur involving individual local medical professionals with individual local religious leaders. This bifurcated system of communication is also easily mapped onto foreign intellectual, medical, religious, funding and aid initiatives. Many AIDS-related publications, for example, target audiences within global communities: evangelical newsletters hold one set of truths, international aid agency Web sites espouse another set, while global health outreach agencies situate themselves squarely within another set. The storytellers of religion, health, and healing regarding HIV/AIDS in Uganda often tell variations while never fully recognizing that they share the same theme. I humbly suggest that it is time to listen to each other's stories.

In an excerpt included on the accompanying CD as Track 7, a performance of the invocation of spirits is led by Nabanji and two women, also witch doctors in Nabanji's community, who join him. The performance occurs in Nabanji's village compound comprised of a group of ancestral shrines. As I began documenting this event with a team of medical doctors, an older gentleman rushed in to join the performance, apologizing for being late. As he explained to me, he had just come from Catholic Mass. That the irony of this statement was noted by the medical doctors who accompanied me suggests yet a further need for conversations about religion and spirituality in this area:

Track 7 **"Dati Itondu mwene inana wooo...Itonda mwere" ("God Himself will know, woo...God Himself")**
Maboni Nabanji and his colleagues

> *Chorus*—God will know, wooo, God will know
> *Verses*—Mother, I have come to see you this early morning
> Hey you, you are welcome
> Today I have come to consult you
> AIDS ate the educated

It has eaten those of Makerere [University]
Sincerely, we are already dead
AIDS has finished us
Sincerely, few will survive
Sincerely, god of gods
Come, we will fight AIDS
Come out of the air now
Ah, I am happy to see you appear now
Sincerely, great father "Maboni"
Come, we will fight AIDS
Sincerely, great father Kiwanuka
All of you come, we will fight the disease

Walya Sulaiman is a Muslim living just outside of Iganga town in eastern Uganda. Since diagnosed almost ten years ago with HIV after the death of his wife, Sulaiman has worked relentlessly to bring education, comfort, counseling, and medical treatment to many other Muslims in his community. I met with Sulaiman on several different occasions. During our final meeting, he asked if I could record his group singing a few songs. He opened the recording session with a prayer, smiling at me as he whispered in my ear, "You know, we often quote your Bible too." In the song performed by PADA on Track 8, Sulaiman and his group reflect on the need to bring discussions of AIDS out in the open:

Track 8 **"Kino kinene kyembwene ekituse ekyatuka"**
("What has come to the villages is very strong")
PADA, Iganga

My clan mates! AIDS came for our village
My clan mates! It came through individuals
It is there even in my clan mates, in the adults it is there
I do not want rumors, you have started rumors
The disease in the community, you do not even have to talk about it
I have heard and I have understood
I have heard the words you have spoken, I have understood, but this is a sour
disease
This virus, even the widow
This virus, even a bachelor
This virus, even the beautiful whom it wants most
This virus, even the ugly persons, it claims them
This virus, even young children, it has claimed them
This virus, it has a hunting mechanism

In the following excerpt from an interview with the traditional healer Maboni Nabanji (see Figure 5.1 and 5.2) in Budwege Village (Iganda),

Figure 5.1 Maboni Nabanji seated before an ancestral shrine in his family compound.

the healer locates the spirit world directly within his everyday healing practice:

Nabanji—Now when I started this work I was a hospital guard in Iganga hospital. We had a traditional ceremony in my clan and the spirits chose and attacked me, and decided that I should leave my work then and become in charge of the clan drums and spirits. That was way back in 1989. From that time the spirits make and administer their cures through me and I administer our herbs to patients. I tried to add my own herbs, and I have also tried to consult my colleagues both in the country and outside in Kenya, Zaire, and Tanzania but I failed to get a passport. However, I do move out to a limited extent for consultations.

I specialize in madness and other psychiatric illnesses. Even if a patient is violent all I have to do is point my stick towards him and he calms down. It is very, very unlikely that a patient will leave my shrine unimproved, whatever the presenting condition. We tried to treat AIDS for quite a long time, but due to the fact that we do not know the origin of the virus, it is still hard for us to cure. However, we administer symptomatic treatment for vomiting, diarrhea esophageal, and ulcers so that a patient can live an additional five years or more with the virus remaining in the body.

Due to the fact that I have worked in a hospital in the past, I have a clearer sense of some issues, such as when a fever is not going down. I call a lab man to take blood from a patient and check for causes. If he identifies any cause then we refer the patient to hospital. I think that both modern medics and traditional healers have handled the AIDS scourge appropriately. With both of us in the struggle I think we have done a lot.

Music has a primary role in AIDS prevention. Singing is the main form of treatment. We play drums and other instruments during the process of diagnosis to discern whether a patient has AIDS, familial spirits, or other possession. When we sing our songs we burn herbs, and then the spirits take over one of us, allow that person to speak out loud what the patient is suffering from. In terms of musical instruments we use drums, we use ensasi (rattles), and we use an olugwale (winnowing tray) when the spirits have come.

Concerning the best way of controlling the spread of HIV, now this is a difficult question. People are difficult. For us, in the songs we sing we ask people to restrict their sexual desires and those who are able to pick these messages have changed. For example, in our village the old people have picked the messages in our songs and have now

Figure 5.2 Maboni Nabanji.

> restricted having sex with just their wives. This is very hard, however,
> for the youth who do not find any interest in our music.
>   The various type of treatment we administer to our patients
> include:
>   Drugs for oral administration
>   Drugs for topical administration
>   We do incision and damage of boils (abscesses)
>   Singing to relax the patient
>   As a traditional healer, how do I tell that someone has AIDS when
> in their normal spirits? I look at the texture of the skin and changes in
> appendages such as their hair. The eyes move inwards into the orbit.
> And here is when we can use drums and singing for diagnosis.

An *olugwale* winnowing tray to which Nabanji refers is traditionally used
to remove what is not wanted in millet, beans, or rice, etc. It is a large, flat
tray made from small, soft sticks, and is commonly used in the Bugwere
region when performing ritual dances. Local herbs are typically placed
in the *olugwale* and then placed on the head for dancing. In the Busoga
region it is called *lugali* (singular) or *engali* (plural). This term comes from
ebigali which refers to anything you put in the basket in *athroine*, small
buildings built for the spirits by witch doctors (see the *athroine* in the
background of Figure 5.3). Monetary offerings are referred to as *bigali* in

Figure 5.3 Residents of Maboni Nabanji's home compound.

order to avoid direct reference to the local term for money. Historically, before they started using baskets they used to use *engali* or *lugali* to put money for local traditional healers who would tell you to ask for what you want while holding your money. After the request was made, the healers would then request that the monies be put it in the basket. Once such an offering is put in a basket it is no longer called "money" but *ebigali*. So when the Bagwere people dance with an *olugwale* on their head, those with health or spiritual problems or issues will put their money there and ask for what they want. People frequently become possessed at the climax of such a dance.

In many African contexts there is a clear reality of multiple engagements of religions. For many people with whom I have been privileged to work—including Walya Sulaiman and Maboni Nabanji—multiple aspects of religion and spirituality inform their worldviews. One can be in-the-world-religiously at highly nuanced levels.

MEETING POINT AND EVERYDAY SPIRITUALITY

Meeting Point is a small NGO located in the Namuwongo district of Kampala. A network of community outreach sites started in 1992 by AIDS activist Noelina Namukisa (see Figure 5.4), the formation of Meeting Point was a direct reaction to the fear many people faced in the 1980s regarding stigma attached to HIV/AIDS. Today, Meeting Point thrives, serving social, medical, spiritual, economic, and psychological needs of count-less children, young girls, and women who find themselves abandoned or helpless, struggling to live in a world of confusing and complicated social and medical issues.

> *Namukisa—Our organization is called Meeting Point because this is the point where all problems, needs, and issues can be addressed and met. This is the meeting point for people living with HIV in this area. Our women's group—Kyamusa Obwongo—was established in reaction to the ignorance of the people of this area. The majority of people living here, mostly women, are illiterate, so that phrase, "Kyamusa Obwongo," meaning "sharpen your brain," was adopted to encourage women to open their minds and allow them to be "sharpened." Before, everyone hid in shame. Now everybody comes out, and this is the point where everyone meets.*

As Noelina suggests, "sharpening your brain," best happens when engaging localize cultural traditions. According to Trinidad Osteria and Gerald Sullivan (1991, 145), educational programs related to AIDS "should be guided by culture... For example, oral-aural approaches are more effective in countries with high illiteracy rates or strong verbal traditions.... It may be that culture could also play a role in maximizing efficient distribution of AIDS education literature."

Figure 5.4 Patrick Anguzu and Noelina Namukisa.

Meeting Point offers an integrated approach to HIV/AIDS, focusing not only on the immediate medical needs of an individual, but on the social problems that accompany family members acting as caregivers as well as children who are often orphaned or abandoned. "Love cannot stop with the patient," according Noelina, "you have to love the entire family." Educating family, caregivers, and neighbors is central to the work of volunteers at Meeting Point.

> *Namukisa—People in the past used to die miserably. You could find a person alone and desperate, lying in her own vomit. Nobody would care for her. Nobody would bathe her. Nobody would give her food. When we started visiting patients, caring for them in loving and compassionate ways, people would model us, and we began to see changes slowly occurring in the way families and friends would react to the disease.*

Many of the changes for Noelina and others involved at Meeting Point are grounded in the faith and spirituality offered by a close affiliation with the Catholic Church. Being open and empathic is based on Christian commandments, according to Noelina. In the following statement, Noelina alludes to a deeply spiritual connection between humanity and divinity in the form of one's person. One "remains a person," according to Noelina even when faced with a life-threatening virus.

> *Namukisa—In fact, in starting this organization we started in a Christian way as followers of Christ, and I think that is why that we feel that we are happy, because when we help these people we feel we are helping Christ himself, because the biggest commandment is you must love one another. This is what Christ left with us. We love our friends because Christ also loved us and died on the cross. So we have to follow God. So our main aim was to care for people living with HIV/AIDS. But in the end we found that when you enter a family and you find somebody who is sick, your love cannot stop with that patient, but you have to love all the family as well. Because they need your help, they need your guidance, they need your love. They are desperate. But when you come in and you show that, for example, maybe there is a great fear that one of the family members is found out to be HIV positive, but when we come in and show that he is still a person even though he is living with HIV, but he's still a person. AIDS does not change a person from his core humanity. But even though he lives with the virus he remains a person.*

Most outreach efforts of Meeting Point target women, primarily because women are at the center of much suffering throughout Africa. In Uganda as in other parts of East Africa, women are responsible for the location and cooking of food, caring for children, and for shouldering many of the social and economic burdens of maintaining a family unit. If women are not literate, according to Noelina, the nation of Uganda will not develop. Thus, her efforts often target women and younger girls.

> **Namukisa**—*Young girls suffer a lot. We take care of girls whose parents die of AIDS and are left alone as heads of families. Maybe there are brothers and sisters that are very young, and often times the girl does not know what to do. These girls are often desperate, and men take advantage of this desperation, offering to give young girls needed soap and sugar in exchange of course for sex. Many men have been using these girls. Meeting Point invited the girls here and we started a tailoring school to help them. Ninety girls went out last year and now they are working. What we want is a girl-child and a mother to have something to do on her own, rather than having to beg. We cannot leave out children, because a nation without children is not a nation.*

Prayer, a purposeful engagement with God, is the most significant aspect of Noelina's work. Her motivation, as is true for her husband Patrick Anguzu and others at Meeting Point, is based in her solid belief in what she refers to as the redemptive powers of Jesus Christ. For Noelina, the hundreds of children serviced by programs sponsored by Meeting Point represent spiritual opportunities to work with Christ, to companion him. As she suggests, "dress [him] when [he] was naked."

> **Namukisa**—*We are Catholics, and since we started we now have a Catholic priest, and we go together on Fridays to visit patients. We go read the Bible together, we pray together.*

> **Barz**—*Do you bring the sacrament?*

> **Namukisa**—*And the priest takes the sacrament. And for me this is the most enjoyable part of my work because we make sure that at least every patient who is dying dies happy after receiving the sacraments. We try by all means and we are very fortunate that all the priests respond immediately when we call them with a need for praying for a dying person. Even the patients, this Friday we shall have the mass here to pray for those who are living and very weak. The first thing is a prayer because we know that without God nothing can go ahead. So, for us this is the most important part in our work, because we know that without God we cannot work. There are a lot of temptations in our work. There is a lot of tiredness. People living*

with HIV/AIDS, maybe they have an experience, myself I know that anytime, any day I can die, but other people do not understand this. They know that a person who has been infected can die at any time, and that they should be ready to die. So, they bring that feeling, that understanding of death to the PLWAs. So, people once they're tested and are determined to be HIV positive, She has no hope, or she loses what hope she has. She thinks, "I'm dying any time." Yesterday I was with a certain child, many of the children around here are living with HIV, but you will not be able to tell, but you go to other families who do not understand, they will refuse to give her food. "After all, she is going to die. Why should I bother myself?" That is what they think. And now, for example, the children become scared because they pick this fear from the adults. So, as a child I become scared. And in fear there occurs a loss of hope. They become stubborn and reckless in their behavior. But, with prayer one can manage. And you bring them nearer with the word of God, reading the Bible together. Like Isaiah 43, "I called you by name, come near me." For me, if I'm reading the Bible together with a patient I feel very happy. And here they can come and say, for example, no one mentions my name here or her name. They call me Mama, you will see everyone calling me mother and you will ask yourselves, who is the mother? Because when we sit together we sit as a child and a mother. Sometimes they refuse or are unable to talk to their own people, their own families, and they say, come, come and we'll talk together, come and I'll tell you that I want my children to remain like this or that. Now, we feel a heavy burden of children. Because everyone who dies thinks that we are the only ones to manage their children according to the love that we have shared. They die confident in us. But, we cannot forget God. Very many organizations have collapsed because most people think that when they start an organization that it is their turn to get rich. He forgets to help the people and helps himself. But, if you put God ahead, knowing so well that what you are giving to a particular patient you give to Christ. Here I go around gathering some old clothes and give to them. They become so happy, because Christ said that you dressed me when I was naked, when I was in prison.

Because many of the women and young girls who come to Meeting Point do not read or write, much information and education occurs within the contexts of music, dance, and drama. Remote locations can be targeted for such sensitization efforts through Meeting Point's musical outreach:

Namukisa—*We communicate our messages primarily through music, dance, and drama. Counseling on our site is also done through* *music and drama. When we organize a play or music, we don't just compose any song or meaningless drama. First we recognize the experiences and needs around us. If we pass along those experiences in drama we find that we help people enormously. We can show a drama demonstrating how younger girls acquire HIV because they want to get rich, to become "smart" at an early age. We can show what happens when women go to witchdoctors instead of testing centers. We can pass along some songs in places where AIDS has hit aggressively. Music is our most powerful tool, Gregory, for affecting change in Uganda!*

Music, however, is much more than a mere didactic or pedagogical tool when employed by Meeting Point. Music and dancing often facilitate opportunities to engage heightened spiritual connections and to move beyond our wounded bodies, to reach out and communicate with a unique and positive attitude:

Namukisa—You know, music makes women happy. They feel at home when they sing, when they dance. They feel that even if they are sick they can "put on the music, put on the drums," and as you know, we can really dance! I don't know how I can express it, Gregory, but you have seen it happen. You have seen women walk in sick and then hours later dance, jumping high in the air, feeling a fresh breath of life! I feel that music—singing, dancing, drumming—is one of the best ways we have of maintaining our community of women and supporting them in their attempts to live positively with AIDS rather than merely being HIV positive.

Women and young girls in Uganda look to Meeting Point and individuals such as Noelina Namukisa for spiritual help, guidance, and support. Many learn that their lives can change through music, dance, and drama as they are introduced to ways in which they can learn to live positively with AIDS.

One day several summers ago after the completion of an interview with Noelina at Meeting Point, we walked through the slums of Namuwongo—known locally as "Soweto." I had forgotten to turn off my DAT recorder and came home to revisit Noelina speaking about her hopes and her dreams, her struggles and her faith.

Namukisa—I'd like to take you to down to see the orphanage where the children stay. These are children who have been abandoned completely. They don't have anybody except me. One young mother hanged herself while she was still a schoolgirl when she learned she was HIV positive, leaving behind a baby of six months. We found the baby lying beside her mother. These are the things we deal with on a daily basis. Every single child has a different story. Some of the parents of these children came to the city to work as house girls, some came to study, some were forced into sex work, others were raped. We are struggling, Gregory, and we trust and have faith that with love, each one will have the opportunity to grow up to be a good person.

CONCLUSION

When I concluded my interview with Maboni Nabanji, I asked if he had any recommendations for the future of AIDS prevention, diagnosis, and care. He quickly responded:

Nabanji—We need to strengthen the coalition between witch doctors, modern medical doctors, mosques, and churches. One way we can effectively promote such a coalition is to learn each other's songs. If we can make sure that people are getting the same accurate messages and information in the church as they are getting from me and from doctors, then, well, we are surely all together in this struggle.

Nabanji's response reflects the interdisciplinary exchange that is demanded (and embraced) by many in both traditional and Western health-care fields.

One person can make a difference. Noelina, Walya, and Maboni are just such people who have empowered themselves to help others and to affect social and economic change in their communities. Each contributes to the care of countless Ugandans by breaking down the barriers that typically separate religion, medicine, and music. In the care and treatment of those with HIV, religion has historically informed many responses, and today many expressive responses contributed to a variety of cultural, medical, and musical interventions specific to AIDS.

Interlude 5
Conversation with Faustus Baziri
Director of VOLSET
Gregory Barz, Vincent Wandera, Godfrey Mukasa

Wandera—Now please, if you do not mind, could you please tell us your names and your organization's aims and objectives?

Baziri—I am Faustus Baziri, I am the coordinator of this organization that is called VOLSET. It is an abbreviation for Voluntary Service Trust Team. VOLSET. We take the first three letters, then two letters, then the last two Ts become one. It is our password.

Mukasa—Thank you very much. Now, what are the aims and objectives of VOLSET?

Baziri—Well, the main aim is to alleviate human suffering. The ideas of the original founder concerned HIV/AIDS in the community. He came from Lubiri and said if we start here, then we could transfer the education to the community, just at the grassroots. So it was to alleviate human suffering related to disease in the rural areas.

Mukasa—Can I know when it started?

Baziri—That is November 2, 1997.

Mukasa—What information, message, relevant to AIDS prevention, is carried out in the music? I understand you have a music department. What information relevant to AIDS prevention is carried out in the music?

Baziri—There are a lot of informations. But one of them is health education. We educate the community. We pass on the message. Music is an organized sound, eh? So, through this sound we send messages to people, and it is quite attractive. As they come to listen they learn, and we believe when they go back that they practice. And, we get feedback that is encouraging.

Mukasa—Now, how much impact can you assess you have had through music?

Baziri—Well, we have this counseling center, and there is an information center. Once we have presented in the community, we get feedback from people coming back here for counseling, for referrals, because we refer them to counselors. People also come and say, "ah, after the presentation I got moved, so I am here to be counseled, to be advised." So, we feel something is being done through music.

Barz—So there is a direct result? Could you give us a specific example of a type of message that is conveyed through music?

Baziri—*This question is welcome. In the community we have HIV/AIDS positive clients. And we advocate for them so that their relatives can give them more support and help them so that they can accept them as they are, so that they can give them support. We advocate. And then we have the orphans. We also put in our dramas and music these messages, so that these orphans are not left uncared for. And then, we have the inflow from the cities and the neighboring towns. They come to stay in the community. And when they come at the village level, they come not always healthy. They are positive, but because of the body breakdown, immunity breakdown, they come to stay this way. And when they stay this way, they do not always control themselves. So we present this music, touching them, educating them to be more human when they come. And then we in the community look at them as our people, receive them, take care of them, stay with them. And that message helps us to prevent HIV/AIDS from spreading in our community.*

Mukasa—*Why do you prefer disseminating information through music, dance, and drama, rather than with speeches and seminars?*

Baziri—*Oh that is wonderful! It is difficult most times, unless you have paid some people some money, to collect them and give them a speech. But it is different when you invite them to watch a play and listen to some music. We include even some video shows. When you invite them to watch a play, see some dance, and hear some music they come without even being invited. And then there are so many, and then we can disseminate information to the group that is already there. So, the reason is attracting them to come, and the easiest way of telling them what you want, without even involving so much as collecting them, is to drum and sing. But when they come, they are there, and they are in your hands, listening, and sometimes they are happy. Sometimes they shed some tears. And by the end of the day, our objectives have been achieved.*

Mukasa—*Now apart from using music to educate and sensitize the community about AIDS, what other work would you give music?*

Baziri—*With our music and drama, plus the video shows, they can act as an income-generating project. Because in a time of peace, when we are not going to sensitize very much, we can organize maybe to go to town if means are available. Then you can make that show. And then people give some money, do some fundraising. You can invite some people and tell them that we have this program, and so people bring something. And we believe it can keep our organization running if we have some money, so when our people go to present, at least they don't present when they don't have lunch. So, I think it can work as one source of generating income.*

Mukasa—*I want to know how you get your compositions, those music compositions that you have?*

Baziri—It is very interesting that within our drama group are those who can compose music. Within ourselves there are those who also compose drama. You only give them the thing, the idea, and then they do it. With the technical support we create it from within ourselves. Maybe in the future, with the funds, we can get those who are advanced to help us to polish, but for now we do it ourselves.

Barz—It is all within the group.

Baziri—Mmmmm.

Mukasa—Don't you borrow from some other groups at times?

Baziri—What is this "borrowing"?

Mukasa—What I mean by borrowing is that you copy a certain piece of music from another group and incorporate it into yours.

Baziri—Well, with borrowing, maybe really just music we do. Because when we present in a religious community, we use this music, church music. They like it very much. But with our drama, and these AIDS messages, we really make our own, and maybe the tapes, when we are presenting a video show, we use the tapes of these other people like the late Juuko. Put them on there, let the people listen to the music. We copy by using our videotapes, so those ones we can copy. But with the presentation, we do it ourselves.

Barz—Now do you have any further recommendations for ways in which music, dance, and drama can be used in AIDS prevention?

Baziri—Okay, here we have a community, a real community, which does not have access to most methods of HIV dissemination. All they have is a radio. You know, they put out on the radio certain announcements. And in this community, they don't even have the batteries. So being a community which lacks some access to privileges which are found in cities, when we present this drama it is easier for them to get what we really want. It is easier to transfer our knowledge through the drama, and the community, down in the village, you give them this message. That is one of the recommendations. So, after you have compared these reports, what next?

Barz—What next? First is to give the information back to groups like VOL-SET, to give them the documentation, to give them the results. Second, is to explore agencies that might be interested in this research, agencies that need to know this information, need to know about what type of information is being given in these songs and for them to see that this is a legitimate mode for communication.

Baziri—Okay. By the way there is one thing before we come to a conclusion. I'm happy that you have taken the initiative of coming to these lower NGOs which are locally just started with the government and with the local government here. And with your coming, we pray that in future you will *also send us this report. I know you have been comparing us with other programs, eh? And then we could also get a report. And from there maybe we can also learn how we can improve on our own performance.*

Barz—*That's my hope, namely that each group can learn from the other groups, so that for example VOLSET can learn from what Good Shepherd is doing.*

Baziri—*And probably another thing I would say to you as you do your research is, the smaller NGOs are oppressed by biggest NGOs. Sometimes you get some announcements about some programs concerning HIV/AIDS, money has come from whatever. But by the end of the day, this group we sit and make a plan, and the big NGOs have the largest share, small NGOs remain small. So we are glad that you took this initiative to come to this level, so that you can find out our problems. And we shall be glad once we get such reports, and then even if we get more visitors that encourages us to say, "Ah! People know. Someone in America knows where VOLSET is." Then we are happy about that.*

6

RE-MEMORYING MEMORY
HIV/AIDS and the Performance of Cultural Memory

Oh AIDS, you killer
You killed my Daddy
So is my Mommy
Oh AIDS, I hate you
I'll never forget you till I die
I'll never forget you till I die

—Sung by Children at the GOSSACE Orphan School,
Golomolo Village

A WALK FROM GOLOMOLO VILLAGE
Excerpt from a Fieldnote

After spending several hours with the children at the school for the orphans in Golomolo Village, Vincent Wandera, Godfrey Mukasa, and I begin the thirty-minute walk from the remote village down to the waterfront of Lake Victoria. We pass through several fishing villages along the way, each connected by winding walk paths. Most of the villages are deserted, their huts and mud-and-stick buildings long abandoned. Vincent points to several dwellings along the way, telling me that there is no one left to live in these homes. The sound of a battery-powered radio interrupts the soundscape—we passed the end of the electricity poles hours before reaching the village on bicycle—and we stop to visit with several young boys in the process of mending large fishing nets. I had not noticed the silence before this moment, but as we continue I am increasingly aware of the absence of sound as we make our way down to the lake. Vincent takes my hand and explains to me that the fishermen used to come up from the lake and rape the girls and women or sometime pay for sex, spreading HIV along their way throughout the fishing villages. Now, Vincent tells me, "Slim has taken everybody."

We pass an old woman sitting on a woven mat outside the entrance to a mud hut. We approach a small compound and Vincent introduces her as "a guardian to many of our children at the school" (see Figure 6.1). I greet her and ask how many children she takes care of. She looks past me and pauses before answering. She says that she can no longer keep track, that she doesn't even know all of their names or from what families they came from. Beginning to tear she tells me that she cannot pass along their histories to many of the children.

TRACK 9   **Sounds of the walk down to Lake Victoria from Golomolo Village**

As we reach the shores of Lake Victoria, I begin to consider the absence of memory, a missing generation that represents missing memories for so many people. As I mumble something about the

Figure 6.1 A guardian to many of "our children at the school."

sadness of all this silence Vincent responds, "That is not the worst of it. There are no aunties left here. There are no aunties to teach the girls about sex. This is how we teach and they are no longer here. What will these girls do, those who are not already infected?" We walk through an area full of abandoned dugout canoes, no longer used. Only a few groups of fishermen, mostly boys, are preparing their nets to go out through the thick water hyacinth out to fishing waters. As we continue to make our way along the shallow waters, I am reminded of one of Vincent's compositions I recently heard performed by the adult HIV-counselors of GOSSACE (Good Shepherd Support Action Centre) at their head office in Kampala. I point to one older canoe that is half submerged in the water and ask Vincent, "a leaking canoe"? He smiles and tells me that he wrote that particular song the last time he was down at the shores collecting children who had gone astray to go back up to school.

RE-MEMORYING AND SOCIAL MEMORY

"I do remember," he said, "only Pooh doesn't very well, so that's why he likes having it told to him again. Because then it's a real story and not just a remembering."

—A. A. Milne 1954, 20–21

IN THIS CHAPTER I advocate for positioning memory within an ongoing process of cultural engagement and change. In many unique ways contemporary cultural performances in Uganda contribute to and enhance the development of multiple memories. Put another way, musical performances facilitate multiple ways of "memorying," that is the purposeful application of giving memory to an idea, thought, or message. Changes in memory along with adaptations of memory—social processes to which I refer somewhat inelegantly in this section as "*re*-memorying"—are often the product of active memory work with intentional manipulation. Understanding memory as a purposeful social activity ("re-memorying")—actively engaging in the recalling of the past within the present—suggests that the passive notion often referred to rather simply as "collective memory" may very well be an artificial construction. An individual's active involvement in recalling the past must be understood, as cultural theorist Mieke Bal (1999, vii) suggests, as a social process that is "continuously modified and re-described even as it continues to shape the future."

The goal of active memory work—maintaining and disseminating objects of social memory—is forefronted in the lives of many Ugandans, women specifically, as many confront their own mortality as well as that of their family members. Many HIV-positive women, frequently the sole heads of families, must consider the futures of their own children and those of their deceased siblings. In this chapter I attempt to come to grips with the very intentional ways in which re-memorying functions as an activity engaged by many women, a process of the engagement of social memory.

THE PERFORMANCE OF MEMORY

Memory is inherently performative, and it is within the *performance* of memory, as Paul Connerton (1991) suggests, that memory is recalled, conveyed, and sustained. The outward projection of individual identity is constantly reflected back in performance, and it is within performances of social memory, specifically within the interaction with others that many aspects of individual memory are both created and affirmed. In many ways, the efforts to preserve and maintain what are typically labeled "collective memories"—what Marita Sturken, Mieke Bal, and others refer to more directly and perhaps more appropriately as "cultural memories"—are often the direct result of some form of performative effort in Uganda, whether it be songs, dances, or dramas. According to Bal (1997, vii), "cultural recall is not merely something of which you happen to be a bearer but something that you actually *perform*, even if, in many instances, such acts are not consciously and willfully contrived." Yet, within any performance of cultural memory a reshaping of the past must necessarily occur, and it is this requisite changing of both the future and present that directly affects a *re-memoried* understanding of the past.

There is much at stake for the individual and for the collective in active memory work—as the case studies presented in this chapter will demonstrate. Many Ugandans are forced to engage memory actively with the process of re-memorying in the absence of entire generations, in the absence of direct links to family, and often in the absence of knowledge of home and community, of ethnic group and clan. Where memory work becomes interactive in Ugandan contexts is in the transmission of memory. Memory is typically formed in the individual according to Edward Shils (1981, 51), within a process that exposes the individual to the memories of others, specifically those older than the individual. The engagement of memory work is a powerful gesture since it is, according to Shils, "an inexpungible part of the human mind and absolutely indispensable to human culture" (94). In Ugandan contexts, as many families experience the loss of spouses, children, parents, and siblings, memory work has had to turn to new, unique re-memorying processes where much is at stake, as I have suggested, for future generations.

In the introduction to *Acts of Memory: Cultural Recall in the Present*, Bal develops a tripartite schema within which we can position the function of performative memories in a given culture. The first category is one that needs little explanation. It is one Bal refers to as an "Ur-narrative," referring directly to the memories we keep tucked away that both form and inform our everyday, routinized habits and conditioned behavior. Such narrative memories are maintained throughout our lives and are born in early childhood: "If you don't wipe your feet, the house gets dirty, your parents become angry, and the trouble begins" (1999, viii). The second category in Bal's schema centers on "narrative memories" that differ from the habitual memories of the first category in that they involve a series of events that are recalled and constructed into a livid story, into a colorful present. The third and final category that Bal introduces focuses on "traumatic recall" in which narrative functions as a healing activity whereby traumatic memories are "legitimized and narratively integrated in order to lose their hold over the subject who suffered the traumatizing event in the past" (viii). Odd as it may seem, traumatic memories occur very much in the present rather than in the past. Such memories when actively recalled, relived, and changed are part of a dynamic process of traumatic re-memorying.

MUSIC AND TRAUMATIC MEMORY WORK

In this chapter I focus on Bal's last category within which we can position the expressive culture of many HIV-positive women in Uganda as an influencing and guiding force in contemporary traumatic memory work. I begin by introducing two issues, one tangible, the other somewhat ephemeral—Memory Books and Musical Performances. Both of these issues represent processes of remembering and re-memorying HIV/AIDS by reconstituting traumatic recall in song texts, introducing different ways of understanding medical interventions, and ensuring continuity through musical re-memories.

By way of introduction, Track 10 on the CD accompanying this text features the counselors from GOSSACE singing "We travel in a leaking canoe," the song title referenced at the end of the fieldnote that opens this chapter. This particular song is a response to the trauma of hopelessness felt among this community of counselors to the sick and dying, most of whom are HIV positive. Of the many traumatic messages communicated within the song, the issue of memory—specifically the loss of critical cultural memory—is presented within one of the most desperate forms of loss, that is the loss of entire generations in many of the communities that GOSSACE services.

TRACK 10   **"Mulyato ebotofu mwetutambulira"**
            ("We travel in a leaking canoe")[46]

We travel in a leaking canoe
Most problems are caused by parents
Parents mostly generate problems for children
When problems occur, tears are shed
It is a delicate situation advising youth appropriately
When the world waves and viruses came,
Ignorantly we perish

A warning to mothers listening now
Gender equality may have contributed to our destruction
When equality was introduced
Women neglected their husbands
Realizing the neglect, husbands lost trust
Wives started loving carelessly
Mothers, the behavior of gender equality is the sole cause
Noting husband's behaviors
Mothers knew the eventuality of catching the killer AIDS

Long ago clans existed
So hard they used to work
Advice was appropriately given to whoever became a youth
What has happened to all these words?
So-called gender equality has contributed to the removal of the good words
How then do you expect anything good, anything different from the behavior
of parents?

Long time ago uncles and aunties were there for those coming up
They could advise
Even fathers and mothers were concerned
Today children parent one another
Gender equality has removed all the concerns
What good then do you expect apart from those acts that
endanger youth's life?

Oh, it is too bad for you parents
You die leaving young ones shedding tears
Oh it is too sad, parents
It is only children now observing funeral rites
Oh, it is bad for the parents who leave young ones shedding tears

Vincent Wandera, the song's composer, addresses the issue of re-memory-ing-as-process in two ways, both of them in direct response to some degree of loss of cultural memory. First, in the song's third verse, the typical duties of clan affiliation are eluded to, primary among which was to provide youth with cultural advice and counsel. The influence of clan structures within ethnic groups has somewhat broken down in this central region of the country due to the death of large numbers of individuals within clans, and now, "what has happened to these words"? Second, Wandera suggests that there is no one left to educate the youth about their clan, their family, their history. According to UNASO (Uganda Network of AIDS Service Organisations), a primary mode for encouraging communication about issues related HIV/AIDS among children is through music, a "powerful tool in helping those emotionally distressed *especially if the songs and tunes are familiar and linked with happy memories*" (*UNASO Best Practice Series* 2002, 3, emphasis added). The suggestion made by UNASO is one validated by Wandera's musical composition, namely that music is one of the strongest ways of "linking" children to the past, to their history, through the rather intentional process of re-memorying (see Figure 6.2 as illustration of the presence of small children in the context of performances of medical interventions intended for adult audiences).

Many groups that organize for purposes of educating youth—such as Wandera's GOSSACE—make intense efforts to address immediate social needs of youth, many of whom belong to what anthropologists George Bond and Joan Vincent identify as a "missing generation":

> Acting out of a sense of moral responsibility for the future of Uganda they [a group of students at Makerere University] were operating in a context

Figure 6.2 Children in Bute Village are present and attentive during a performance led by Aida Namulinda.

of knowledge that configured the AIDS pandemic as an inevitable process of decimation that would leave their nation with no leaders, a lost elite and urban middle class, a destroyed national economy, a missing generation—in short, a cataclysmic view of their universe. (1997b, 101)

In the final stanza of Wandera's "We travel in a leaking canoe," the roles and responsibilities of uncles and aunties are also suggested to be unfilled. These roles were traditionally to educate and counsel adolescents as they prepare to enter adulthood. With no parents, no uncles or aunts, youth, according to "We travel in a leaking canoe," must parent themselves and one another, mirroring what Bond and Vincent suggest happens when an entire generation goes missing.

A similar social construction is outlined in the song text that opens this chapter. The young, orphaned children from Golomolo village in the Mukono District (see Figure 6.3) sing of AIDS killing both parents. Yet in this text the children assert a need to remember, to cling to memories, to retain cultural information, albeit within a song text that has a potentially double meaning regarding what the children will deliberately not forget—AIDS or their parents—"I'll never forget you till I die."

Speaking to a group of villagers in the Rakai District in 1990, legendary Ugandan popular musician Philly Bongoley Lutaaya—one of the first public figures, musician or otherwise, to acknowledge his HIV status

Figure 6.3 Young, orphaned schoolchildren of Golomolo village.

openly—made a similar statement, urging all children in the assembled crowd to make sure that they learned more information about the areas from where their families came, to never forget lest their family's tradition and history disappear (*Frontline: Born in Africa* 1990).[47] Similarly, in an earlier interview in 1989, Lutaaya urged a deliberate reordering of social memory regarding AIDS, a re-memorying of the disease:

> There is no sense in looking for guilt or origin when it comes to AIDS. What matters is that it can affect any one of us; you, your best friend, your neighbor, your children. What makes it so difficult to master this dreadful disease, for which there is no cure, is that it is so closely related to one of our most important desires, our sexuality. My message to all of you and especially the youth is therefore to learn as much as possible about AIDS and to love responsibly. Those who have already contracted AIDS are the other side of the coin. Very often we are rejected and left alone with our disease, our needs, fears and suffering. Don't desert us! We need and are entitled to as much care, compassion and understanding as any one of you. AIDS should not be fought by just a few, to be able to overcome we have to fight it together. (1989, 681)

The decade from 1985 to 1995, often labeled the first decade of AIDS in Uganda—although the virus surely existed before this time—represents the introduction of new interventions, an acceptance of multiple systems of knowledge acquisition (local and global), and a reconciliation of older "re-memoried" conceptualizations of AIDS with newly invented memories of the disease. The absence of memory is reflected in the following song text recorded at Meeting Point. In the song's text, homes become "bushes," meaning that houses have been abandoned due to the loss of complete family units, save for the orphaned children, many of whom are taken care of by agencies such as Meeting Point. There is no one left, suggests the song, to teach many of these children how to "fight'" the disease, and thus the performers of the song adopt the role of teacher and of family members in their efforts to provide "shields, spears, and powerful guns" with their words.

"I can hear"
Meeting Point Kampala

Solo—I can hear, I can hear wailing and people crying for help
We are all in danger, Ugandans
Those who are still alive to fight the diseases that wants to destroy us, let us
pull up our socks
Many diseases have come to torture us and mercilessly kill both the old and
the young
Now is the time for those of us who can see into the distance to stand and
fight our hunters

For sure it is true that the Lord must be annoyed and that we have sinned
against Him
We sinned but we do not know how
Even when created we did not know God's plan for creation
Look how he has put temptations to work within us, ordering us to do things
he has told us not to
We are like rats in a person's home surrounded by traps or poison for us to eat
We eat in peace to our satisfaction, and then slowly we die
It is now clear that we too are in danger, we are being finished, we are dead
Look at the cities that were once filled with people

Chorus—We have become only a handful, we are being finished dead
Everywhere you go you hear wailing and crying

Solo—Woe to us, Woe to us. Woe to parents who bury their offspring
Our heads drip with pain, who will bury us?
Who will help us when we are old, in the future when our bones are old?
Ah, wasteland, those villages that used to be inhabited
It has taken all the parents and babies, a home quickly becomes a bush
Let us plead with God almighty, I would not like you to deny it
Keep quiet, I will teach you
I am teaching you how to fight
Go fight this side with our...
Shields, spears, and powerful guns, our enemy is a skilled fighter
Trust one another
All the other people are infected except your beloved

Those left in the villages able to "see the distance"—whether they are related to orphaned young children or not—are often in positions where they must fight for continuing survival. The increasing number of child-headed households in rural areas is alarming, and the complete absence of cultural memory is a frequent theme in songs such as "I Can Hear."

In Herman Basudde's popular song "Ekiwuka ekyaga muntamu" deep cultural memories of HIV/AIDS in Uganda are invoked within the context of a dream experienced by the performer. The dream, a narrative tool used by Basudde to lead his listeners to an integration of historical and contemporary knowledge of the disease, focuses on a lizard-like insect that invades the Basudde household, threatening all with which it comes into contact. The lizard enters by force and becomes lodged in a "saucepan," a particular image rooted in the women's domestic world and also slang for a women's vagina. Breaking the saucepan in the process of killing or overtaking the lizard would deny any further access to food, or more directly to sex, what women offer to men. The insect is eventually mutilated, struck over the head with a piece of wood and ultimately killed. But, the saucepan is also destroyed in the process. Such has been the strength of the lizard's effect.

I include Basudde's extended song text below—the first stanza of which was discussed earlier in chapter 4—in an English translation (the original is in Luganda) to demonstrate the degree to which singers such as Basudde depend on localized knowledge, reflecting an engagement of historical cultural memories within a process of re-memorying the disease in contemporary contexts. The elaborate text is a cautionary tale that attracts its listeners because of its ability to recall, re-memory, and reinvent—all part of the same musico-memory process.

"Ekiwuka ekyaga muntamu"
("The insect caught in the saucepan")
Herman Basudde

Solo—I had a dream at our home during the night and I was so very afraid
I had a dream at our home during the night that passed and I was so scared
I did not sleep again so I remained awake till daybreak
When daylight came I did not waste any time
I went directly to my mother to interpret the dream and tell me the meaning behind it
I dreamed there was an insect in the saucepan at home
The insect looked like a lizard
It was as big as a kitten but its tail led me to believe it was a poisonous insect
We converged to look at it critically
No one had the guts to suggest that we should kill it or beat it to death
When you hit the insect-lizard you could easily break the saucepan
And then we would not get anything to eat
This is because the insect was in the saucepan used to cook food
When we saw that the insect had taken over our saucepan one of us picked up a piece of wood
He hit it so hard on the head that the insect died
But the saucepan had also been badly destroyed
We looked at each other because we had lost the saucepan
When I asked my mother to explain to me the meaning of the dream this is what she said
Please sit and listen and you will know what kind of mind I have
In which I store lots of good things that I cannot easily expose
You know my conversations need people to listen who are settled
No one should disturb me by jumping up and down in their seats
Let me start by telling you that by the time I finish, even the disabled here will be dancing
You know my friends, things are bad nowadays, especially during this period of our youth

God made a fence [woman], and He put only one path through it [the vagina]
which is very small
And there is the only one that leads you inside the fence,
that is through the path
Once you get through the fence, you can eat anything you like
When you have sex with a woman the enjoyment is tremendous
But getting back out through the fence is difficult because you cannot always
find your way
Yet, the fruits that God put on the other side of the fence were tested long ago
Back when the trees were still free
The trees where we used to pick the fruits are now dry and very aged
The young trees have all been fenced off by God, so it is difficult
to get any fruit
We remain with large appetites
If you try to see through the fence, you can see much that is ripe and
ready to be eaten
When you force yourself into that small path that goes into the entrance
to the fence
You'll find that God put it in a very hidden place
But if you enter, you can pick any fruit you want, chewing and swallowing
easily
When you lose your appetite then you can stop eating
Then you have to pass back through the narrow path again because it is the
only way out
People who try to give up on women are very few
Even those who give up do so for only a little time until they find that they
must again continue
The tree that bears fruit has much ripe fruit, even young flowers
that are just budding
Even you who said that we should abstain in order to escape AIDS
You will soon feel the need to go back through the fence
The taste of the fruit is too sweet and nice
That no one who eats the fruit is able to stop
The day you see someone who says no to sex
That is when you see someone who enjoys sex but has not yet
contracted AIDS
The next day you wake up early
You take out your stick [penis] to pick as many fruits as possible
Then go back home to pick fruit [to have sex]
This time when you go back the owner of the fence will release
her trap [AIDS]
You will never come back
By this I mean that you are already dead
Sometimes you come back with wounds all over your body

Just because you ate fruit that was rotten and full of maggots
I have interpreted my dream for you
AIDS will kill us all
Ah, you cannot imagine!
Chorus—Fellow men, always try to eat good things like chicken, which is rich
and nutritious
Kasozi, who are you working for?
You should try to take some beer because life is short
We are surrounded by dead bodies or dead people
Let us just eat and feed well
There is nothing much we can do
Solo—This dream has people interested in "playing sex" with many women
that cannot be cured of AIDS
When you think of abstinence you think of a person you think is going to get
AIDS and fails to get it
This is going to help the owner of the farm get those who go to pick fruit every
day and every month
The seed of the AIDS virus is very hard
A person with AIDS will only be noticed when they are about to die
Now talking about AIDS, you are just wasting time
Because between you, me, and the rest of the world, no one is HIV negative
or AIDS free
What still encourages me is that I do not see any wounds on my stick [penis]
But I cannot tell a lie to the people I pass by that I am AIDS free
So now my fellow dead bodies, let us encourage each other
Here I address those who think they too are healthy and living for
many more years
Do not prepare for the death of friends
Instead, prepare for your own death
Because tomorrow you could wake up with wounds all over your body
You entered into the fence
You remember last time when you were not sure that AIDS was there
Now, because you have gone for so long without playing sex
You are going to count yourself among the healthy
You make us laugh—the AIDS virus is too strong and hard
If you want to kill it, you need to work hard and fetch water to draw it in
Now if your HIV virus is slow, do not feel overly healthy
It takes only one night for your virus to germinate
Even though you have four nights left, do not feel so healthy
Your virus will soon come up and so will the signs and symptoms
Everyone I look at here is already dead, so my friends take my advice
Remember the insect that fell in the saucepan
Between a person who abstained and the one still having sex—no one
is AIDS free

Check the back of your shirt that is now too big for you
And Topista's skirt is falling off and she has put on a big belt
It is too sad my fellow dead people
I have looked for a healthy person and I could not find any
Herbalists worked hard to find medicine for AIDS
We have failed to find it and now let us stick to one sexual partner
When we die, those of us who loved sex, the young ones who are AIDS free
will take over
God will make a new world, just as Sodom and Gomorah were destroyed
During Noah's time they were not educated,
and God left some creatures and only then was He happy
What can we do to convince God that we are sorry for stealing
the fruits in the fence?
I will die like this at home just because I "moved out" with very many women
Even though I stopped and now stay at home most of the time
And I am now counted among the humble people
So what comes next now that only God knows if I will survive or if
I'm already dead?
I ask those who will bury me not to delay
I will also do the same for anyone who dies
I do not feel any signs, but I am not sure whether I am HIV negative
Also you standing over there, we are in the same boat
It is because you pretend that we are blind
When someone asks you to measure the speed at which he is moving, and you
also go that same speed
The speed at which AIDS is killing us is too high
Now we are asked to change
Do not be conservative with your wealth
When you get money, please do something.
When you get enough to put up a house, please do so
Do not wait for a lot of money that could build a very nice house
I ask you to marry tomorrow
AIDS treats a man who has no wife so badly
AIDS mostly kills men without wives
They go to Sseggueu for sex in the morning and evening to Mouya
What can he do since he has no wife?
The Baganda people who understand this language
[Basudde is singing in Luganda]
You have the obligation, I know
You cannot lie to the young ones, telling them that you no longer play sex
when you do not sleep at home
If you know you have AIDS then you must get married
The one you marry should also have AIDS
If by chance you are both negative, be faithful to each other and
you will live longer

We have agreed, my dear fellow dead bodies
Those who abstain and also those who still play sex with many women
Stop that habit of pointing at your friends saying,
"Oh, it is sad that man has AIDS"
You passed each other on the way home, and you were both playing sex
with the same woman
The bus dropped one there, and the other one came back with that very bus
Let us try hard and see that we die in a dignified way
Let us also help our fellow dead bodies who are so badly off
Let us ask God to prepare for us
He can never cure AIDS
If you did not know this, know it from today
He will call those who did right but not those who were bad instead
of doing nothing
Everyone prepare what you will tell God
This is what I have done
I do not know what you will tell him, neither do you know what I will tell him.
Let me try, and I hope I will never lose my sleep
Look at your shirt, it is becoming bigger and bigger
Topista's skirt is all most falling off and she ties it with a big belt

Localized memories are re-memoried in Basudde's song as historical memory processes are intentionally located within contemporary
(albeit problematic) medical discourse. Basudde challenges his target
audience—typically men who consume his music either in discos or
social clubs—to reconsider older notions of the *Slim* disease while simultaneously appealing to all men to adopt behavioral changes that could
in many cases save lives. If the messages are not always couched within
a gender appropriate or politically correct way, they nevertheless speak
clearly to several generations of urban men who have found themselves
in the position of responding to the challenge of re-memorying AIDS in
the best way they know how, that is in historical, localized ways.

MEDICAL ETHNOMUSICOLOGY AND
CULTURAL RE-MEMORY

Witch doctors, traditional healers, and herbalists throughout Uganda
represent for many a meeting point where the production of historical
memory and the reliance on traditional, localized systems of knowledge
interact with Western-influenced medical interventions and sensibilities.
The assertion of new cultural memories—such as those demonstrated in
Herman Basudde's song—represents the act of re-memorying new issues
and new diseases within greater, more globalized cultural contexts. A culturally sensitive organizational approach to the integration of globalized
techniques drawing on local and foreign medical perspectives of health

and healing is now practices by THETA (Traditional and Modern Health Practitioners Together Against AIDS and Other Diseases), an organization in Uganda initiated in part by medical anthropologist Rachel King in collaboration with *Médicins Sans Frontiéres* (Doctors Without Borders). The central tenets of the original THETA initiative encouraged an ongoing collaboration and networking between traditional healers (often misunderstood and mislabeled as "witch doctors" even if the sobriquet is embraced by healers themselves) and conventional health practitioners, and brought together so-called Western and African perspectives. As an organizational effort, THETA corresponds directly to the publication of Edward Green's groundbreaking study, *AIDS and STDs in Africa: Bridging the Gap Between Traditional Healing and Modern Medicine* (1994), in which he suggests specific ways in which Western medicine can and should benefit from collaboration with African traditional systems of faith and healing. In a recent review of the role of traditional healers and their role in treatment of HIV/AIDS in sub-Saharan Africa, writer Matthew Steinglass suggests that transcultural organizational responses to disease can affect (and in fact have affected in the case of THETA) significant change regarding the integration of traditional healing—representing the historical memory of a community—with scientific applications of medicine and healing:

> The program [THETA] initially trained just seventeen healers, but it did so intensively: fifteen months of training, three days a month. Before the program, according to [Rachel] King, healers were "reluctant to discuss AIDS with their clients, because they feared losing them." After the program, healers promoted and distributed condoms to their clients, counseled them on "positive living," and *staged AIDS-education performances using music and theater*. (2001, 33, emphasis added)

As Steinglass suggests, communication through musical and dramatic performances were central to the efforts of healers associated with THETA from its inception, and it was within the contexts of indigenous forms of music, dance, and drama that AIDS became further localized in the re-memorying process engaged by many Ugandans.

Healers have all too often been conceptualized as a contributing force to Africa's overall AIDS problems rather than as agents for change or as providers of individual solutions and localized interventions for accompanying issues such as opportunistic infections. The role of ethnomusicology—specifically medical ethnomusicology—within a glance on this historical health-care issue is somewhat problematic. From my field research with rural traditional healers in Uganda, one personal response that I have had to come to grips with is my own reaction that is frequently manifested in jumping in to defend and justify the need for such practitioners. Simultaneously, I fully appreciate the fact that healers (including several with whom I have worked) have seldom had access to all the currently available "science" regarding AIDS, and thus have not always been as informed in their diagnoses and treatment recommendations as they otherwise could be. Steinglass suggests that a similar disconnect occurs among contemporary medical anthropologists: "Anthropologists used to consider traditional healers a vanishing breed in need of protection. Today, anyone who talked that way would be laughed out of the lecture hall" (2001, 31).

Healers are typically understood within a bipartite (or sometimes even a more complicated) social stratum—herbalists (traditional healers) versus spirit- or diviner-mediums (witch doctors). At the grassroots, however, the duties and roles of healers and the expectations of healers by their clients often cross boundaries as both frequently prescribe natural medicinals, interpret dreams, counsel, and attempt to address issues of possible spirit possession. Based on personal observation, however, all forms of healers incorporate the process of re-memorying through the reinsertion of culture memory into individualized contexts of diagnosis and treatment, as well as in the performance of healing rituals. The rooted position of patients or clients within local communities is frequently reinforced in reassertions of deep, re-memoried cultural healing.

As Steinglass suggests, the practices of many traditional healers contribute directly to the retention of cultural memory of most Ugandans, and this is critical for understanding ways in which individual health-care choices made in the name of Western medicine are often (mis-)understood as either "alternative," inaccessible, or expensive.

> [W]hile Africans rely on doctors and hospitals to treat many illnesses, most believe that traditional healers are better than doctors at curing sexually transmitted diseases. At least part of the reason is that unlike doctors, healers tend to take a "holistic" approach, treating the patient's spiritual and physical well-being together. With a terminal disease like AIDS, the spiritual side becomes very important. (2001, 32)

Steinglass posits that the holistic approach to individual health care adopted by many African traditional healers not only appeals to many in African contexts, but it also makes emotional and economic sense. Additionally, many traditional healers utilize various forms of music, dance, and drama in their health education outreach. One group that depends heavily on its ancillary performing troupe is TASGA (Tokamalirawo AIDS Support Group Awareness) directed by Mzee Mutebi Musa (see Figure 6.4). A charismatic man, Mzee Musa is passionate about marshaling as many resources as he can for the promotion of the health and well-being

Figure 6.4 Mzee Mutebi Musa, traditional healer, director of TASGA.

of his community on the outskirts of Kampala. As a recognized leader in the traditional healing community, Musa maintains, supports, and trains a music and drama group comprised mostly of AIDS widows and orphans. The members of the TASGA performing troupe frequently offer critical information to audiences concerning various medical issues confronting a given community, often elaborating on the issues already presented by the healer. In the song below—given in English translation—information concerning specific, physical ways of differentiating between TB (tuberculosis) and AIDS are detailed.

TASGA Music and Drama Group

Solo—Hello friends, where have you come from?
Chorus—We have been far away
There were several things we went for
There was a workshop
Forgive us for not telling you what we had gone for
The workshop was on the difference between HIV and TB
Solo—Why didn't you tell me?
Chorus—Did you think that I would stop you?
Forgive us, friend, we ask you
Allow us to tell you part of what we learned
Let's start with the signs and symptoms on both sides as a reminder—
"Looking alike doesn't mean you are relatives." TB?

TB is an English word for bacteria that infects the body through inhalation
That's where the suffering comes in, but the symptoms are almost similar
Let's give them to you and you will see
Another thing, you can be vaccinated against TB, but not against AIDS
Signs, signs, open your ears
Loss of strength, skin rash, loss of weight, chronic fevers, headache
Abdominal discomfort, prominent superficial veins that look ugly
are the signs
Let's also mention the types of TB
There is abdominal TB, pulmonary TB, and TB of the brain [meningitis]
OK, TB even causes psychoses
But the most important thing is that it can be vaccinated against
The advice TASGA gives is that when you start the treatment do not relax
Destroy your friendship with TB
Avoid smoking and alcoholic drinks
"Take your food on time"
That was the theme of the workshop
How can you avoid this pulmonary tuberculosis?
It is possible if your children are immunized
Do not spit saliva everywhere
We recommend early treatment for those infected
Complete the dose
And most important is sensitization and counseling. Because?
It is good
People can learn a lot more in seminars
TASGA, TASGA, TASGA
In full, Tokamalirawo AIDS Support Group Awareness
TASGA, TASGA

In this song, a restructuring of medical memory occurs. The members of the chorus synthesize a group of symptoms for the audience into one medical condition, and then conclude by prescribing a treatment plan for avoiding TB. A re-memorying of the symptoms of this disease occurs within the context of TASGA's performance, as the audience interacts with the performers in a re-ordering of the cause and effect of HIV.

In the following interview with Mzee Mutebi Musa, medical and spiritual care are both integral work in his healing practice. The performance of memory has been significantly altered, he suggests, due to increased interaction with THETA.

> *Musa—My names are Mutebi Musa but I am commonly called "Tokammalirawo" and my group is called TASGA I began this work in 1967 when I was young. My grandy showed me the bush*

and herbal medicine for treating ailments among men, women, and children. That is when I started my work, and I loved it so much. I have developed over time those medicines formerly found in clay. I changed them because some people could not handle the skin medicine. I began putting it in petroleum jelly, then I bottled the liquid type also.

Now I am consulted on any health problem because I am now affiliated with the THETA organization. They taught me about counseling HIV-positive patients and those with other health problems. After introducing myself to fellow villagers they began immediately to consult me. Today I cooperate on cases I cannot handle or on those that I have failed. The THETA organization told me to refer cases I cannot deal with to others. In addition, some medical cases require scientific methods like rehydration by drip. I refer dehydrated patients to Mulago Hospital. Most problems I get after introducing myself as an AIDS counselor concern HIV and AIDS matters. I have an AIDS support group of women who are widows. They frequently rehearse and perform.

Since I work hand-in-hand with THETA, they bring modern medics to train us in counseling and different conditions, because formerly we were treating swollen hand and thinking we were treating a spell. But the medics have taught us the signs of diseases, that someone could have a disease not caused by a spell or spirit. We have learned this in this process. Now like with herpes, we now know that herpes is not a spell.

Music and dance have played a significant role in the fight against AIDS, so much. When we go to teach, music, dance, and others act as a trap for mobilizing people. For example, if they were to begin now even those walking along outside would branch off. When they come, as we had informed them that there would be a seminar, drama that is to say, one can learn in several different ways. Wherever we teach, people have asked us when we are coming back? And we also use music in treating AIDS victims. You see when these AIDS victims are singing, even one who came very weak would be able to respond. You see, for us, our treatment is in two ways. Physical care and spiritual care. When one sings eventually she gets relieved. Sometimes he is forced to dance and forgets about the pain.

Barz—What word in your language would you use to refer to your work?

Musa—Traditional doctor.

Barz—How do you get to know that one has AIDS?

Musa—*It sometimes depends on the kind of disease I have treated. For instance fever. If I treated it and it persisted I would advise the patient to go for a blood test for both malaria and typhoid. Then if after treating them there was no improvement I would suspect that there was a problem. I usually persuade them to go for a blood test, and then after testing positive, I would know what kind of patient I am treating. I then eventually use my traditional medicine.*

Barz—*Do you treat to heal?*

Musa—*AIDS cannot be healed, but I insist on seeing that one live longer, to carry on because some have children. For instance, if one had a son of fifteen years, then he must live for another ten years. By the time he dies the son will have grown because death is a certainty. Even one without AIDS can die. As for me, I do not heal HIV/AIDS, but I do heal the symptoms.*

Barz—*What do you think will be the status of the AIDS/HIV situation in five or ten years to come?*

Musa—*If there is no support for teaching people more about AIDS, many will die of AIDS, as I mentioned earlier. Many have continued to ask questions, and this shows that people will continue to be infected and they will eventually get used to it. Before, one did not feel free to be close to people or to eat with them. My advice is, if people are not taught, AIDS will increase.*

"Traditional doctors" such as Mutebi Musa continue to contribute significantly to the overall health and spiritual well-being of many Ugandan AIDS patients. In addition, they often now contribute directly to the reframing of cultural memories regarding curative and palliative care regarding HIV/AIDS.

In *Body and Soul* (2001), a documentary that focuses on the need for integration of spirituality in the treatment of AIDS in South Africa, one traditional healer, Dr. Conrad Tsiane, relates that AIDS has re-ordered pleasure and fear for many in a similar way to the efforts of groups such as TASGA:

> I had a question the other day from a very young man who told me, "I understand that you are a very powerful traditional healer." I said, "yes." He said, "why not negotiate and talk with ancestors so that they can stop this?" I told that guy very straight that, "you know, I don't think that this is punishment from God, and I don't think that this is a punishment from ancestors." That boy said to me, "It seems to me that everything that is nice and enjoyable is terrible." I said, "why?" He told me that because this AIDS epidemic that is with sex, "everyone's going to die." (2001)

In significant ways musical performances can also facilitate a re-ordering of that which is conceptualized as "old" and "new" with "good" and "bad" along with the associations that pertain to cultural memories. According to Rev. Mankekolo Mahlangu-Ngcobo, a South African pastor now living in the United States, "many people in Africa ... still believe in ancestors. The question is, how can we work together to prevent HIV and AIDS instead of merely condomizing Africa, I believe there are other spiritual, African ways in which we can come together to bring hope, help and healing to Africa" (2001, 47). Mahlangu-Ngcobo suggests an essential "African" way of incorporating the spiritual world as it is understood and embraced by many African communities by invoking the presence of ancestors. Reinserting "AIDS-Talk" within historical trajectories that incorporate a re-memorying of the position of the disease has already proven to be a highly effective approach now increasingly adopted by many community-based organizations (CBOs) and faith-based organizations in Uganda.

Rev. Jackson Muteeba, the director of IDAAC (Integrated Development Activities and AIDS Concern) in Iganga town, told me on one occasion that in addition to being received as entertainment, music also "helps people to *remember* certain things, past or future. Now when it comes to the client, it refreshes him, soothes the mind they say, acting like a catharsis, blowing out their inside feelings and in most cases, people can change how they feel." According to Rev. Jackson, the musical facilitation of a catharsis, which in its Aristotelian sense accomplishes purification of the emotions through drama, allows spiritual practice to occur. It is this cathartic "change" brought about by a musical or dramatic experience that ultimately allows a process of re-memorying, and perhaps a mystical connection to spirits or ancestors to occur. Vincent Wandera, director of GOSSACE in Kampala and Mukono affirms this.

> **Barz**—*So, apart from using music to educate people about AIDS, what other reason can you give for using music personally?*
>
> **Wandera**—*Music, it works as something to convert and fight the stress. Especially for people living with HIV you can get stressed up, but listening to music, it brings back your memories, it restores the spirits in your body.*

Wandera's comments succinctly address the central issue developed in this chapter—the role of performances of cultural re-memorying in the support and expansion of the efforts of localized systems of health and healing regarding HIV/AIDS. The very present role of spirits and ancestors in the lives of many Ugandans, as Wandera himself concludes, transforms musical performances into active events of re-memorying regarding the culture of HIV/AIDS.

MEMORY BOOKS

> NACWOLA's Memory Project responds to needs and problems of parents and children living in AIDS affected families. It aims at empowering HIV infected parents to support their children to survive parental loss with less trauma. Parents are supported through training to disclose their HIV status and ill health to their children, plan for their future by establish-ing child guardianship arrangements, and provide documentation of important family history and precious memories in the format provided by the Memory Book. (*NACWOLA Brochure* 2002)

In this section I extend the chapter's focus on re-memorying as a social process by introducing the cultural phenomenon most often referred to in Uganda as the "Memory Project." Among East African CBOs, NGOs, and a large variety of faith-based groups, active memory work—specifically those efforts conceptualized within the rubric of Memory Projects—pro-vides opportunities for remembering and memorializing by reconstitut-ing memory in song texts, introducing culturally appropriate medical interventions, and ensuring the continuity of community through musical memory. Members of the National Community of Women Living with HIV/AIDS (NACWOLA), for example, frequently provide counseling, emotional support, and practical assistance through a variety of initia-tives. NACWOLA's Memory Project initiative supports and encourages the creation of child-specific Memory Books that include sections on a parent's favorite songs, important rituals, rites of passage, and music associated with the clans and ethnic groups of the mother.[48] In addition, song texts that include lyrics related to HIV/AIDS—plus general hymns and choruses—are woven into individual Memory Books for didactic rea-sons and to reinforce the ability of music to contribute to active memory reinforcement for youth. NACWOLA members often speak publicly and reveal their sero blood status to their families and friends in order to *live positively* rather than merely living as one who is *HIV positive*.

As recently reported in the *New York Times*, memory work, specifi-cally in the form of creating elaborate Memory Books, is of increasing importance, especially for women who will be leaving behind children in situations where guardianship of children is not guaranteed. *Times* reporter Marc Lacey relates the story of one young mother's engagement of memory work to communicate to her son her hopes and desires for his future:

> Rebecca Nakabazzi's son Julius is about to become an AIDS orphan. Right now the shy 11-year-old lives at home with Ms. Nakabazzi, who is frail and feverish but still very much a doting mother. But all too soon—it could be weeks or months or even years—she will die and the number of AIDS orphans in Africa, estimated at 11 million, will increase by one. Ms. Nakabazzi is taking no chances when it comes to Julius's memory of her. During her remaining time with her son, she is preparing a book of memories that she hopes he will treasure throughout his life. "I want you to study and to go to university and to be responsible," Ms. Nakabazzi, a 30-year-old former hairdresser and seamstress now too sick to work, has written in her book, advice she wants him to remember when she is not here to deliver it in person. (2003)

Memory Book activities specific to HIV/AIDS began in 1992 in London when they were first introduced as an active re-memorying process by Barnado's, a children's charity organized to help parents of African origin as well as those with origins in the United Kingdom who were HIV positive. An original purpose of Barnardo's was to bring together parents of diverse cultural backgrounds whose HIV status was a common thread. Support groups within Barnardo's soon discovered that greater than the parents' concern with their own lives was the need to ensure that children were properly informed about the development of their parents' diseases and informed about the early lives of their parents, their family's origins, and the identities and locations of their relatives. Above all, many early participants wanted creative venues within which they could express their own beliefs and values, as well as their aspirations for their children's future.

In Uganda, Memory Books were first introduced as a method by which HIV-positive mothers could document their lives in order to re-memory their history, culture, and family particulars, establishing increased familial communication, as the following from the Save the Children Web site suggests:

> In Uganda, the National Community of Women Living with AIDS (NACWOLA) and Save the Children developed the Memory Project. This project aimed to relieve the mental stress of children and to improve the coping mechanisms of families through increased family communication. At the core of the project is the creation of memory books. Parents create a book for children to retain after their death containing memories of their lives, traditions and family history. The Memory Project has developed a training programme that has reached approximately 20 districts throughout Uganda. The Memory Project involves far more than the creation of a scrapbook for children. It encourages parents to disclose their HIV status and opens up channels of communication between parents and children. (2004)

Adopted by NACWOLA in Uganda in 1996, the Memory Book project quickly became a means by which Ugandan parents living with HIV—most often mothers—could achieve greater openness in their relationships with their children. The books also played a very central role in the documentation of memory.[49]

Each Memory Book in the NACWOLA model is divided into thirty sections. For many women, the book quickly moves beyond "scrapbook" creation. The prescribed Memory Book model begins with sections such as, "Your Birth" and "As a Baby you..." and includes a section on a parent's favorite song(s). In addition, song texts concerning HIV/AIDS are woven into many individual Memory Books for seemingly didactic reasons, that is to educate young children about ways to avoid exposure to the virus, coping with issues related to mother-to-child transmission of the virus, etc., providing a practical approach for children to avoid having happen to them what happened to their parents. Thus, the Memory Books serve as concrete and accessible means of transmission for preserving cultural memory within an active process of re-memorying:

> People find it difficult to tell their children that they're HIV positive. Many don't. TASO are involved in a project to train parents to write a 'memory book' for their children. It's like a scrapbook, full of family photos. The parent writes about where she came from, her lineage and describe herself. She includes her dreams for the child. She might also mention how she got, or suspect she got, infected, to try to deal with the issue of blame. The book's aim is to help the child build an identity. When the parent dies it may be the only evidence of where they came from. It's better for the child if the parent writes it with him because he'll understand more. But it's not easy. Many parents write a memory book and leave it with a friend to give to their children after they die.
>
> The Memory Book Project is run jointly by TASO, Save the Children and another Ugandan NGO called the National Community of Women Living with HIV/AIDS (NACWOLA). Beatrice Were, who runs the latter, has been HIV-positive for eight years. She knows how hard it is to write a memory book. She has two children and is half way through her first one for her older child. It takes time to gather all the information you need from far-flung relatives and it costs money to have family photos printed to make it beautiful. Only a fifth of the 150 women trained to make memory books in NACWOLA's recent pilot project in Kampala had actually completed one a few months later. (Guest 2001, 36–37)

For many women, Memory Books are also a way of giving voice to the profound and often dangerous silence surrounding the disease in many Ugandan families (Pillay 2003, 114). The following points detail the general expectations of typical of Memory Books in Uganda:

- There are specific guidelines for composing an individual Memory Book, but there is flexibility regarding how issues are ordered and prioritized.
- The Memory Book is typically produced in a photocopied, loose-leaf format.
- Individual Memory Books are to be created for each child in a family, thus five children dictate five Memory Books.
- If there are sad or highly emotional issues that are uncomfortable to disclose, a brief letter can be enclosed with the Memory Book which can then be entrusted to a family friend.
- In addition to the Memory Book, it is recommended that a box of collected memorabilia be assembled for a child that would include: video and audio tapes, files that include school reports, first drawings, necklaces and bangles, birth certificates, ceremonial dresses, father's *kanzu*,[50] etc.
- If unready to turn a Memory Book over to a child, someone close to you should be identified to keep the book. This person should be knowledgeable about your life in case the child has questions concerning contents of the book.
- Appropriate time, care, and attention should be given to the production of a Memory Book.
- For those that have the resources, a Memory Book can be put on video tape.
- The Memory Book can be laminated to protect individual pages.

In the fall of 2002, I conducted an ethnographic survey focusing on the role of music in relation to Memory Books. Due in part to the highly emotional nature of the interviews that were conducted, I kept my sample to thirty individuals, including both men and women.[51] Each respondent had already completed one or more Memory Books for their family. While one individual had eight living children (necessitating the production of eight separate Memory Books), the average number among the respondents was 3.2 living children. The participants in this study ranged in age from 26 to 40, although several admitted to not knowing exactly how old they were—33.2 was the median age for respondents.[52]

While interviews focused heavily on the Memory Book Project, the results of the survey nevertheless also provide much detail concerning the different ways music functions in the memories and re-memorying that occurs within individual families and clans. Concerning the individual understandings of Memory Books, the concept was translated during interviews most often as either *Ekitabo Eky'Ekijjukizo* in Luganda or *Kitabo cha Kumbukumbi* in Swahili, both translating as Book of Remembrance. Various ways of understanding these books by the respondents are given below:

- A book written by parents with their children that includes the family history, the parents life history, the child's likes and dislikes, health issues, hopes for the child (for example, to become a doctor or professor), memories of childhood.
- A book by parents for their children about life experiences, background, ancestors, facts about the family and the family's home, family traditions and special events, education of parents.
- This book has the family history and information about the backgrounds of and contact information for relatives.
- This book is written by a parent or guardian, documenting the background of both mother and father, and includes information about the child's trustee if the parent dies.
- A collection of important information for our children under eighteen years.
- A book to enable one to remember events of a particular family.
- A book to tell children about their family's culture, religion, and traditions.
- This book is written by parents, relatives, or friends to preserve vital information about a family's background.
- It is the book that helps your child understand what has happened to the mother and father and to know about the cultural background of the parents.
- A book that documents the family, tribe, country, and clan history.
- A book that enables parents to save the family's history for their children.
- A book written to document background information concerning the clan of a parent and developmental issues related to a child.
- A book written by the one whose responsibility it is to pass along the historical background of the family.
- Children will know facts about their family from their parents not from 3rd parties, relatives, or family friends.
- It will help children relate their past to the present.
- This book helps build a solid social identity for a child who needs to understand their family history and have accurate details of their early childhood.
- This book will teach children what to do and where to go and the right person to approach in case of a problem.

Almost without exception, those interviewed first heard about the Memory Project through some form of outreach effort by NACWOLA, primarily through facilitation by Save the Children UK. Save the Children initially provided seminars in Uganda, hosted by NACWOLA in 1998 and spearheaded by Beatrice Were, NACWOLA's first coordinator. Additional early efforts to infuse active memory work in the re-memorying process with families was introduced by the Centenary Club of the home care program affiliated with Nsambya Hospital in Kampala and by AWOFS (AIDS Widow Orphans Family Support), a group also hosted by Nsambya Hospital.

Typically included in a Memory Book are specific tools for later facilitation of the re-memorying process that will occur after the death of a parent. In the following section, I draw on the blank Memory Book given to me by a member of NACWOLA. This book was first developed and distributed by Barnardo's in 1995. The pages that are to be filled in by a parent—in this case developed especially for a mother—include sections such as the following:

> *"The Story Of Your Family"*—This page is intended to include a description of significant moments in the history of a family, both in the past as well as contemporary events. Items to be included are details of the present home, information (age, names) of siblings and pets, as well as details about other people who may have lived in the family's house or compound.
>
> *"Other Important Facts About The Family"*—This is an area where specific details concerning places and dates of important life events may be included, such as deaths, births, baptisms, marriages, divorces, etc.
>
> *"Your Birth"*—Details concerning the place, date, and time of day of a child's birth are to be included in this section. The weight of the child, who was present, and information concerning how a child was named (and who was responsible for the naming) are also included.
>
> *"As A Baby You…"*—This section encourages a parent to reflect on the early years of a child, including information about early sleeping and eating patters, any significant early illnesses, who the baby first looked like, etc.
>
> *"The First Time You…"*—Documentation can be provided in this section for important milestones in the life of a child, such as when walking first occur, the loss of a first tooth, when talking began, when schooling starting, etc.
>
> *"Growing Up"*—An opportunity to tell stories that move beyond facts and important dates to include general observations of what has happened in the child's life since infancy.

"*School Days*"—Details can be provided in this section that will help the child remember names and addresses of all school experiences. Names of teachers and school friends should be included, as should information about favorite subjects, examination history, and activities or sports in which the child was involved.

"*Your Interests*"—This section can provide details about general interests of the child over time, as well as specific hobbies and activities engaged at different developmental stages, such as sports, clubs, teams, etc.

"*Your Likes And Dislikes*"—Favorite foods, music, clothes, and people can be included in this section.

"*My Favorite Memories Of You...*"—The purpose of this section is not only to document special aspects about the child that appealed to the parent, but also to provide the child with an opportunity to recall and re-memory the past through the favorite memories of the parent.

"*My Hopes For Your Future*"—Any aspirations the parent may have for the child can be enumerated in this section. Advice and counsel can be included as well as reminders on how to live a good and decent life can be included.

"*People Who Are Special To You*"—Names, addresses, and detailed contact information for important people in the child's life (neighbors, family doctors, relatives, and family friends) should be included.

"*Your Health*"—Details about what aspects of vaccinations, illnesses and other health-related issues that can be obtained from a family doctor should be included. Other general information, including details on how to locate the doctor or health-care professional in possession of the child's health records should be given.

"*Information About Your Mother*"—This is a highly individualized section that can include basic background information on the mother of the child. In addition, more detail can be provided concerning how, for example, the mother met the father of the child, etc.

"*About My Childhood And Where I Grew Up*"—Children will especially appreciate knowing about the childhood of the mother, including details about language, food, culture, etc. The inclusion of photographs will help the child appreciate the early development of the mother's childhood.

"*My Education*"—Children will appreciate understanding how they themselves mirror or are different from their parents by reading an outline of what the parent excelled in, were hopeless in, or were interested in at school. Providing complete educational histories of the parents can also be motivational for children to continue their studies.

"*My Working Life*"—This section allows the mother to provide a detailed description of her employment history or the development of her skills in additional to detailing her ambitions and to what extent she was able to act on those ambitions.

"My Health"—Information of any hereditary illnesses can be passed along in this section, as can complete contact information of health-care professionals who know more about the mother's illnesses can be included. Disclosure of the mother's HIV status can also be included in this section.

"What I Do In My Free Time..."—In this section, the mother has the opportunity to document what she engages on a daily or occasional basis to occupy herself in a pleasurable way, including hobbies, so-cializing, reading, etc. Such information can help a child creatively (re-)imagine the everyday life of a mother after her death.

"Special Interest/Talents"—Details of what a mother is known for can be included here, such as music, love of children, linguistic abilities, cooking, etc.

"My Likes and Dislikes"—A summary of things or times of the year that were special to the mother, that might include books, music, holidays, etc. Similarly, situations, people, or things that did not appeal to the mother should be included.

"Thoughts On Life and Things I Believe In"—Religious or faith traditions can be documented in this section, allowing a child the opportunity to experience and understand the beliefs or personal philosophy of the mother.

"Special Memories"—Important events in the life of the mother that might help the child recall at a later time the special occasions of the mother.

"Important Friends"—This section provides contact information for friends who were close to the mother so that in the years to come a child can make contact with friends of the mother for further information or to discuss memories the child might have of the mother.

"Special To Me"—This section provides the opportunity to include the lyrics of the mother's favorite song, poem, recipe, or prayer.

"Information About Your Father"—An opportunity to provide similar details for the father's life as has already been provided above for the mother's life.

"Information About Your Relatives"—Specific details of ages, names, and contact details for siblings as well as family relations should be provided.

"Our Family Home"—This section provides a description of home and neighborhood as well as nearby landmarks that could potentially help the child in the future in case of dislocation.

"Family Traditions and Special Events"—This sections allows the mother to provide information pertaining to specific cultural, ethnic group, familial, or clan activities that will help the child understand the customs, beliefs, and spiritual practices that were important to the mother.

"*The Family Tree*"—Two "trees" are provided to allow the mother to trace the family of origin for the child as well as to extend "branches" to indicate the important nonfamilial relationships she has had in her life.

"*Maps*"—General maps of Uganda and Africa are provided to allow the mother to detail where the family originated and where they are located within a greater African context.

A global initiative, The International Memory Project, was recently introduced to other areas of Africa in large part due to the success of the Memory Project in Uganda. In Uganda, Memory Books have served many functions in the communities of women who have collaborated in the training and execution of these memory devices. One of the principle outcomes has been the use of the tool in the disclosure of a mother's HIV status to her children. One hundred percent of those surveyed for this research responded that details of their HIV status had been included in their Memory Books and that full disclosure for many was made easier through the engagement of such directed memory work. Memory Books have often functioned as a nonthreatening mode for transmitting knowledge of the disease within the context of remembering and re-memorying the life of the mother, breaking the silence typical of parent-child discourse about HIV/AIDS.

Memory Books have guided many parents in creative ways to open up the world of HIV/AIDS to greater family discussions. The inclusion of music in the form of song lyrics, reflections on performances of music, dance, and drama, as well as memories of important rites of passage related to the culture of the mother's clan or ethnic group are some of the more significant aspects of the Memory Books for many of children. The sounds of their mothers are made permanently alive within the pages of these books, as they re-memory the songs and dances their mothers once performed, providing not only information and details of the child's family of origin, but perhaps more importantly a source of identity that emerges only within re-memories.

THE PERFORMANCE OF MEMORY

In this section I focus on the performance of memory, specifically ways of understanding transitions in memory, a process of re-memorying introduced in musical performance to communicate changes in understandings and conceptualizations of HIV/AIDS. Based on my interaction with women and the Memory Book Project, I am convinced that it is worthwhile to reflect on how memorying can be understood as a layering of the memory process. I include and draw on a specific narrative text to support my reflections in this section.

In the Ugandan novel *The Invisible Weevil* (1998), author Mary Karooro Okurut uses frequent flashbacks as a rhetorical device with several of her characters to demonstrate changes that have occurred in memory formation over time regarding HIV/AIDS. The author also assigns her principal characters to different generations in order to unravel ways in which memory varies in different ways from youth to old age. *The Invisible Weevil's* main character, Nkwanzi, is torn throughout the novel as she negotiates between remembering how her family understands the AIDS scourge and with remembering how her own understanding has developed. For Nkwanzi re-memorying is a highly emotional, indigenous response to changes in historical memory. Okurut's novel is one of the most important literary efforts to document familial effects of the AIDS pandemic in Uganda. In the novel's opening sections, Genesis, the husband of the novel's main character, Nkwanzi, is brought back to his family in his home village to die, as was the practice with many early AIDS patients in Uganda. In fact, the return to the village, the font of all memory, still typically occurs for many at the end stage of the disease.

Various ways of remembering the disease are introduced in the opening section of *The Invisible Weevil* until the novel's *mzee*, spiritual elder, introduces a new foreign term, referring to HIV as "ACQUIRED," set aside in capital letters. The *mzee*, keeper of the older village memories and cultural traditions, invokes a re-memory, forcing us to re-read all other memories of the history of the disease thus far presented in the text through a new focus, namely as an acquired immune deficiency. Even the book's title refers to an older, localized memory, a way of understanding HIV as an invisible insect that has imbedded itself in the human body. In a fascinating denouement, the novel concludes with a song text. After a series of horrific events Nkwanzi finds herself listening to the radio one day when she hears the "happy voices of school children" sing the following song:

> For a number [of] decades now
> More dead than alive were we
> Africa's Pearl[53] a laughing stock
> Ugandans in exile ashamed
> To acknowledge their native roots—
> But now in openness we live
> The gun demystified [sic]
> And AIDS no longer a mystery.
> It too shall be conquered. (205)

This performance of the school children's song in the novel confirms not only for Nkwanzi but also for the readers that HIV/AIDS has become internationalized among Ugandans who now realize they are a part of a global curiosity concerning the disease. AIDS in the new "openness"—i.e., "living positively" and being open about one's HIV status—is remembered both as a "gun," one of the oldest ways of understanding the virus, as well as a demystified "AIDS."

GENDER AND RE-MEMORYING

Why focus on the performance of memory as a unique phenomenon within women's cultural production in Uganda? The answer is both disciplinary and political. For several generations, ethnomusicologists have spent much energy documenting the rich musical traditions of Buganda, Busoga, and other kingdoms, chieftainships, and territories of Uganda. That many of the musical traditions have been in large part performed and produced by men should be predictable and comes as no surprise. (I too have fallen into the trap on more than one occasion of hiring local *male* informants and *male* translators to locate and record *male* musical traditions. In retrospect, I should have anticipated this trap on numerous occasions.)

In many regions of East Africa (as elsewhere in the world), specific gender roles are prescribed, inherited, transmitted, or adopted for and by men and women in traditional village music making, specifically within everyday or specialized traditional performance. There may be behaviors and beliefs that might appear at first glance to be very different from one's own in various areas. Women, for example, are typically discouraged from playing, and some cases not allowed to play musical instruments in eastern Uganda. Many men in this area believe that women should never play instruments; men play instruments and women dance. Some men are of the opinion that women should be discouraged from even touching musical instruments, especially drums, or passing near them; they tell women not to sit on drums, let alone play a drum. Many young women still grow up in villages with the understanding that they are not supposed to touch any musical instrument, and specifically discouraged from sitting on drums, for fear of spoiling the drum during the period of a menstrual cycle. If they do touch a drum, it is considered a social taboo. In fact, even today in many villages in eastern Uganda I have been told that if a woman jumps over an instrument she will become barren, never being able to produce children. Instead of telling women directly not to sit on a drum during times of menstruation due to possible harm to drums caused by leakage, men often times merely tell women that they are not allowed near the drums.

In urban centers, many of these beliefs are today openly challenged, especially in schools where boys and girls are instructed simultaneously on many different musical instruments. Yet, many gender-specific cultural beliefs are deeply rooted. As Centurio Balikoowa, a musician raised in village culture in eastern Uganda but now living in the urban capital, notes below:

> **Balikoowa**—*Women and girls avoiding playing drums has nothing to do with reality. But historically women did not have access to many things, and they used to not put on those undergarments, so if it was time for that thing and they sat on a drum, it was believed that it would spoil the what? The drum. But, over time, this translated into a deeply felt belief.*
>
> **Barz**—*How do the parents of the girls in schools in the larger cities feel about them performing?*
>
> **Balikoowa**—*Now, for those parents who still have those funny beliefs from the villages, they are not at all happy with their young girls playing the instruments. But, we are trying to educate them that these things represent no problems. But they somehow still aren't convinced. They ask themselves, how can that girl play that instrument? We are trying to get that funny idea out of those people's minds. The youth understand, but those older people, they still maintain those beliefs. While it is allowed in the schools it is still a problem. It is not gone yet.*

Positioning stigma, myth, and taboo in any discussion of memories and re-memories of AIDS must take into account issues of context-based gender studies in Uganda. Women developing earlier menstrual cycles, distancing from family networks of sex education, and lack of a generation of "aunties" to take young women "into the bush" for sexual training before marriage all lead to the development of new performances of cultural memories associated with HIV/AIDS that are informed by historical, prescribed gender identities.

CONCLUSION

I believe that it is of the utmost importance that everyone involved in the day-to-day experience of AIDS-related work, in whatever capacity, should keep records of every example of injustice, inhumanity, and insult occasioned in the course of the epidemic. It is sad that many of those who have suffered most are no longer around to tell their stories. We owe it to them, and to ourselves, to remember that many others will live through these bad times to see justice done. (Watney, *Policing Desire*, 150)

Written in reaction to public policy (or lack thereof) in Britain, Europe, and North America primarily, Simon Watney's activistic stance regarding historical memory certainly resonates with many of my experiences in Uganda. This call to remember mirrors the efforts of many at the grassroots in Uganda working to see that processes of re-memorying contribute to significant social change.

Perhaps one of the most obvious roles of memory in fighting HIV/AIDS as it relates to musical performance is the ability of music to trigger memory. Many CBOs using music to communicate their messages, rely on the ability of music to "stick" long after they've gone. As one of the members of the group, Bright Women Actresses in Bwaise suggests below, the memory of a song's performance can recall the message of that particular song. And for many women who sing, this is what they hope for.

> **Barz**—*What has been the impact of music on anti-AIDS campaigns?*

> **Member of the Group**—*Music has done so much, you know. People can appear indifferent, yet they will have learnt something. This happens many places we've been to with this women's group. In an audience it is hard for people to go away with no lesson learned, at least one person will learn. Many listen to what we sing and when he gets tempted to love a young girl he remembers the songs...*

Memories and the social processes of engagement that I have labeled as "re-memorying" are both significant products of musical performances that are closely associated with HIV/AIDS outreach efforts in many regions of Uganda today. The case studies that support this chapter provide illustrations of several ways in which re-memorying occurs, drawing on references to both earlier ways of memorying the virus and newer, externally informed ways of understanding the epidemiology of the disease over the past twenty years.

Interlude 6
TASO Drama Group Testimonies

As we have learned over time, perhaps the best way to reach these people is through traditional theatre. On holiday and weekends, when people are free from work or religious activities, huge crowds throng the townships. When a drama group presents a free, open-air performance using the street language and portraying real-life situations to highlight a problem, people can identify with it in terms of their own lives. A clever group of artists can make a strong impact on its audience.

—Mouli and Rao 1992, 236

IN THIS FINAL INTERLUDE I present the testimonies of four members of the TASO (The AIDS Support Organization) Drama Group (see Interlude Figure 6.1). On several occasion I had opportunities to visit, record, and interview members of the Drama Group affiliated with TASO's main branch located at Mulago Hospital in Kampala. During the course of one of my interviews, the individual members introduced themselves to me by way of offering their personal testimonies. Testimonies such as those transcribed below are frequently used by the Drama Group in their sensitization and outreach efforts with youth in schools and in remote villages, allowing individual members the opportunity to "make a strong impact" on their audiences as Mouli and Rao suggest above regarding the use of theatrical performance in AIDS educational outreach in Zambia.

As Rand Stoneburner suggested in a recent National Public Radio interview (2004) with commentator Brenda Wilson, intimate "one-on-one" interactions, where one person feels comfortable telling another about behavioral choices that can be made and adopted to save one's life, have been one of the most effective means of reaching a broad range Uganda's population.

Wilson—Stoneburner says something happened in Uganda in the 1980s that has happened nowhere else in Africa, a system of social networking centered on AIDS. People passed the message from person to person. It led young people in Uganda to abstain from sexual activity and men and women to reduce their number of sexual partners. HIV began to decline even then.

Stoneburner—We feel that there's something about a personal message that may have more value. It's not that the government isn't important in triggering this message, but when they can open up enough space to allow people to express their concerns and advise each other on behaviors, the message has more impact.

While permission was given to record and transcribe the testimonies of the TASO members that follow, I nevertheless have altered the identities of each group member due to the fact that each shares and reveals quite a bit of personal information that could potentially cause shame or embarrassment out of the original context of disclosure.

> **Richard**—*My name is Richard. I am now thirty years old and I discovered I had contracted HIV some twelve years back, and during that time there was a lot of stigma. I did not know much about HIV/AIDS until I went for HIV/AIDS counseling in search of treatment so that I could live for even the following two years, and that was back in 1990. So after the counseling I decided to join TASO so that I continue to get ongoing support in terms of medication, counseling, and social support which involves interacting with friends who are in the same situation. So later I decided to join TASO's Drama Group to deal with my worries, because I was so stressed. Even now, after twelve years, I do feel some stress. But, I now know how to control it and how to deal with it. And another important thing, as to why I joined the Drama Group, is to pass on the messages to other people, because I looked at HIV like pregnancy. A lady, a girl, or woman can be pregnant, but this pregnancy is not something you can hide from anyone. Because each day, day by day, it is growing. So the same thing applies to HIV. Because people were pointing at me 'cause I lost a girlfriend. So they were saying, "Richard is soon gonna go, Richard is soon dying." So, after the counseling I decided that I would go back to my community to inform the public about HIV/AIDS and what I feel so they can learn from me and so they can come and support me instead of talking behind my back. So, I found that I was supported by the Drama Group, because I couldn't do it alone. So, I joined the friends who were drumming, singing, dancing, and doing dramas, sharing various experiences, very personal experiences about HIV/AIDS. So, I felt that I had a right to live because I was not alone. We went around passing along these messages. At first people were not coming out to us because we were HIV positive. Or they would not sit near us, or they we would not shake our hands. I was amazed that people eventually came in such numbers, not only to me, but to the entire Drama Group asking questions about our personal experiences and what living with HIV/AIDS meant to us. They asked questions like, one time somebody asked to me, "What does if feel like having HIV moving in your blood." So they think that HIV is something that you can feel in their bodies. So questions like that we tolerate and we answer them. And, as you know, most of the people here did not go to school. So it is only through music, yes through music, dance, and drama that you can not only attract these audiences, but people also get to learn as they listen to songs, nice songs, which sometimes are soulful, but at times they are encouraging, and they instill hope in the people. So I feel great to be in the Drama Group. Yeah.*

Figure Interlude 6.1 TASO Drama Group members and counselors hold hands as they sing.

Edward—My name is Edward. I was born in 1974. I joined TASO in 1998 after finding myself positive. This came after I was living in a hostel during my studies where I picked it. So this happened, but I could not confirm that I was positive until a friend urged me to go on and take the test to confirm my status. So when I went for the test—which took me two weeks—unfortunately, when I went for the results, it was positive. So I broke down. I thought, what I can do next? I thought maybe that I was going to die the next morning. So, what I decided to do was to join TASO. There was one friend who was working with TASO. I talked to him and he told me that you can come and join TASO, and there was somebody who can come help you. So, I also decided to come, to go and join TASO. When I went there, OK, my health was not quite in a good way 'cause I was so debilitated. So when I went there, they welcomed me and gave me a counselor. So, in that session, the counselor talked about positive living, how you can avoid stress, re-infection, balancing the diet to prolong your lifespan, all of which I adopted. And after that I started getting medication from TASO. I kept coming to TASO to get medical assistance. So, when I used to come there my counselor once told me about the Drama Group. He told me that in this center there was a Drama Group, and if I had the time I could come and join the Drama Group. The motivation of the Drama Group is to go to the public and sensitize youth and other peoples about the pandemic. So if you are willing to do this, if you are willing to join the Drama Group, you can go and join it and speak to the public and tell them about the pandemic.

So I also decided to join the Drama Group and go into the community to sensitize about the pandemic. Apart from sensitizing the public about the HIV pandemic, we also really come together with our friends who are also positive. Sometimes, we share our life experiences, or if we have other problems. So those are some of the benefits of being in the Drama Group. And, when you go to the communities, we try to bust open the opinions. When we go we even test. So we find that people may feel that they are stigmatized. They come down and say, "I want to go for a test, but how? What can happen?" You say, "Oh, it's OK. You go and you take the test, and if you find yourself positive, you can come back to us." So the drama community tries to calm down the stigma, and we bust open opinions. So those are the few things we do in the Drama Group.

Generous—My name is Generous. I am forty-three years. I was born in 1959. I had my blood tested in 1994 and found myself HIV positive. By then I was not in my home district. My district was in war. They used to spread HIV/AIDS. And yet I was a leader. I had leadership. I was the Secretary for Women in my district. So, at the time people used to say that those who were infected shouldn't be seen and that they shouldn't teach our children because they are infected. So, when I tested the blood I chose not to join TASO. I thought maybe those at home would find out that I am infected. I could not stand the thought of even talking to them if they know that I was infected. So I kept it to myself there until 1998 when I became very weak and had the symptoms and signs of HIV/AIDS. So, I decided to join TASO. When I came to TASO I used to stay at home because of the separation with my family. I used to feel loneliness, crying all the time. I had children, five of them, and the father died. So, I did not know who would look after those children. So, I stayed at home all the time to think until I was advised by my counselor to join the Drama Group so that I wouldn't be staying at home all the time thinking of them, crying all the time, failing to do anything for myself. When I joined the Drama Group I found my girlfriends, they were enjoying their lives. When they sang I listened. The messages were coming. I was not the only one who was infected. So I enjoyed staying with them. And when I used to come, I used to forget. I used to leave all the problems at home and come to Drama Group. Another thing, with the Drama Group we visit the district where I come from where they don't know much about AIDS, but there are very many who are infected, and they don't want to come out. So, I knew that when I joined the Drama Group we would get the chance to go to my district and everyone would enjoy hearing the music. People from my place especially enjoy music, dance, and drama. I think they enjoy music more than speeches. When we tell them that it is time for the leader to speak, you see people leave to look for something to eat, and what what. But when the drums begin, they come back. That's where our messages are passed along. And, what leads me to come back is that here I am with my friends. I feel free and I don't think. I forget about HIV/AIDS.

Grace—*I'm called Grace. I am also a member and client of TASO. Let's talk about myself. I went to school, one of the premier boarding schools in Uganda. And I liked music very much. This school was one of the best schools training students in music, dance, and drama. And I also started getting myself in such activities so that I could sing and do something at least for myself. I had friends and they had boyfriends. After contracting the virus I tested myself in 1990. I joined TASO. But when I joined TASO, there were so many other activities that were going on in TASO. There is counseling, there's medical, there was the Drama Group. So many activities were going on in TASO. What I did, after being counseled I was referred to one of the centers, and this was the TASO Drama Group center. And they told me what was going on in TASO Drama Group. What I very much wanted to know was what I could do in the TASO Drama Group. They told me that these are the people who can help you get yourself into activities so that you can cope with the virus. The members encouraged me and I started asking myself, what can I do? Because I had pain. Because of the suffering and stigma around my home. What I did was I tried to plan what I should do. When I saw this Drama Group and the many activities going on, I tried also to apply what I learned from my school and joined the music group. That's why I joined, so that I can express myself through the music, express my pain and whatever, transforming these messages to the people, in the communities especially about positive living. Because the counseling could give positive living, but through music, dance, and drama, you can give more positive living to the people, so that they can cope, so that they can get rid of the HIV virus. And another thing, because I was a student, I very much wanted to go to the schools to tell my fellow students that this is our problem. I find so many encouraging friends and they encourage me, I encourage them, because we share different views, our pain, we share so many secrets in our lives. So, I very much have learned so many things concerning what TASO has to offer, through music, dance, and drama. But it was all that because of the counseling and the training that we got from our counselors and because of TASO being there.*

CONCLUSION

"Getting the Message Across Without Music Is Sometimes Shaky"

> When a lion comes to the village you don't make a small alarm.
> You make a very loud one. When I knew of this problem of AIDS,
> I said we must shout and shout and shout and shout.
>
> —President Yoweri Museveni
> *AIM Scope: One Year On* 2002

ARVIND SINGHAL HAS STATED on many occasions that African communities must continue to "shout," as President Museveni suggests in the above statement, in order to address a very real and profound loss of health stability in many contemporary African contexts. The metaphor of "the shout" is one that illuminates the potentiality for social change for Singhal. As he has posited, "Breaking the silence on AIDS by 'shouting' loudly allows a nation, a community, or a family to step up from words to deeds. Uganda, for instance, has mobilized its civil society—schools, churches, mosques, mass media—to spread the word on AIDS" (2003, 233).

Throughout this text I have highlighted the role of music in efforts to shout in Uganda. Rev. Jackson Muteeba, director of IDAAC in Iganga suggests that music has the power to penetrate "deep into you" and that musical mobilization at the level of grassroots outreach efforts produces "real feelings" and musical performances communicate essential "life messages." Rev. Jackson, whose efforts are essential in the rural village networks in the eastern Busoga area surrounding Iganga town, emphatically

215

reiterates that "getting the message across without music is sometimes shaky," an aphorism I reiterate as a heading for this concluding section.

> **Rev. Jackson**—*You find that sometimes when they are singing, some people may not be so much willing to listen, but the music comes as an entertainment. But then it goes deep into you, especially when you know people who are suffering from it. I'm avoiding using the word "victim." The real person who is affected who is living with AIDS is seeing something. It comes out as a real feeling that he is having. So the whole message is that someone receives this as a life message because music remains in one's brain, and it is a very strong tool for communication because it remains in the brain and someone will continue to meditate.*

> **Barz**—*How do you think that we should apply music to the messages that we are putting across? Why not just talk to the people or hold seminars? Why should we supplement this with music?*

> **Rev. Jackson**—*Because music per se, is a kind of entertainment, and for people that don't have time to sit down and listen they can make time for music. They can record and go with it and whenever they have time refresh themselves again. Because when you talk, somebody must be interested enough or must have a pen to write down information. And in some communities they are not literate enough to that level. So, getting the message across without music is sometimes shaky.*

Music, according to Rev. Jackson, can be cleverly disguised as entertainment, and this is critical in the attraction of the largest possible audiences for the health-care outreach provided by groups such as IDAAC throughout the country.

BEYOND UGANDA

In the conclusion of this book, I hope I will be forgiven for venturing just a bit beyond the borders of Uganda, if only to demonstrate the effectiveness (of consequent lack of affect) of music within HIV/AIDS intervention programs elsewhere in sub-Saharan Africa. Rather than survey individual African countries for their culture-specific responses—clearly beyond the scope of this study—I first share below excerpts of a recent discussion with Abimbola Cole, a doctoral candidate in ethnomusicology at UCLA, in which the uniqueness of the cultural responses of another African country hard hit by HIV—Botswana—is detailed.

Barz—Have there been responses by religious institutions? Para-statal, non-governmental responses? In some sub-Saharan African countries the governmental response has not always been the strongest or the most noteworthy. Often other cultural institutions wield more effective power. What is the situation in Botswana, how does it compare to other African nations?

Cole—In 2001, the Government of Botswana collaborated with the Bill and Melinda Gates Foundation and The Merck Company to establish the African Comprehensive HIV/AIDS Partnerships (ACHAP). Since its inception, ACHAP has become a major force in tackling Botswana's HIV/AIDS pandemic. There are a number of ACHAP affiliates throughout the country such as MASA—the organization responsible for administering Botswana's free antiretroviral drugs—and the National AIDS Coordinating Agency—the organization that prepared Botswana's national framework on HIV/AIDS. There are also NGO-based organizations that ACHAP now supports such as CEYOHO—a youth center—and the House of Hope—a center for orphans. ACHAP seems to have the most far-reaching and powerful response to HIV/AIDS in Botswana. In addition to playing a major role in the distribution of ARVs, ACHAP works with PSI and Lover's Plus, one of the largest local condom companies, to ensure that condoms are readily available across Botswana. So far my research has focused on ACHAP and its subsidiaries.

Barz—How about the arts sector? I'm curious to know whether such a sector exists as a separate entity, that is, do other public outreach entities include or separate out the arts? What I'm getting concerns my observations that the arts are typically included in the outreach efforts of many African AIDS outreach programs, not labeled as "arts," but rather understood as public health initiatives.

Cole—When I first arrived in Botswana, I had the chance to speak with a staff member at the National AIDS Coordinating Agency. I explained to him that during my time in Botswana I wanted to do research on HIV/AIDS and the musical arts. He explained the concept of Botswana's multi-level, multi-sectoral response to AIDS. Then he identified several different sorts of sectors and the arts sector was among them. There are definitely programs outside of the arts sector that use arts in their outreach programs. For instance, companies such as Air Botswana, Cresta Hospitality, the Independent Electoral Commission, and Budget Rent-a-Car sponsor concerts that educate the public about HIV/AIDS.

Barz—Is the phenomenon you discuss a national response, or are there local, ethnic, parastatal, external responses also worth noting? I am curious about the notion of a unilateral, national response that collectively communicates a response in totality.

Cole—The national response to HIV/AIDS has been shaped by a number of external forces. Several million dollars have been invested into Botswana's HIV/AIDS programs by organizations in Europe and North America to assist within the country. Money has come from the Centers for Disease Control and Prevention, the European Commission, the Swedish International Development Agency, the United Nations, World University Service of Canada, and World Health Organization. The money has been channeled into various HIV/AIDS programs.

Kathleen Noss, another doctoral student in ethnomusicology at UCLA, engages in similar work in Kenya regarding HIV/AIDS and music. Her approach is similar to that of Cole. In a recent conversation, Noss confirms the need to approach an understanding of institutional power within educational outreach efforts focusing on HIV/AIDS in Kenya.

Noss—My work in Nairobi focuses on the use of music in community education campaigns to address HIV/AIDS and children's rights, both "hot" topics in Kenya now. A few years ago, a Ugandan artist with whom I had been working in Nairobi—Edward Kabuye of the Talking Drums of Africa—told me about his group's participation in a USAID-sponsored national AIDS awareness festival. Through contact with him and my own research on Kenya and other areas of Africa I became aware of the great number of collaborations between artists and organizations for educational purposes—collaborations in various forms: sponsorship, partnerships, etc. My study in Nairobi examines how and why organizations are drawing upon artists and the arts for their work, as well as how artists are also using music on their own for educational purposes. Of course, a number of other issues also come up in such a study—views on the music scene in Nairobi today, donor dependency, politics, etc.

The continuing field research efforts of Cole and Noss in Botswana and Kenya will further document local responses to HIV/AIDS within musical contexts in other parts of Africa. Approaching an interpretation of the "shouting" that occurs in other cultural contexts is a much needed exercise not only among the scholarly community, but perhaps more importantly to inform funding agencies and the outreach efforts and projects they help subsidize.

BACK TO UGANDA

Before bringing this text to a close, I insert one more voice, that of one of the most historically popular musicians in Uganda, singer Paulo Kafeero. Kafeero sings openly about his personal fears and reactions to the AIDS pandemic, frequently weaving reflections on the impact of AIDS on the musical community in Uganda into his song texts. Embedded within the threads of these weaves, however, are often conflicts regarding gender stereotypes and the ways in which the virus is passed along. Kafeero typically maps issues related to HIV/AIDS directly onto religious and spiritual morality, as demonstrated in the extended text of his song, "*Turabye nobulamu buno ovwakokony*" ("It is sad that life is too short"), quoted below. Rather than ignore such socially problematic texts, I include Kafeero's lyrics in their entirety below as an illustration of the problematics inherent in the broad popular appeal of artists such as Kafeero among audiences today in Uganda.

"Turabye nobulamu buno ovwakokonyo"
("It is sad that life is too short")
Paulo Kafeero

It is sad that life is too short, yet we work so hard to see that we go on with life
Yet no one knows where life comes from and no one knows where
life goes after death
I got so scared yesterday in the middle of the night when I thought about
the time of death
AIDS kills us for nothing wrong that we did, I have discovered that
we die for nothing
It is too bad that life is too sweet and nice and we lose it so easily without
anyone's knowledge
All these earthly things that make us do all sorts of things
They are just fog or water vapors in the atmosphere
Paulo, whenever I think about those things, all the money I save, I feel I
should use it all just by taking beer
There is nothing that we are buried with, can you imagine
We all know death is natural and God given but we cannot get used to it
When a person disappears it is quite a short distance, but when you look into
a grave it is quite far away
It is too sad the way we die nowadays because homes are destroyed
And the children are left behind with nothing at all, and they always cry to get
something to eat
AIDS has killed very many young men who look nice in suits without having
any money
I will be buried in the bushes and will be thrown to the maggots to enjoy my
flesh for free

Where all my friends have gone I will go there too because of this AIDS
I think about the graveyard where I will be thrown to the maggots and
I will smell like shit
Where my mother went is where I will go just because of this bad AIDS,
it is too sad
AIDS is hunting us like the god of hunters does to animals
AIDS raises the original level of our shoulders in an abnormal way
AIDS disturbs all creatures and it has killed many
AIDS kills even those who have lost all their weight and have only bones left
Even the small ones, AIDS kills them
Women who are still in the labor ward die and leave their babies behind
because of AIDS
Even the very old who walk around with walking sticks, AIDS kills them with
their bald heads
If AIDS can kill people with bodyguards then it is very powerful
All property you have worked for a long period of time can be taken by people
not related to you
They cannot tell where it came from, oh this AIDS, AIDS you make us walk in
isolation
You make us lose a lot of saliva from our mouths like monsters
Where you are sending us you, AIDS, the place is so terrifying and
not good at all
You cannot change the time of death even though you change your blood
Others are taken to London to the expert doctors, but nothing can be done
God, you brought us a lot of pain, you make us quit the world to
go to the grave
AIDS makes you suffer a lot
AIDS likes those who decorate their good houses
It kills them before they can enjoy life in their houses
AIDS can find you at your wedding as your bridegroom dies,
can you imagine?
All those things that make us hate each other, we should leave them
To leave this world it takes just a blink of the eye and you are already gone
AIDS stored many rich people in their graves and they have never come back
Normal people will all die and you cannot tell how you will be when
you get AIDS
On my burial day come with the guitar, bury me and I will go forever
and ever
Wherever there is a nice woman there is AIDS and all men feel very small
because AIDS is there
If AIDS can kill a cat that can see in the dark of night it is very tough
AIDS with all your authority help us and let us raise our children
You kill us and we leave them when they are helpless
Where you take us is bad and too sad

You look at people who were once nice and you cannot believe it
Ash comes off their bodies like burning wood
All those who were healthy are now too thin and skinny, oh this AIDS
AIDS can easily read your will, and instead of the parent dying first,
the heir dies too
Your child who was giving you all that you need is killed
We should know on which day any of us will die, but instead we find people
dead along the road
Even those who fly airplanes, AIDS kills them from way up there and they
cannot avoid it
I wish AIDS was the only hunter, and that it was not assisted by wrong and
mentally confused people
AIDS puts prostitutes out there to win our hearts and lure us into sex,
oh this is bad
I really cannot understand women nowadays who love us for our money only,
that is the problem
One can easily find oneself with a woman who is totally sick and as you die
she takes your property
We always get scared whenever one of us dies, the hour of death comes with a
lot of words
Some say that so-and-so is the one who killed him or her, anyway that is the
world we are living in
That is why I always look drunk, because when death comes everyone be-
comes so stupid
You disorganize people who have been friends just because you are mad
Maybe AIDS kills owls because they make noise all night trying to let us know
that one of us will die soon
Some insects also announce the death of a person, people cry so much when
taking their loved ones for burial
God bless his soul and he will never ever come back, so forget about him
I fear AIDS because it can turn around and kill my own friends
Even cleaners are killed by AIDS, nothing is disgusting to AIDS
In the grave there is no stage, so where will you, AIDS, put us since
you cannot build
Now what can we say when you even kill the builders
AIDS killed Simbwa, my good plumber who stayed at my small home
A man who was very calm and very gentle and a joker too
AIDS has a very big band where he stays down there in the grave
He killed very many musicians in a very bad way
Jim Reeves died and he was not buried
AIDS is a very strong disease and very tough
If Hitila [Hitler] died who was a strong soldier what about you, why did you
kill Sseseko [Mobuto]
And you took him when he was standing, you kill presidents just like goats

> People say very mean words such as it is good that he died because
> he had too much pain
> As if any of us has ever died and knows what happens in the grave

The efforts to educate and publicly shout out the issues should not be mocked or criticized. Rather, analyses of such song lyrics can help us understand how misunderstandings and fear regarding AIDS can be easily regenerated and planted in the large communities of listeners attracted to individual popular musicians, an area of study ripe for further research and analysis.

TOWARD A MEDICAL ETHNOMUSICOLOGY OF AIDS IN AFRICA

Throughout this text I have relied on ethnographic case studies grounded in the experiences of my field research to introduce and develop principle themes that contribute to the development of a medical ethnomusicology of AIDS in Africa. These themes, often relegated to the restrictive confines of individual chapters, were in fact often unleashed as they pervaded much of my research experience on this topic. The first and perhaps central theme introduced in this text has been omnipresent in much of my thought on this topic from the start. This theme underscores the need to move beyond the medical model when approaching the cultural contexts of HIV/AIDS in Uganda. The fact that HIV/AIDS is more than a medical crisis in Uganda and elsewhere in sub-Saharan Africa, reinforces the need to approach the disease as a culturally defined and determined social phenomenon. Numerous efforts in the past to study the AIDS pandemic in Africa have concentrated primarily on medical issues, ignoring, as I suggest in chapter 1, the multiple layers of meanings that frequently accompany the indigenization of AIDS in local African contexts. That AIDS may assume the position as the third or fourth most important presenting issue for an individual Ugandan is understandable when poverty, development, education, and other health-care issues are taken into account. By positioning musical interventions within the domain of general care and treatment, we approach a broader understanding of and appreciation for localized responses to HIV/AIDS in Uganda.

A second theme, introduced in chapter 2, positioned music's relationship to the study of AIDS in Africa within the Ugandan concept of "positive living." Early efforts of medical ethnomusicology were suggested to contribute to a greater appreciation of such relationships by unraveling localized experiences of health and healing underscored by music, dance, and drama within local performances related to HIV/AIDS. Contributions of medical ethnomusicology focus on deep culturally performative factors in regard to the history and causes of HIV/AIDS in Uganda. The case studies presented in the second chapter support an analysis of musical strategies and responses that local Ugandan villages and communities have developed over time to respond to cultural conceptualizations of HIV/AIDS. The use of music as medical intervention among women's groups was a third theme that was introduced in the text. In chapter 3 a variety of song texts and case studies were introduced to document the everyday confrontation with AIDS experienced by many women. That musical efforts of women's groups have contributed to the decline in HIV infection rates in many areas, both rural and urban, can no longer be denied; the songs women sing offer persuasive power and support for encouraging ongoing community medical interventions throughout the country.

A fourth theme that was developed in detail drew on the indigenization of local terminologies related to HIV and AIDS within contemporary musical performances by individuals and groups. Historically rooted within song and other performance texts, specific terms have emerged and are maintained in contemporary local performances. In chapter 4's exercise of "Naming of Parts," localized conceptualizations surrounding HIV/AIDS and condoms in Uganda were documented and analyzed in an attempt to demonstrate how local performance traditions respond to medical interventions that are both local and foreign.

In chapter 5, the roles of religious and faith-based initiatives in regards to care, treatment, and counseling in Uganda regarding HIV/AIDS were introduced. Problematic histories of religious interaction with the disease were suggested in order to demonstrate the dramatic responses of individuals who take matters into their own hands, often moving beyond denial and fear to perform their spiritual acceptance in a voice "that AIDS can hear." Today many faith-based initiatives actively facilitate connections with spiritual matters regarding HIV/AIDS, providing long-needed opportunities to connect mind, body, and spirit. This theme was supported with the sentiments of traditional healers and Christian and Muslim community leaders who have introduced musical interventions of faith, hope, and healing regarding HIV/AIDS. The sixth and final theme introduced in this text concerned a cultural practice I referred to as "re-memorying," a process that details the engagement of active memory work within many contemporary musical performances. Re-memorying as a social process was supported with the analysis of song texts and with a focus on the Memory Project's production of musical memories within the construction of Memory Books.

CONCLUSION

Drama and music groups led by women and youths affect significant change in Uganda today, and at no place greater than the grassroots. The government is often not able to act, but women's groups especially working without funding have been most successful. It is repeatedly surprising for the urban-trained medical doctors with whom I work that efforts to fight the virus and disease in rural villages are primarily in the form of musical responses and dramatic initiatives. On multiple occasions, when these same doctors asked women *living positively with HIV* why they persisted in their efforts to contribute to local medical interventions, why they continued to dance when they had such little energy, the answers they were given remain profound; Ugandan women do not want other women and youths to experience what has in many cases been *forced* on them, and they will use whatever power they can access to introduce social and political interventions, no matter how small the reward.

Aida, Noelina, Vilimina, Florence, and countless other women in Uganda dramatize the need for better-informed communities, dance for continued health education of youths, drum to attract the attention and participation of men, and sing the songs that turn people's heads and cleverly trick them into listening. In their carefully constructed and medically informed musical performances, women today are not only *singing for life,* they are also *saving lives.*

AFTERWORD

IN MY QUIET, TEMPERATURE-CONTROLLED and hermetically sealed office in Nashville, Tennessee, I often close my eyes and recall specific songs and stories, testimonies and dramas recorded and transcribed over the years performed by friends and colleagues in Uganda. Last year a first-year medical student and I met in my office to discuss the unique responses of religious NGOs in individual African countries to HIV/AIDS. In mid-conversation she stopped me and blurted out, "Don't you ever cry?" My reaction was quick and in retrospect inappropriate. I rather nonpassionately told her that in my research and "scientific" work with HIV-positive colleagues *my* responses and reactions have never really been all that important or interesting and that I have never wanted the focus to be on me or *my* work. I suppose I was suggesting that her question did not really matter. Wrong answer. I cry. Fast forward. Different time. Different student. Same office with a doctoral candidate. During a conversation about a particular song's lyrics concerning the lack of access to ARVs in many parts of Uganda, I became overcome emotionally. I chose not to apologize to the student. When I was asked if I would be all right, I took my time before responding that I would not, nor would I ever be "all right." The student paused before saying, "Good answer."

In my office I surround myself with photographs and with the recorded sounds of many individuals and groups performing—singing, dancing, telling stories—to remind me daily of why I do what I do and for whom I am doing it. A photograph taken by the student whose photographs grace the pages of this ethnography—Jonathan Rodgers—in Bute Village

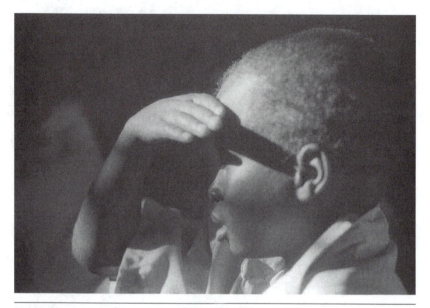

Figure Afterword 1.1 Young boy in Bute Village.

continues to inspire me. My frequent gaze in its direction takes me constantly deeper into my memories as it continues to kindle new thoughts concerning interactions between HIV/AIDS and music in Uganda. The image is simple and there is no obvious "music" or message present in the photograph—no one is singing, no one is dancing, no one is performing. Rather, for me this black-and-white photograph communicates the hope among those who listen, the potentiality that is inherent within any musical performance in Uganda.

The young boy in the image has just returned from a long day attending primary school and through the blaze of the setting sun he watches a performance of women in his home village offering an HIV/AIDS informational session within the context of a drama. The intense attention he pays to the performance led by song leader Aida Namulinda is telling. I have followed this boy's gaze throughout *Singing for Life* as I have watched, absorbed, responded to, and interpreted the use of music, dance, and drama as medical interventions in Bute Village and throughout Uganda.

Over the years I have taken many photographs, made countless sound recordings, and conducted scores of surveys and interviews in Uganda. In retrospect, when all these materials are lumped together in ever increasing piles around my office they seem to be nothing more than mere documentation. More substantial for me has been the accumulation of experiences, memories, and ongoing relationships that support the paths of my personal experiences with HIV/AIDS in Africa since the 1990s. Along these pathways I have been privileged to walk with strong and motivated men and women, many of whom have passed away since we first began accompanying each other. Together we have experienced suffering, death, and loss in everyday situations of homelessness, rejection, and poverty that still easily shock and appall. I have never grown accustomed to everyday pain and hopelessness, particularly in grassroots areas where disadvantaged women have little input concerning decisions they must make in their daily lives. I have encountered women in confusing, seemingly abusive relationships in which everyday despair and poverty frequently necessitate engagement in unwanted sexual relationships. I have watched women enter into such cultural abuse out of necessity in order to help clothe children, pay school fees, or provide their children with the food to survive until the following morning.

That many voices in Uganda continue to *sing for life* no longer shocks me as it once did—it inspires me now more than ever. The sounds of children *singing*, the experiences of women *dancing their disease,* and the knowledge that more and more men and women are learning to *live positively* with HIV/AIDS continue to move me as I continue along my own life's journey. And at times I cannot help but imagine and hope that someday the destination each of us reaches in our personal response to HIV/AIDS in Africa will remind us all of a horrific disease that we once lived with, a destination decorated with collages of photographs of beautiful, smiling people we once knew, a destination made holy with the sounds of the recorded voices that sing of a long-forgotten pandemic.

I close this book with the voice of the Secretary General of the United Nations, Kofi Annan who challenges me, as he challenges many others, to continue in our pursuits for care, education, and counseling regarding people already infected with HIV and those yet to be infected:

> All of us must recognize AIDS as our problem. All of us must make it our priority. We cannot deal with AIDS by making moral judgments, or refusing to face unpleasant facts—and still less by stigmatizing those who are infected, and making out that it is all their fault. We can only do it by speaking clearly and plainly, about the ways that people become infected, and about what they can do to avoid infection. (*Keeping the Promise: Summary of the Declaration of Commitment on HIV/AIDS,* United Nations General Assembly, Special Session on HIV/AIDS 2001)

APPENDIX

This text has been formed and informed by the time, direction, and sentiment of many people working at the grassroots in HIV/AIDS care, counseling, and prevention in Uganda. There is little I can do to repay the debt of gratitude for the time and attention I have received from countless individuals I have encountered over the years. I can however, assign credit where it is due by officially acknowledging the assistance and guidance given to me by those individuals and groups. Those listed below have given permission to have their identities acknowledged as contributors to my research.

INTERVIEWS
Women's Groups
Virimiina Nakiranda, (Kibaale)
Bakusekka Majja (Igunda)
Bwoyidha Oyega Club (Bute)
Buwolomera Dev. Ass. (BUDEA)
Baligeya Club (Kityerera Village)
Tulamuke (Bugwe/Busiki)
NACWOLA (Iganga)
Bukona Village Community Members
Kanihiro Group (Kitabi/Bushenyi)
Bright Women Actresses (Bwaise)
NACWOLA Drama Group
Makula Women's Group

Kotida Nabukela (Namsama, Munsumbi, Wakiso District)
Rashida Sendagi (Entebbe, Mpala Village, Wakiso District)
Nagawa Jane Florence (Kanyanga, Kampala, Kikaya Zone A)
Betty Namyanzi (Makerere West, Kampala Zone C)
Justine Nakiggwe (Kyebando, Kampala Distrct, Elisa Zone)
Nanyanzi Prossy Luziga (Namugongo, Kampala District, Lubya II Zone)
Nakamya Lillian (Mengo, Kampala District, Kisingiri Zone)
Joyce Mubiru (Bunanwaya, Wakiso District, Ngobe Central Zone)
Were Martha (Makindye II, Kampala, Katwe II Parish, Kiganda Zone)
Sarah Nakkazi (Nkanibya, Kampala District, Gogonya Zone)
Sarah Bakamansa (Sana-Namasuba, Wakiso District)
Nabuma Robinah (Busega, Kampala District, Kibumbiro B Zone)
Nambi Efrance (Makerere, Kampala Banda Zone)
Margret Sewankambo (Nsambya West Zone, Kampala District)
Kyomugiswa Sylvia (Kazo Central Zone, Wakiso District, Kawempe)
Nalongo Kityo Rose (Seeta Gongobe Zone)
Namubiru Grace (Lubya Kyadondo, Kampala)
Betty Naluwoza (Kagoma, Wakiso District, Kawempe)
Fatuma Namanda (Muyenga Kanyoza Zone, Kampala District)
Nakabuye Jane Frances (Maganjo Kagoma, Wakiso District)
Ntege Margeret (Naluvule Zone 1, Nansana, Wakiso District)
Bakanansa Jasinta Breanda (Kagoma Maganjo "B." Wakiso District)
Namutebi Hadija (Bulenga Kikayaz Zone, Wakiso District)
Kalungi Faith Atwoki (Mulago Nalwewuba Zone)
Kayondo Faridah (Kampala)
Nandita Daisy (Kawempe Division, Kampala District)
Namukwaya Harriet (Mulago, Katale Zone, Kampala)
Josephine Nachiana
Proscovia Jokod
Betty Naluwoza
Margret Sewankambo
Sarah Nakazzi
Namutebi Hadijja
Florence Bagunywa Nkalubo
Margret Babuulyakuseka
Vilimina Nakiranda
Nawaikoke Village Women

Popular Musicians

Joanita Kawalya (Afrigo Band)

Youth Groups

Good Shepherd School (Golomolo)
Lubiri Triangle Youth Group

Kabowa Youths
Giant's Group (Kampala)
Jumbo Theatre Group (Kampala)
Ambassadors of Hope (Bunamwaya)
Negro Angels Balamayika
Kashenyi Model Primary School (Ishaka)
BAPET (Kampala)
Kitogo George Ndugwa
Steven Busuulwa (Makerere College School)
Makerere College School (Group of Students)
Nsimbe Daniel (Lubiri, Youth Alive)
Onama Caesar (Makerere College School)
Apollo Mbowa (Makerere College School)
Ssebunja Senyojnjo Mubende (Makerere College School)
Lukwiya Bernard (Makerere College School)
Ouma Myko (Makerere College School)
Tumwesigye Zeddy (Kansanga Primary School)
Centurio Balikoowa (Police Children School)
Lukwago Abdu (KAYDA, Katwe Youth Development Association)
Faisal Nsubuga (KAYDA)

Religious Groups

Bukato Christian Fellowship
Fr. Joe Lumanyika Nsubuga (Nsambya Sharing Hall)
Betty Muhangi
Ethery Mubiru
Luzife Prossy
Lillian Nanyonga
Charles Luka Makanga
Mutebi George William
Nakazibwe Florence
Kibalizi Edward
Mubiru Twaha Ngogelatefanana
Namanda Fatuma
Tebandeke Samuel
Kitende Mary
Kabera Ntale Godfrey
Nafule Winne
Alinaffe Christopher
Betty Naigaga
Lubwama Irene
Kateregga John
Joyce Namagembe
Musimami Idi Mobarak
Lukyamuzi Francis
Birabwa Beatrice Annie

Augustine Sebuuma
Monica Uzamukunda
Ssangu Irene
Kaweesa Jane Florence
Kajubi Lasto
Kiwanuka David
Leoben Mubiru

NGOs

Namirembe Post-Test Club
PADA CMS Trading Center, Bukoyo
Good Shepherd Support Center
TASO Mulago
TASO Drama Group
Meeting Point (Namuwongo)
MUDINET (Mukono)
VOLSET (Nakaseke/Luwero)
Rev. Jackson Muteeba
Walya Sulaiman
Godfrey Mukasa
Vincent Wandera
Sebastain Sentamu
Noelina Namukisa Anguzu
Festus Baziri
Anne Kaddumukasa, TASO
Tony Kasule, TASO

Witch Doctors/Traditional Healers/Medical Doctors/Herbalists

TASGA (Kampala)
Dr. Alex Muganzi
Ruth Namusaabi
Apofia Naikoba
Maboni Nabanji
Mutebi Musa
Haji Luttakome Ssentamu
Nanteza Sandra
Majjemba Zaitun

Non-Affiliated Individuals

Mata Nasani Byansi (Iganga)
Charles Kasumba (Kanyanga, Kampala District)
Kibwiika Edward (Kawempe, Kitagoba Zone, Kampala)
Ndyemala Fred (Mulago, Katale Zone, Kampala)
Joseph Mugasa (Makerere College School)

NOTES

1. Similarly, music, dance, and drama figure prominently in post test clubs (PTC), especially those associated with the Philly Lutaaya Initiative (PLI): "Youths meetings (PTC/PLI Youth) take place on Saturday at 2:00 p.m. and these have many activities...Quiz, music and drama competitions with neighboring youth's clubs also keep the youth busy and thinking actively" (Katusiime 2002, 10–11).
2. Music is given priority of place in the published descriptions of the outreach efforts of many major NGOs in Uganda. MUDINET (Mukono District Network of People Living with HIV/AIDS), for example, one of the primary NGOs offering services in Mukono district highlights this position: "MUDINET involves itself directly in the fight of HIV/AIDS by offering services such as home visiting, offering both pre and post test counseling, educating the community on HIV/AIDS through music dance and drama, organizing HIV/AIDS seminars, giving public testimonies." (*UNASO NEWS* [Newsletter of Uganda Network of AIDS Service Organisations] 2002, 8).
3. For more detailed accounts of this earlier work *see* Barz 1997a, 1997b, 1997c, 2000a, 2000b, 2002, 2003a, 2203b, 2004, 2005a, and 2005b.
4. For a similar response, see the online *Economist* article, "AIDS and Artists Holding Up a Mirror: Writers, Painters and Film-makers Struggle to Respond" (2004).
5. "Epidemiology" used this way refers to the way in which a distribution and determinants of a disease and injury in human populations is studied.
6. For a thoughtful overview of issues related to development, population, and growing urbanization throughout contemporary Africa, especially as these issues relate to HIV/AIDS, see Gordon 2001. The small Southern African kingdom of Swaziland now maintains the highest HIV infection rate among the adult population, a staggering 38.8 percent, which according to Michael Wines and Sharon LaFraniere "now tops Botswana's as the world's highest. The death rate has doubled in just seven years" (2004).
7. Anthropologists George Bond and Joan Vincent provide a detailed cultural history of HIV/AIDS in Uganda in their article, "AIDS in Uganda: The First Decade" (1997b). In this article they outline the progression of anthropological perspectives of AIDS in Uganda from its beginnings as a biomedical paradigm to a community paradigm, and then finally to a critical paradigm. In my own study I suggest an additional, fourth perspective that has emerged in the new millennium, a contemporary global African paradigm.

8. Museveni maintains that the NRM is not a political party per se, but rather a movement that claims the loyalty of all Ugandans.

9. In the United States—with a total population of 294 million—890,000 people live with either HIV or full-blown AIDS. The transmission of the virus in the United States has historically been through bodily fluid exchanges occurring through homosexual contact or as a result of IV drug injection.

10. Bumiller 2003.

11. This aspect of ABC is known locally as "zero grazing," meaning that one should not have multiple sex partners outside of a primary relationship, i.e., one should not "graze" outside one's pasture.

12. Greg Behrman reports that at one time 66 percent of the child population in Uganda was positive with the HIV virus (2004, 14).

13. The United Nations tends to locate countries in the following three categories: industrialized countries, developing countries, and least developed countries. Uganda is typically located with the final category, least developed countries, while its closest neighbors, Kenya and Tanzania, fall in the developing countries category (see *Young People and HIV/AIDS: Opportunity in Crisis* 2002, 48).

14. "Opportunistic infections" refers to a type of illness or infection affecting someone with a weakened immune system, such as someone who is HIV positive. "Opportunistic infections are responsible for up to 90% of all AIDS-related deaths" according to the *AmFAR AIDS Handbook* (Ward 1999, 417).

15. IDAAC—Integrated Development and AIDS Concern, Iganga, pronounced "Ai-dæk."

16. TASO—The AIDS Support Organization.

17. I raise this issue not to confuse the issue of how closely individual rhythms are associated with specific dances throughout East Africa "[M]usic and dance [are] always closely interlinked. It is interesting to note that many drum rhythms bear the same…" (Busuulwa Katambula n.d., 10).

18. Throughout this and other chapters, I argue for an understanding of the authority given to localized responses regarding HIV/AIDS in Uganda. For a detailed analysis of a very different social response network in Brazil that has largely been international see Bastos 1999.

19. For further information on Kumunhyu, see Kirungi 2001.

20. Lusoga, bowl lyre.

21. Lusoga, long drum.

22. The term "prevalence" regarding HIV is used to refer to the number of HIV positive individuals at a given point in time. This is typically expressed as a "prevalence rate" which references a percentage of the total population.

23. The figure for 1999 is from Bennell 2003. The figure for the 2003 prevalence rate is from the UNAIDS Report, "AIDS Epidemic in sub-Saharan Africa" (2004). All other prevalence rates are from the 2003 "STD/HIV/AIDS Surveillance Report."

24. The open secret policy mirrors in some ways the "Silence = Death" metaphor early AIDS discourse in the United States. For further analysis of this issue see Edelman 1989.

25. "TASO is Going Forward," *A Decade of Hope: TASO Uganda*, vol. II, TASO Mulago Drama Group. Recorded by Dungu Productions Studio. Produced with the support of the Phoenix Trust, England.

26. For an in-depth and deeply personalized history of the TASO movement see Kaleeba 1991, a memoir written by one of the founders of TASO, Noerine Kaleeba. Dennis Altman suggests that the responses of CBOs such as TASO are "often strongest in countries with relatively few resources, such as Uganda or Zambia" (1994, 14).

27. The term, client, is used in Ugandan medical and social contexts to refer to one who is either HIV+ or has AIDS and is registered with one of the larger social service agencies or organizations such as TASO, Mildmay, Nsambya, Meeting Point Kampala, etc.

28. For further documentation on "living positively" with AIDS see Hampton 1998 and Ruzindaza 2001.
29. According to the Uganda AIDS Commission, stigma is "the negative thoughts about a person or group based on prejudiced position. Stigma does not naturally exist, it is created by individuals and society and builds on power relations and reinforces social inequalities" (World AIDS Campaign 2002/3 Information Leaflet).
30. I, of course, realize the problems inherent in labeling this process as "simple" within the interviews. Several people in fact had to have known about me and my work, anticipating many of my questions. Yet, I maintain that the question to which I referred was received as outside the main goals of the healthcare interviews.
31. For an extended interview with Faustus Baziri see the Interlude 5.
32. *TASO Uganda: The Inside Story* 1995, 30.
33. The "Drama Group" is a cover term. The group mostly performs songs and dances, although dramas are also a part of their repertoire.
34. This one-time drug has been highly politicized in other countries such as South Africa which according to anthropologist Virginia van der Vliet has been "wrestling with the most basic drug provision issue—the use of AZT or nevirapine (viramune) to prevent HIV-infected pregnant women passing on the virus to their babies" (2004, 64).
35. There are, however, questions of ethics related to this issue. "Introducing antiretroviral drug programmes for the prevention of mother-to-child transmission in countries where antiretrovirals are not available for the treatment of HIV-positive people more generally has raised sometimes heated debate about the ethical implications. The question is asked: If a mother's access to antiretroviral drugs is limited to the period of pregnancy and labour, does this amount to treating the mother for the sake of her baby alone? In fact, the question is based on an erroneous perception, for an antiretroviral drug used for the purpose of preventing MTCT of HIV is not really a treatment, but a 'vaccine' for the infant" (*Intensifying Action Against HIV/AIDS in Africa* 2000, 83).
36. In Uganda the disease and virus (AIDS and HIV) have both in fact been referred to as "*Slim*" longer than they have been referred to as HIV/AIDS. See Serwadda, Mugerwa, and Sewankambo et al., 1985.
37. See D'Adesky 2004, 403 4n, quoting *IRIN HIV/AIDS Weekly* 2001 as stating that "[UNICEF] notes that AIDS was responsible for 12 percent of deaths in Uganda in 2001, surpassing malaria and other diseases among individuals aged between fourteen and forty-five. An estimated 1.7 million children under fifteen has also lost one or both parents to AIDS."
38. "*Kisoga*" is the adjectival form of reference for the culture of the Basoga people of Busoga.
39. "Mzee" is a typical term of respect used for male elders or a father.
40. With apologies to poet Henry Reed's "Naming of Parts" from his *Lessons of the War*.
41. The AIDS Support Organization.
42. This small focus group of Makerere College School students included Kitogo George Ndugwa, Onama Caseser, Apollo Mbowa, Ssebunya Senyonjo Mubende, Lukwiya Bernard, and Owuma Nyko.
43. Terms for HIV/AIDS in other regional local languages not covered in the present study emerged in song and drama texts including in the Samia language—*Esikosa, Ahawuka, Sirimu, Esisaanyawo, Esya boosi, Esizunga, Esilwaye*; in the Acoli language—*Two acwi, Cilimu, Two mateki*; in the Arua Lugbara language—*Sase Kavera, Kinylonbo, Kisasebo, Oci, Amadezua, Sindani, Aci gba eribo, Sirimu, Azo onziri, Izi'izia, ondri'ndria*, and *Azo amani diari*.
44. See section "Personification" below for this term.
45. Other terms for condoms arose in the contexts of songs and dramas in regional languages. In the Acoli language—*Roc-ngoro, Kwot, Kondomu, CDs, Mupira*; in the Lugbara language—*Jurua, Katara, Bumboot, Drai'yaku, Gombeere'ombani, Enyi Ombani, Sokisi, Mupira*;

in the Samia language—*Esi doniawo obulamu, Ahapiira, Sina kerdera ye, Ahamasu, Engabo, Esibidiira, Kondomu, Amakesi ka'baswungu, Sokisi, Ebirato byo Hulwana.*

46. Music and text by Wandera Vincent. English translation by Wandera Vincent and Gregory Barz.

47. Popular musicians in Uganda and elsewhere in Africa have long used their access to the media to educate and to heighten people's awareness of HIV/AIDS. Other creative artists, such as writers, have lagged behind in this effort as South African writer Nadine Gordimer suggests in one of the first collective efforts by writers to address this lacuna: "Musicians have given their talents to jazz, pop, and classical concerts for the benefit of the 40 million worldwide men, women, and children infected with HIV/AIDS, two-thirds of whom are in Africa. We decided that we too should wish to give something of our ability, as imaginative writers, to contribute in our way to the fight against this disease from which no country, no individual is safely isolated" (2004, x).

48. The Memory Project is also engaged by groups such as TASO, GOSSACE, and Save the Children in Uganda, among others.

49. Original financial support came from Save the Children, and the ancillary materials supporting the Memory Book project are now available in Luganda, KiSwahili, and Luo, in addition to English.

50. A *kanzu* is a floor-length white robe worn by men on special occasions such as weddings.

51. Of the total number of respondents, twenty-four were from the Baganda ethnic group (with a wide distribution among the following clans: Nnyonyi, Mbogo, Mamba, Nte, Nkima, Fumbe, Ngonge, Ngeye, Mbwa, Nsenene, and Mpewo). The remainder were Bafumbira (Nte clan), Banyolo (Njobe clan), Rwandan (Kasimba clan), Banyankole (Nkima clan), Basamya (Njovu clan), and Basoga (Ngabi clan).

52. This survey was cofacilitated by Vincent Wandera and Godfrey Mukasa and was conducted in the language most comfortable to the informant—most often Luganda or English.

53. Winston Churchill referred to Uganda as the "Pearl of Africa" after his famous visit to the territory. Today the pearl is a common metaphor for the country.

WORKS CITED

1990 *Frontline: Born in Africa*, A Frontline/AIDS Quarterly Special Report.

1995 *TASO Uganda: The Inside Story, Participatory Evaluation of HIV/AIDS Counselling, Medical and Social Services 1993–1994*. Kampala and Geneva: TASO and WHO.

2000 *Intensifying Action Against HIV/AIDS in Africa: Responding to a Development Crisis*. Washington, DC: The World Bank.

2001 *Body and Soul*, video, vol. 4 of "Steps for the Future": California Newsreel, San Francisco, CA.

2001 "Plan of Action: The Ecumenical Response to HIV/AIDS in Africa". Nairobi, Global Consultation on the Ecumenical Response to the Challenge of HIV/AIDS in Africa.

2001 "Uganda: Government Decentralizes Access to Anti-AIDS Drugs." *IRIN HIV/AIDS Weekly* 35(July 13).

2002 *AIM Scope: One Year On*. Kampala, The Uganda AIDS/HIV Integrated Model District Programme.

2002 *A Conceptual Framework and Basis for Action: HIV/AIDS Stigma and Discrimination*. Geneva: UNAIDS.

2002 "An Overview of Child Counselling." *UNASO Best Practice Series* 1(2): 2–4.

2002 *Coming to Say Goodbye: Stories of AIDS in Africa*, video. Maryknoll, NY: Maryknoll World Productions.

2002 *Fact Sheet 2002: Sub-Saharan Africa*, UNAIDS.

2002 *Fight Stigma! Reach Out to Positive People. 2002/3 World AIDS Campaign/World AIDS Day*. Kampala: Uganda AIDS Commission Secretariat.

2002 *Keeping the Promise: Summary of the Declaration of Commitment on HIV/AIDS*. New York, United Nations General Assembly, Special Session on HIV/AIDS.

2002 Mudinet. *UNASO News* [Newsletter of the Uganda Network of AIDS Service Organisations, 5.

2002 *NACWOLA: National Community of Women Living with HIV/AIDS in Uganda*. Brochure. Kampala.

2002 THETA—Working with Traditional Healers to Increase Access to HIV/AIDS Prevention and Care in Uganda. *UNASO News* [Newsletter of the Uganda Network of AIDS Service Organisations, 5: 6-8.

2002 *World AIDS Campaign 2002/3 on Stigma and Discimination*. Kampala: Uganda AIDS Commission Secretariat.

2002 *Young People and HIV/AIDS: Opportunity in Crisis*. New York: United Nations Children's Fund.

2003 *Global AIDS: Facing the Crisis*. Pamphlet. Elkhart, IN: Church World Service.

2003 "President Warns Religious Leaders On HIV/Aids," December 2, *New Vision*. Kampala.

2003 "STD/HIV/AIDS Surveillance Report," STD/AIDS Control Programme, Ministry of Health, Kampala, Uganda; http://www.health.go.ug/docs/hiv0603.pdf.

2004 "AIDS and Artists Holding Up a Mirror: Writers, Painters and Film-makers Struggle to Respond." *Economist* December 29, http://www.electronic-economist.com/books/PrinterFriendly.cfm?Story_ID=3518612.

2004 "AIDS Epidemic in sub-Saharan Africa." UNAIDS Report.

2004 *Save the Children UK*, http://www.savethechildren.org.uk.

2004 *TASO Uganda Ltd.*, general brochure.

2004 *UNAIDS 2004 Report on the Global AIDS Epidemic*. Geneva, UNAIDS.

Altman, D. 1994. *Power and Community: Organizational and Cultural Responses to AIDS*. London: Taylor & Francis.

Babiracki, C. 1997. "What's the Difference? Reflections on Gender and Research in Village India." In *Shadows in the Field: New Perspectives for Fieldwork in Ethnomusicology*, edited by G. Barz and T. Cooley. New York: Oxford University Press.

Baer, H. A., M. Singer, and I. Susser. 1997. *Medical Anthropology and the World System: A Critical Perspective*. Westport: Bergin & Garvey.

Baker, R. 1994. *The Art of AIDS*. New York: Continuum.

Bal, Mieke 1997. *The Mottled Screen: Reading Proust Visually*. Stanford: Stanford University Press.

Bal, M., J. Crewe, and L. Spitzer. 1999. *Acts of Memory: Cultural Recall in the Present*. Hanover, NH: University Press of New England and Dartmouth College.

Barfield, T., ed. 1997. *The Dictionary of Anthropology*. Oxford: Blackwell.

Barnett, T., and A. Whiteside. 2002. *AIDS in the Twenty-First Century: Disease and Globalization*. London: Palgrave Macmillan.

Barz, G. 1997a. "Confronting the Field(Note) In and Out of the Field: Music, Voices, Text, and Experiences in Dialogue." In *Shadows in the Field: New Perspectives for Fieldwork in Ethnomusicology*, edited by G. Barz and T. Cooley. New York: Oxford University Press.

———. 1997b. "Chasing Shadows in the Field: An Epilogue." In *Shadows in the Field: New Perspectives for Fieldwork in Ethnomusicology*, edited by G. Barz and T. Cooley. New York: Oxford University Press.

———. 1997c. "*Kwayas, Kandas, Kiosks*: A Tanzanian Popular Music." *Ethnomusicology Online* II, http://research.umbc.edu/eol/2/barz/.

———. 2000a. "Politics of Remembering: Performing History(-ies) in Youth *Kwaya* Competitions in Dar Es Salaam, Tanzania." *Mashindano! Music and Competition in East Africa*, edited by F. Gunderson and G. Barz. Dar Es Salaam and Oxford: Mkuki na Nyota and African Books Collective.

———. 2000b. "*Tamati*: Music Competition and Community Formation: an Epilogue." *Mashindano! Music and Competition in East Africa*, edited by F. Gunderson and G. Barz. Dar Es Salaam and Oxford: Mkuki na Nyota and African Books Collective.

———. 2002. "No One Will Listen To Us Unless We Bring Our Drums!: AIDS and Women's Music Performance in Uganda." *The aWake Project: Uniting Against the African AIDS Crisis*. Nashville, TN: W. Publishing.

———. 2003a. *Performing Religion: Negotiating Past and Present in Kwaya Music of Tanzania*. Amsterdam: Editions Rodopi.

———. 2003b. "'I Am Able To See Very Far But I Am Unable To Reach There': Ndugu Gideon Mdegella's *Nyimbo za Kwaya.*" In *The Interrelatedness of Music, Religion and Ritual in African Performance Practice*, edited by D. Avorgbedor. Lewiston, NY: Mellen Press.

———. 2004. *Music in East Africa: Experiencing Music, Expressing Culture.* New York: Oxford University Press.

———. 2005a. "Soundscapes of Disaffection and Spirituality in Tanzanian *Kwaya* Music." *The World of Music* 47(1): 5-24.

———. 2005b. "We are from Different *Makabila*, But We Live Here as One Family': The Musical Performance of Community in an East African *Kwaya.*" In *Chorus and Community*, edited by K. Ahlquist. Champaign: University of Illinois Press.

Bastos, C. 1999. *Global Responses to AIDS: Science in Emergency.* Bloomington: Indiana University Press.

Bateson, M. C. 2003. "Lives of Learning." *The Chronicle Review, The Chronicle of Higher Education.* July 25, Section 2: B5.

Baylies, C. 2004. "Perspectives on Gender and AIDS in Africa." *AIDS, Sexuality and Gender in Africa: Collective Strategies and Struggles in Tanzania and Zambia*, edited by C. Baylies and J. Bujra (1–24). London: Routledge.

Behrman, G. 2004. *The Invisible People: How the U.S. Has Slept Through the Global AIDS Pandemic, the Greatest Humanitarian Catastrophe of Our Time.* New York: Free Press.

Belcher, A. E., D. Dettmore, and S. Holzemer. 1989. "Spirituality and Sense of Well-Being in Persons with AIDS." *Holistic Nursing Practice* 3(4): 16–25.

Bellamy, C. 2002. "To African Religious Leaders' Assembly on Children and HIV/AIDS", Speech delivered in Nairobi, Kenya. Source: UNICEF Press Center, http://57.69.14.59/media/media_9438.html.

Bennell, R. 2003. "HIV/AIDS in sub-Saharan Africa: The Growing Epidemic?" http://www.eldis.org/fulltext/BennellHIVAfrica.pdf.

Birabwa, S. 2002. "Dimensions of HIV/AIDS in Uganda." *Arise: A Women's Development Magazine Published by ACFODE*, special edition: 41–42.

Bond, G. C., J. Kreniske, I. Susser, and J. Vincent. 1997. "The Anthropology of AIDS in Africa." *AIDS in Africa and the Caribbean*, edited by G. C. Bond, J. Kreniske, I. Susser and J. Vincent (3–9). Boulder, CO: Westview Press.

Bond, G. C., and J. Vincent. 1997a. "Community Based Organizations in Uganda: A Youth Initiative." In *AIDS in Africa and the Caribbean*, edited by G. C. Bond, J. Kreniske, I. Susser, and J. Vincent (99–133). Boulder, CO: Westview Press.

———. 1997b. "AIDS in Uganda: The First Decade." In *AIDS in Africa and the Caribbean*, edited by G. C. Bond, J. Kreniske, I. Susser, and J. Vincent (85–97). Boulder, CO: Westview Press.

Breitinger, E. 1999. "Introduction." In *Uganda: The Cultural Landscape* (9–20). Bayreuth, Germany and Kampala: Bayreuth African Studies and Fountain Publishers Ltd.

Browner, C. H., B. R. Ortiz de Montellano, and A. J. Rubel. 1988. "A Methodology for Cross-Cultural Ethnomedical Research." *Current Anthropology* 29(5): 681–702.

Browning, B. 1998. *Infectious Rhythm: Metaphors of Contagion and the Spread of African Culture.* New York: Routledge.

Bujra, J. 2004. "Target Practice: Gender and Generational Struggles in AIDS Prevention Work in Lushoto." In *AIDS, Sexuality and Gender in Africa: Collective Strategies and Struggles in Tanzania and Zambia*, edited by C. Baylies and J. Bujra (114–32). London: Routledge.

Bumiller, E. 2003. "Uganda's Key to White House: AIDS." *New York Times,* June 11.

Campbell, C. 2003. *Letting Them Die: Why HIV/AIDS Prevention Programmes Fail.* Bloomington: Indiana University Press.

Connerton, P. 1991[1989]. *How Societies Remember.* Cambridge: Cambridge University Press.

Cook, A. S., J. J. Fritz, and R. Mwonya. 2003. "Understanding the Psychological and Emotional Needs of AIDS Orphans in Africa." In *The Children of Africa Confront AIDS*, edited by A. Singhal and W. S. Howard (85–104). Athens: Ohio University Press.

Cooley, T. J. 2003. "Theorizing Fieldwork Impact: Malinowski, Peasant-Love, and Friendship." *British Journal of Ethnomusicology* 12(i): 1–17.

D'Adesky, A.-C. 2004. *Moving Mountains: The Race to Treat Global AIDS*. London: Verso.

Defert, D. 1996. "AIDS as a Challenge to Religion." In *AIDS in the World II: Global Dimensions, Social Roots, and Responses: The Global AIDS Policy Coalition*, edited by J. M. Mann and D. J. M. Tarantola (447–52). New York: Oxford University Press.

Doumbi-Fakoly. 1992. "African Literature: Witness to its Time." In *A Leap in the Dark: AIDS, Art and Contemporary Cultures*, edited by A. Klusacek and K. Morrison. Montreal: Véhicule Press.

Edelman, L. 1989. "The Plague of Discourse: Politics, Literary Theory, and AIDS." *The South Atlantic Quarterly* 88(1): 301–17.

Epstein, H. 2004. "The Fidelity Fix." *The New York Times Magazine*, June 13, 54-59.

Eschen, A. 1993. *Community-Based AIDS Prevention and Care in Africa: Building on Local Initiatives: Workshop Report: Berlin, June 5, 1993*. Presented by The Population Council and The Wellcome Foundation.

Farmer, P. 1992. *AIDS and Accusation: Haiti and the Geography of Blame*. Berkeley: University of California Press.

Francis, R. A. 1989. "Moral Beliefs of Physicians, Medical Students, Clergy, and Lay Public Concerning AIDS." *Journal of the National Medical Association* 81(11): 1141–47.

Frank, M. 1995. *AIDS Education through Theatre*. Bayreuth, Germany: Bayreuth African Studies.

Friedson, S. M. 1996, *Dancing Prophets: Musical Experience in Tumbuka Healing*. Chicago: University of Chicago Press.

———. 2003. "The Disease of the Prophets: The Musical Construction of Clinical Reality." In *The Interrelatedness of Music, Religion, and Ritual in African Performance Practice*, edited by D. K. Avorgbedor (155–89). Lewiston, NY: Mellen Press.

Gordimer, N., ed. 2004. *Telling Tales*. New York: Picador.

Gordon, A. A. 2001. "Population, Urbanization, and AIDS." In *Understanding Contemporary Africa*, edited by A. A. Gordon and D. L. Gordon (189–216). Boulder, CO: Lynne Rienner Publishers.

Gow, J., and C. Desmond. 2002. "Time for the Next Steps." In *Impacts and Interventions: The HIV/AIDS Epidemic and the Children of South Africa*, edited by J. Gow and C. Desmond (207–8). Pietermaritzburg: University of Natal Press and UNICEF.

Green, E. C. 1994. *AIDS and STDs in Africa: Bridging the Gap Between Traditional Healing and Modern Medicine*. Boulder, CO: Westview Press.

Greenwood, D., S. Lindenbaum, M. Lock, and A. Young. 1988. "Introduction to Theme Issue on Medical Anthropology." *American Ethnologist* 15(1): 1–3.

Griffin, G. 2000. *Representations of HIV and ADIS: Visibility blue/s*. Manchester: Manchester University Press.

Grundfest Schoepf, B. G. 1997. "AIDS, Gender, and Sexuality during Africa's Economic Crisis." In *African Feminism: The Politics of Survival in Sub-Saharan Africa*, edited by G. Mikell. Philadelphia: University of Pennsylvania Press.

Guest, E. 2003. *Children of AIDS: Africa' Orphan Crisis*. London: Pluto Press and University of Natal Press.

Guthrie, M. 1967–71. Comparative Bantu: An Introduction to the Comparative Linguistics and Prehistory of the Bantu Languages. London: Gregg International Publishers.

Hampton, J. 1998. *Living Positively with AIDS: The AIDS Support Organization (TASO), Uganda*, rev. ed. London, Nairobi, and Colchester: ActionAid, AMREF, World in Need.

Hope, K. R. 1999. "The Socioeconomic Context of AIDS in Africa: A Review." *AIDS and*

Development in Africa: A Social Science Perspective, edited by K. R. Hope (1–35). New York: The Haworth Press.

Hunter, S. S. 1990. "Orphans as a Window on the AIDS Epidemic in Sub-Saharan Africa: Initial Results and Implications of a Study in Uganda." *Social Science and Medicine* 31(6): 681–90.

Joinet, B. 1994. *The Challenge of AIDS in East Africa, Part One: Basic Facts.* Dar es Salaam: self published.

Kaahwa, J., G. Wadulo, J. Muganga, and E. Breitinger. 1999. "Theatre for Development in Uganda: Strategies for Democratisation and Conscientisation." In *Uganda: The Cultural Landscape*, edited by E. Breitinger (207–25). Bayreuth, Germany: Bayreuth African Studies and Fountain Publishers Ltd.

Kaleeba, N. 1991. *We Miss You All—Noerine Kaleeba: AIDS in the Family.* Harare: WASN (Women and AIDS Support Network Book Project).

Kalindile, R., and M. Mbilinyi. 1991. "Grassroot Struggles for Women's Advancement: The Story of Rebeka Kalindile." In *The Unsung Heroines*, edited by B. Koda and M. Ngaiza. Dar es Salaam: Dar es Salaam University Press.

Katambula, B. n.d. "Music Development in Uganda." *Music Education*, edited by S. W. Muwonge. Kampala.

Katusiime, M. R. 2002. "'Counseling Gave Me Courage Like a Gisu Boy Waiting for the Circumcision [sic] Knife': I Was Ready to Take the HIV Test." *AIDS Information Centre AIC News* (Kampala, Uganda), 2: 9–11.

Kauffman, K. D. 2004. "Why is South Africa the HIV Capital of the World? An Institutional Analysis of the Spread of a Virus." In *AIDS and South Africa: The Social Expression of a Pandemic*, edited by K. D. Kauffman and D. L. Lindauer (17–30). New York: Palgrave Macmillan.

Kirungi, F. 2001. "Uganda Beating Back AIDS: Leadership, Education and Openness Are Keys To Progress." *Africa Recovery* June: 26–27.

Kisliuk, M. 1997. *Seize the Dance! BaAka Musical Life and the Ethnography of Performance.* New York: Oxford University Press.

Kleinman, A. 1980. *Patients and Healers in the Context of Culture: An Exploration of the Borderland between Anthropology, Medicine, and Psychiatry.* Berkeley: University of California Press.

Koen, B. D. 2003. *Devotional Music and Healing in Badakhshan, Tajikistan: Preventive and Curative Practices.* PhD dissertation. Ohio State University.

Lacey, M. 2003. "African AIDS, and Helping Orphans Remember." *New York Times* (online edition), April 2, http://www.nytimes.com/2003/04/02/international/africa/02UGAN.html?ex=1118462400&en=93322b7c5a8dc4ae&ei=5070.

Lucas, I. 1995. *Growing Up Positive: Stories from a Generation of Young People Affected by AIDS.* London: Cassell.

Lyons, M. 1997. "The Point of View: Perspectives on AIDS in Uganda." In *AIDS in Africa and the Caribbean*, edited by G. C. Bond, J. Kreniske, I. Susser, and J. Vincent (131–46). Boulder, CO: Westview Press.

Macpherson, M. 1999. "Makerere: The Place of the Early Sunrise." In *Uganda: The Cultural Landscape*, edited by E. Breitinger (23–36). Bayreuth and Kampala: Bayreuth African Studies and Fountain Publishers Ltd.

Mahlangu-Ngcobo, M. 2001. *AIDS in Africa: An African and Prophetic Perspective.* Baltimore: Gateway Press, Inc.

Mahoro, F. 2002. Benefits of Being a Member of Post Test Club/Philly Lutaaya Initiative. *AIDS Information Centre AIC News* (Kampala, Uganda), 2: 15–16.

Manyindo, S. K. 1996. *An Exploratory Organizational Study of AIDS Programming Approaches by UNICEF, USAID, CHDC, TASO and UAC in Uganda.* M.S. thesis, University of Cincinnatti.

Marcus, G., and M. Fischer. 1986. *Anthropology as Cultural Critique: An Experimental Moment in the Human Sciences.* Chicago: University of Chicago Press.

Mbilinyi, M., and N. Kaihula. 2004. "Sinners and Outsiders: The Drama of AIDS in Rungwe." In *AIDS, Sexuality and Gender in Africa: Collective Strategies and Struggles in Tanzania and Zambia,* edited by C. Baylies and J. Bujra (77–95). London: Routledge.

Mbowa, R. 1998. "Theatre for Development: Empowering Ugandans to Transform Their Condition." In *Developing Uganda,* edited by H. B. Hansen and M. Twaddle. Oxford, Kampala, Nairobi, and Athens, OH: James Currey, Fountain Publishers, East African Educational Publishers, Ohio University Press.

McCarthy, G. 2004. "*The Social Edge* Interview: Author and Missionary Educator Diane Stinton". *The Social Edge.Com,* December 2004, http://www.thesocialedge.com/archives/gerrymccarthy/2articles-dec2004.htm.

McIlhaney, J.S.J. 2004. "Evidence That Demands Action: Comparing Risk Avoidance and Risk Reduction Strategies for HIV Prevention"(Powerpoint Presentation), http://www.pacha.gov/meetings/presentations/p0304/p0304.html.

McKee, N., M. Aghi, R. Carnegie, and N. Shahzadi. 2003. "Sara: A Role Model for African Girls Facing HIV/AIDS." In *The Children of Africa Confront AIDS,* edited by A. Singhal and W. S. Howard (171–92). Athens: Ohio University Press.

Merson M. H., J. M. Dayton, and K. O'Reilly. 2000. "Effectiveness of HIV Prevention Interventions in Developing Countries." *AIDS* 14 (Suppl. 2): S68–84.

Mike, C. and Members of the PSW. 1999. "Performance Studio Workshop: Igboelerin East." In *African Theatre in Development,* edited by M. Banham, J. Gibs, and F. Osofisan. Oxford and Bloomington: James Currey and Indiana University Press.

Milne, A. A. 1954. *Winnie-the-Pooh.* New York: Dell.

Mlama, P. M. 1991. *Culture and Development: The Popular Theatre Approach in Africa.* Uppsala, Sweden: Scandinavian Institute of African Studies.

Moshtael, N. 1996. *The Global AIDS Strategy and the Power of Community Responses to HIV/AIDS: A Case Study of the AIDS Support Organization (TASO) in Uganda.* PhD dissertation. University of Oregon.

Mouli, C., and K. N. Rao. 1992. "Performance and AIDS in Zambia." In *A Leap in the Dark: AIDS, Art and Contemporary Culture,* edited by A. Klusacek and K. Morrison. Montreal: Véhicule Press.

Muller, D., and N. Abbas. 1990. "Risk Factors: Cofactors in Heterosexual AIDS Transmission in Uganda." In *Cofactors in HIV-1 Infection and AIDS,* edited by R. E. Watson. Boca Raton, FL: CRC Press.

Namukisa, N. 2002. *Annual Report.* Kampala, Uganda, Meeting Point Kampala.

National Public Radio. 2004. Analysis: Study Suggests Why Uganda Has Been So Successful in Reducing HIV Rates.

Okurut, M. K. 1998. *The Invisible Weevil.* Kampala: FEMRITE Publications Limited.

Osteria, T., and G. Sullivan. 1991. "The Impact of Religion and Cultural Values on AIDS Education Programs in Malaysia and the Phillipines." *AIDS Education and Prevention* 3(2): 133–46.

Patton, C. 2002. *Globalizing AIDS.* Minneapolis: University of Minnesota Press.

Pillay, Y. 2003. "Storytelling as a Psychological Intervention for AIDS Orphans in Africa." In *The Children of Africa Confront AIDS,* edited by A. Singhal and W. S. Howard (105–18). Athens: Ohio University Press.

Preble, E. A. 1990. "Impact of HIV/AIDS on African Children." *Social Science and Medicine* 31(6): 671–80.

Reed, D. B. 2003. *Dan Ge Performance: Masks and Music in Contemporary Côte d'Ivoire.* Bloomington: University of Indiana Press.

Reed, H. 1970. *Lessons of the War.* New York: Chilmark Press.

Roseman, M. 1984. "The Social Structuring of Sound: The Temiar of Peninsular Malaysia." *Ethnomusicology* 27(3): 411–45.

———. 1988. "The Pragmatics of Aesthetics: The Performance of Healing Among Senoi Temiar." *Social Science and Medicine* 27(8): 811–18.

———. 1991. *Healing Sounds from the Malaysian Rainforest: Temiar Music and Medicine.* Berkeley, CA: University of California Press.

———. 1996. "Pure Products Go Crazy: Rainforest Healing in Nation-State." In *The Performance of Healing*, edited by C. and M. R. Laderman (233–69). New York: Routledge.

———. 2000. "The Canned Sardine Spirit Takes the Mic." *The World of Music* 42(2): 115–36.

Ruzindaza, C. 199?. *Living Positively with AIDS: An African Experience.* Nairobi: Paulines Publications Africa.

Schoub, B. D. 1999. *AIDS and HIV in Perspective: A Guide to Understanding the Virus and its Consequences.* Cambridge: Cambridge University Press.

Serwadda, D., R. D. Mugerwa, R. K. Sewankambo, A. Lwegaba, J. W. Carswell, G. B. Kirya, A. C. Bayley, R. G. Downing, R. S. Tedder, S. A. Clayden, R. A. Weiss, and A. G. Dalgleish. 1985. "Slim Disease: A New Disease in Uganda and its Association with HTLV-III/LAV Infection." *Lancet* 2(8460): 849–52.

Shils, E. 1981. *Tradition.* Chicago: University of Chicago Press.

Shoumatoff, A. 1988. "In Search of the Source of AIDS." *Vanity Fair* 51(7).

Shuey, D., and H. Bagarukayo. 1996. "AIDS: Despair, Or a Stimulus to Reform?" In *AIDS in the World II: Global Dimensions, Social Roots, and Responses: The Global AIDS Policy Coalition*, edited by J. M. Mann and D.J.M. Tarantola (122–24). New York: Oxford University Press.

Singhal, A. 2003. "Communication Strategies for Confronting AIDS." In *The Children of Africa Confront AIDS*, edited by A. Singhal and W. S. Howard (230–45). Athens: Ohio University Press.

Steinglass, M. 2001. "It Takes A Village Healer: Anthropologists Believe Traditional Medicine Can Remedy Africa's AIDS Crisis. Are They Right?" *Lingua Franca* 11(3): 28–39.

Stoneburner, R. L., and D. Low-Beer. 2004. "Population-Level HIV Declines and Behavioral Risk Avoidance in Uganda." *Science* 304(30 April): 714–18.

Sturken, M. 1997. *Tangled Memories: The Vietnam War, the AIDS Epidemic, and the Politics of Remembering.* Berkeley: University of California Press.

Ulin, P. 1992. "African Women and AIDS: Negotiating Behavioural Change." *Social Science and Medicine* 34(1): 63–73.

van der Vliet, V. 2004. "South Africa Divided Against AIDS: A Crisis of Leadership." In *AIDS and South Africa: The Social Expression of a Pandemic*, edited by K. D. Kauffman and D. L. Lindauer (48–96). New York: Palgrave Macmillan.

Vanderpuye, K., and J. Amegatcher. 2003. "Participatory HIV Intervention with Ghanaian Youth." In *The Children of Africa Confront AIDS*, edited by A. Singhal and W. S. Howard (149–58). Athens: Ohio University Press.

Vansina, J. 1985. *Oral Tradition as History.* Madison: University of Wisconsin Press.

Vatsyn, E. 1986. "Spiritual Aspects of the Care of Cancer Patients." *CA—A Cancer Journal for Clinicians* 6: 110–14.

Voeten, H. A., O. B. Egesah, M. Y. Ondiege, C. M. Varkevisser, and J. D. Habbema. 2002. "Clients of Female Sex Workers in Nyanza Province, Kenya: A Core Group in STD/HIV Transmission." *Sexually Transmitted Diseases* 29(8): 444–52.

Wakiraza, C. 2002. "Reintegration of Street Children: A Critical Look at Sustainable Success." In *Poverty, AIDS, and Street Children in East Africa*, edited by J.L.P. Lugalla and C. G. Kibass. Lewiston, NY: Mellen Press.

Ward, D. E. 1999. *The AmFAR AIDS Handbook: The Complete Guide to Understanding HIV and AIDS.* New York: W. W. Norton.

Watney, S. 1994. "Missionary Positions: AIDS, 'Africa', and Race." *Practices of Freedom: Selected Writings on HIV/AIDS.* Durham, NC: Duke University Press.

———. 1996[1987]. *Policing Desire: Pornography, AIDS and The Media.* Minneapolis: University of Minnesota Press.

Whyte, S. R., and H. Birungi. 2000. "The Business of Medicines and the Politics of Knowledge in Uganda." In *Global Health Policy, Local Realities: The Fallacy of the Level Playing Field*, edited by L. M. Whiteford and L. Manderson. Boulder, CO: Lynne Rienner Publishers.

Wines, M., and S. LaFraniere. 2004. "Hut by Hut, AIDS Steals Life in a Southern Africa Town." *New York Times*, November 28, 1.

INDEX